# BORN TO RUN

Campaigning American Style

Series Editors
Daniel M. Shea, Allegheny College
F. Christopher Arterton, George Washington University

Few areas of American politics have changed as dramatically in recent times as the way in which we choose public officials. Students of politics and political communications are struggling to keep abreast of these developments—and the 2000 election only fed the confusion and concern. *Campaigning American Style* is a new series of books devoted to both the theory and practice of American electoral politics. It offers high quality work on the conduct of new-style electioneering and how it is transforming our electoral system. Scholars, practitioners, and students of campaigns and elections need new resources to keep pace with the rapid rate of electoral change, and we are pleased to help provide them in this exciting series.

### Titles in the Series

*Born to Run: Origins of the Political Career*
by Ronald Keith Gaddie

*Life after Reform: When the Bipartisan Campaign Reform Act Meets Politics*
edited by Michael J. Malbin

*Political Polling*
by Jeffrey M. Stonecash

*High-Tech Grass Roots: The Professionalization of Local Elections*
by J. Cherie Strachan

*Campaign Mode: Strategic Vision in Congressional Elections*
by Michael John Burton and Daniel M. Shea

*The Civic Web: Online Politics and Democratic Values*
edited by David M. Anderson and Michael Cornfield

### Forthcoming

*Negative Campaigning*
by Richard R. Lau and Gerald M. Pomper

*Running on Empty?: Campaign Discourse in American Elections*
edited by L. Sandy Maisel and Darrell West

*The Rules: Election Regulations in the American States*
by Costas Panagopoulos

# BORN TO RUN

## Origins of the Political Career

RONALD KEITH GADDIE

ROWMAN & LITTLEFIELD PUBLISHERS, INC.
*Lanham • Boulder • New York • Toronto • Oxford*

ROWMAN & LITTLEFIELD PUBLISHERS, INC.

Published in the United States of America
by Rowman & Littlefield Publishers, Inc.
A wholly owned subsidary of The Rowman & Littlefield Publishing Group, Inc.
4501 Forbes Boulevard, Suite 200, Lanham, MD 20706
www.rowmanlittlefield.com

P.O. Box 317, Oxford OX2 9RU, UK

British Library Cataloguing in Publication Information Available

**Library of Congress Cataloging-in-Publication Data**

Gaddie, Ronald Keith.
    Born to run : origins of the political career / Ronald Keith Gaddie.
        p.  cm.—(Campaigning American style)
    Includes bibliographical references and index.
    ISBN 0-7425-1927-9 (alk. paper)—ISBN 0-7425-1928-7 (pbk. : alk. paper)
    1. Political candidates—United States.  2. Political campaigns—United States.
I. Title.  II. Series.
JK2281.G33  2004
324.7′0973—dc21                                                    2003013487

Printed in the United States of America

♾ ™ The paper used in this publication meets the minimum requirements of
American National Standard for Information Sciences—Permanence of Paper for
Printed Library Materials, ANSI/NISO Z39.48-1992.

# CONTENTS

# FOREWORD

Political science professor Keith Gaddie has always taken a keen interest in his students. It is not surprising that when some of these students were considering mounting a political campaign, they came to him for advice. Keith's interest in their ambitions led him to tag along as they campaigned throughout the state. He keenly and objectively observed the characteristics of these budding politicians; he probed their motives and their values. His observations ultimately led to the writing of this book.

*Born to Run* presents us with nine case studies from five states. The politicians profiled in his book have varied economic and political backgrounds and come from both urban and rural districts. They have their own sets of beliefs and political party connections. Some have more advanced education than others. Some have long-term political ambitions for higher office while others have more limited goals. One thing they have in common is age. All of these candidates are young. Gaddie clearly illustrates how this "youth and inexperience" (to paraphrase Reagan) can be exploited for political purposes to the benefit or detriment of the candidates.

In addition to my role as a university president, I teach an introductory course in American politics each semester. I am always heartened to see students in my own classes express a desire to get involved and give something back to their communities. This generation is a very caring generation. These young people contribute a great deal of their time volunteering for community service. They organize and participate in blood drives, renovate homeless shelters, serve food to those in need, pick up trash along the roads, tutor younger students, and help in many ways. They are continuing and enhancing the great American tradition of volunteer service which has been one of our greatest national strengths. Alexis de Tocqueville understood its importance and wrote about it more than 170 years ago. These students are eager to make the world around them a better place.

As someone who also started in politics at a relatively early age, I was curious to read about the experiences of these young candidates. There are a lot of similarities between their careers and mine. Some of them faced an uphill battle, and won the election despite the odds. Others had carefully laid the groundwork ahead of time, which allowed them to pick up endorsements and raise the money necessary to clinch the party nomination. Addressing civic organizations during luncheons, having breakfasts with groups of friends at small coffee shops, and passing out flyers are still part of the process. Unfortunately, the price of running a campaign has skyrocketed, even in local and state races.

When I first ran for a legislative seat in the late 1960s, a political candidate could expect to pay no more than three or four thousand dollars to wage a successful campaign bid. Some of my early fund-raisers included old-fashioned bean dinners. I was thrilled to bring in a couple hundred dollars after some of these events. When I ran for governor, I distributed flyers throughout various towns asking potential contributors to leave the lights on at their front door the following evening if they were willing to contribute to my campaign. We raised funds with literally a door-to-door effort. Some donors would be able to make more substantial contributions, but most gave small amounts. Today, the amount of money needed for a serious campaign at the state legislative level in some Oklahoma races has reached six figures. For the new politicians profiled in this book, expensive campaigns are the norm, yet they all understand that fund-raising alone is not enough to be successful in politics.

Professor Gaddie offers an intimate glimpse into the campaign process. He allows us to walk alongside candidates as they talk to people in the streets, at their homes, and at fund-raising events. His inside portrait of campaign life is invaluable to any would-be politician who needs to understand the difficulties and hard work that are an inherent part of the campaign trail.

Reading this book, I was reminded of my first political campaign. I was twenty-five and still in law school. I was presented with an opportunity to run for an open seat in the Oklahoma House of Representatives. I remember sitting in my car trying to muster up the courage to knock on my first door. I got out and walked up to the house while rehearsing in my mind everything I would say. When the door opened, I started with, "Hi, I'm David Boren and I'm running for—" Before I could finish, this gracious woman said that she had known my aunt for years and invited me to come in for some fresh-baked cookies. My rehearsed speech gave way to relaxed conversation and I realized I had gained a supporter. Several years later, I became the governor of Oklahoma and found myself riding through this same neighborhood where this woman lived. I had my driver pull over. I got out of the car, knocked on her door, and once again, she offered me some fresh-baked cookies. I thanked her for her help in starting my political career and told her that I might never have been elected governor had it not been for her kindness. Thankfully, my first experience was a good one. I might have veered away from politics if it had not been.

I was able to relive some of these experiences recently, as my son Dan ran for the seat I once held in the state House of Representatives in the 2002 elections. He wanted to run his own campaign with his own set of issues. I tried to avoid giving unsolicited advice. As a father, I found myself often resorting to the same thing Keith Gaddie did, and that was to observe. I was relieved to see that hard work and voter contact, at least in local races, is still more important than money. I am sorry to say that large campaign funds are harder to overcome in congressional and statewide races, though Dan won the election with 65 percent of the vote. By contrast, the margin of victory in my first race was much smaller—about 1 percent!

Gaddie captures the ups and downs of campaigns—the realities of slammed doors, negative advertising, and the thrill of people agreeing to put up yard signs in their front lawns. He writes vividly about election night and the joys accompanying an electoral victory. The reader can share in the excitement of these candidates and their families when they learn that they will be occupying a seat in the capitol. He then documents the early steps of some of these newly elected public officials. Many of these freshmen had successful first years in office. While they made some mistakes, most learned from the school of hard knocks and were able to become effective legislators.

One of the most important lessons learned is the importance of timing. This sense is usually something gained over longer periods of time, after dealing with many bills and many legislative sessions. Younger politicians can benefit from the experience of more senior officials, just as new members or potential members of a state legislature can benefit by the experiences chronicled by Gaddie.

Gaddie effectively integrates the literature on campaigns and voting to see how it squares with his observations. From this scholarship, Gaddie draws his own conclusions. He notes how young and vigorous candidates can compensate for the resources of their more established opponents. He looks at the importance of issues, campaign strategy, and following the established political norms within one's district. He shows us how age ceases to be an issue once a youthful candidate becomes integrated into the institution in which he or she has been elected to serve. Gaddie also examines the role of ambition and its evolution among the politicians he observed. His observations lead us to the conclusion that personal ambition alone without a sincere desire to serve is not enough for success in the long run.

Gaddie's technique of being "in the mix, but not in the way" allows him to get to see these candidates up close and in a way that is not often captured by archival research. This type of scholarship is invaluable. Political scientist Richard Fenno stated as much during one of his presentations as a participant in the Julian Rothbaum Lecture Series at the University of Oklahoma. Gaddie also quotes this from Fenno in the appendix:

> Glimpses from the campaign trail . . . remind us that it is, after all, flesh and blood individuals, real people we are talking about when

we generalize about our politicians . . . there is something to be gained by occasionally unpacking our analytical categories and our measures to take a first-hand look at the real live human beings subsumed within.

Fenno further said that, "Representative government has local roots and a bottom-up logic." That is the perspective of observational research like Gaddie's. Even those candidates who start their careers by running at the statewide or national levels must have a keen understanding of that fundamental truth if they are to succeed.

As someone who has practiced politics at the local, state, and national level for almost thirty years, I find that there is often more art in politics than science. Some human interactions and relationships cannot always be measured quantitatively. The best way to understand the political process is to observe it first hand. Gaddie offers us an important opportunity to do just that. There are important lessons contained in the stories that he tells.

—David L. Boren, President, University of Oklahoma

# ACKNOWLEDGMENTS

M ARK TWAIN ONCE OBSERVED, "There comes a time in every rightly constructed boy's life when he has a raging desire to go somewhere and dig for hidden treasure." This book started in my mind in 1998, when Kenneth Corn called me up and said, "I'm running for the legislature." Then Shane Hunt called a day later and said the same thing. The tumblers turned in synch in my mind, screaming to me that this was the chance to go digging for the hidden treasure of what Joseph Schlesinger termed "the hopes which lie in the hearts of young men" and to see, up close, how political careers start and how political fortunes are built. Here before me was the chance to examine how young people become candidates and how as candidates with little in terms of résumé or experience they start their careers and then build their political reputations.

For the next five years I met young candidates and legislators, observed their actions, and followed their progress. I bothered them with phone calls, tracked them in the papers and the media, and talked to political informants. Some of them I met as they first ran for office; others, just after they had won office. This book is about the rites of passage of nine people, from ambitious amateur to candidate, to lawmaker, and then in pursuit of higher ambitions. Not all of them initially succeeded. One grew weary of officeholding; two aspired to higher political callings. But all shared one trait: At a young age, these people stepped forward and said to their communities, "Here I am. Make of me what you will. I will serve."

Instead of practicing political science at the hard edge of the desk, I was tromping through neighborhoods with candidates, traveling miles and miles from campaign event to campaign event, attending backroom meetings or getting drawn into debate prep. My frequent flyer cards are a bit fuller, and I put a lot of miles on my old Chevy Suburban. The travels turned into a rediscovery of the bits of democracy we forget about, like neighborhood fish fries, summer political party picnics, and visits with old folks and people in their homes. After the initial election trips, the study evolved from watching young politicians as a unique centerpiece on the campaign trail, to observing their socialization, their development of expertise, and their pursuit of power, influence, and reputation. Time on the campaign trail was traded for time in legislative offices and committee meetings, and then traded again for time on the campaign trail.

My first and greatest thanks must go to the nine people who are the foundation of this book: Matt Dollar, Shane Hunt, Joe Handrick, Adrian Smith, Thad Balkman, Stephanie Stuckey-Benfield, Michael V. Saxl, Kenneth Corn, and Jon Bruning. Their hospitality and accessibility over the past five years were crucial to telling this story, and I look forward to long conversations in the future.

All the folks who read bits and pieces of the book or who helped me prepare to visit their states deserve special thanks, including Sunil Ahuja, Hal Bass, Gary Copeland, Tony Corrado, Robert Cox, John Hibbing, Larry Hill, Malcolm Jewell, Cherie Maestas, Sarah Morehouse, and Brian Taylor. When the draft was complete, Chuck Bullock, Rhodes Cook, Richard Fenno, Ron Peters, Jos Raadschelders, and Joe Stewart read it from cover to cover and offered numerous comments and insightful suggestions that improved the manuscript. Robert Hogan at LSU was generous in sharing survey data from his study of state legislative candidate campaigns, and I am especially grateful for his assistance not only in sharing the data but in performing the data runs for the analysis interspersed throughout the book. A sabbatical from the University of Oklahoma allowed me back onto the campaign trail. My editor, Jennifer Knerr, took a chance on this book when it was half-written.

My spouse, Kim, and children, Collin, Alec, and Cassidy, endured my frequent absences, and I appreciate their love and support as I finished the book.

I want to make a last, personal observation about the road that led to this book and thank three people who showed me a road worth traveling. When I was an underperforming undergraduate at Florida State University, the best undergraduate teacher I ever saw, Glenn Parker, assigned a little orange and brown book titled *Home Style* in his course. I could not put it down. When I stubbornly insisted on going to graduate school, Glenn steered me to Chuck Bullock at the University of Georgia, who took me in, undisciplined and rough, and made a professional, and a friend, out of me. Then, there is Dick Fenno. After knowing his writings, I came to know him during the past decade. When I read *Home Style* for Glenn's class, my reaction after finishing was "*That* is what I want to do." And, finally, I am able to do so.

So this work is dedicated to Glenn, Chuck, and Dick, with thanks from a grateful student, and also to the memory of Senator Larry Dickerson (1956–2002), who lived the words of Appius Claudius: "Every man is the artisan of his fortune."

# Political Ambitions, Political Careers

> Political scientists know a lot about America's politicians. But there is a
> lot we do not know.
>
> —Richard F. Fenno

T HE QUESTIONS OF WHO candidates are, where they come from, and
why they succeed or fail continue to hold the attention of political
analysts. The American political system is candidate centered, and
Americans have always had an appreciation for powerful personalities and
celebrity, for candidates who knew how to take to the stump and capture our
attention. We are a campaigning people. We hold more elections, more often,
for more offices, and at more levels of governance than any society on Earth.
Linda Fowler and James McClure (1989) observe that "the maze of constitutional federalism and political pluralism in the United States can divert even
a strong ambition, if it is not narrowly focused . . . the United States offers
the politically motivated a cornucopia of public offices, spreading out in all
directions and exerting substantial influence over many public questions.
Energetic politicians can find real power in many places [besides Congress]"
(3). There are so many such outlets for various ambitions. David Nice counts
over eighty thousand governments in the United States (Nice and Frederickson 1993), and the number of Americans in elective office is in the six figures
(513,200), from those serving on boards of special districts to county commissioners to state and federal legislators to the presidency.[1] The system
affords numerous opportunities to serve, and numerous opportunities to
choose.

All of this electioneering takes place in an environment of diffuse and frag-
mented political power, where party is important but not necessarily predom-
inant. Individuals and groups matter in the American system because parties
are weak, and elected officials have tremendous latitude to define their political role and how they discharge their official duties. It makes ambitious, energetic young candidates possible. It is this evolution of the American political
system from a system of parties to a system of highly independent entrepreneurs that requires students of campaign politics to take an individual, candi-
date-based approach to understanding candidate recruitment, candidate

emergence, and the development of political careers. The decline of parties places the initiative squarely with the candidates (e.g., Monroe 2001). As a consequence, the calculus of individuals plays a tremendous role in determining who will run. To recall the observation of Alan Ehrenhalt (1991), "We ask who sent our leaders, and the answer is easy: They sent themselves." If we want to understand the emergence and development of our leaders, we should go listen to them and observe them, preferably before their subsequent experiences cloud their recollections and flavor the retrospective evaluations of the origins of their careers.

This book is an exploration of the early political careers of nine politicians, a report from the field on the beginnings and progress of some lives in politics. Joseph Schlesinger (1966) observed in *Ambition and Politics* that "the hopes which lie in the hearts of young men running for their first office are secret" (7). Are they secret? Or should we just ask or look more closely? We have some notion of why politicians seek office. We can use knowledge gleaned from interviews, observation, and informed inquiry as a starting point to describe and understand the development of the public life, as politicians perform and react in the pursuit and assumption of office, and in pursuit of political ambitions. Linda Fowler (1993) declares that "ambition is the dirty little secret of American politics. As much as we despise politicians who openly display ambition, we could not do without them and their intense desire for political power" (186). Politically active, ambitious persons are the self-starters who make American electoral politics possible; a close examination of those ambitions and goals, and the actions that accompany their pursuit, merit our periodic and continued examination.

## Matt Dollar, Georgia, 2002

Matt Dollar is the ultimate nice guy next door. Tall, on the thin side, with curly black hair, he has the youthful appearance one associates with a young person just out of college and embarking on a career. But, unlike a management trainee at IBM or the advertising intern at Coca-Cola, Matt Dollar is on the political fast track. He just won election to the Georgia House of Representatives, and, at twenty-five, is the youngest Republican in the General Assembly from District 31.

As an undergraduate, he took advantage of the Georgia Hope scholarship, which paid for tuition and books at a state college for qualifying Georgia residents, and used the scholarship to attend the "big school" up the road, the University of Georgia. "When I went to college," Matt told me in his family's suburban Cobb County home, "I had zero interest and knowledge about politics. Then, I took the 101 government class with Paul Gurian and thought, 'I'll give this political science a try.'" He took a major in the area and also spent two semesters as an intern in the General Assembly, working for state senators on different committees. He was "just biding time" when he finished a political science degree at the University of Georgia in 2000. He joined the legislative staff of the General Assembly when "the bug bit me. As I was watching the legislative process, I started thinking, 'You know, I can see doing this in twenty years.'" Dollar developed a quick understanding of the legislative process, which activated in him a sense of public service that also hosted an inkling of political ambition.

Dollar acted on his nascent ambitions more quickly than he expected. In the summer of 2001, the legislative redistricting created a new, open seat in rapidly growing east Cobb County. Dollar had grown up in the district, and as he examined the new maps and reflected on his three years at the General Assembly as an intern and later as a professional staff member, he began to think about the things a candidate needs. "So what does a candidate need? OK, there's money. And time. And energy and stamina. You have to be able to make commitments of these things to win." Dollar did not spend a lot of money ($5,000 or so) in the first primary, and he was outspent by his other opponents. But what he did have more of than any other candidate was time and energy. "I am twenty-four years old, and I think to myself, 'I do not have a mortgage, I do not have any kids, I do not have a marriage, and I don't have a career to take care of. I have nothing but time and energy.'" And he could dedicate that time and energy to working the district to gain election. "I figured, I could dedicate two or three months just to campaigning. And, if I could do that, I might just win, because none of these other candidates could do that. I'm young and healthy. The rest of the candidates were older, and they had less time to commit. There was no way they could go door to door in a Georgia summer." The other candidates also "had run before. They had traditional connections and experience . . . so, youth and inexperience became energy and excitement. . . . People voted for me because I seemed genuine."

## Suburb of Dreams

Cobb County is one of the bastions of American conservatism. Northwest of Atlanta, straddling I-75, Cobb County is a grown-up bedroom community. Once farm country and later the site of the largest industrial manufacturer in Georgia (Lockheed), the county has developed in the last twenty years into an almost unbroken expanse of subdivisions, minimansions, and strip malls. Multilane highways follow routes that were once cow paths, and traffic is in a constant snarl, with commuters leaving earlier and earlier to get home later and later from jobs that are farther and farther away.

The county historically divided at an old landmark, the "Big Chicken" at the Colonel Sanders franchise on U.S. 41 at Roswell Road. Peter Applebome (1996) describes it aptly in *Dixie Rising*: "'West of the Chicken' traditionally meant pickups with gun-racks, old Marietta, Dobbins and Lockheed, and rock-ribbed conservatism. 'East of the Chicken' meant new cul-de-sac subdivisions, Saabs and BMWs, and the corporate transplants and endless sprawl of state-of-the-art suburbia" (36).

East Cobb is still the more affluent part of the county; this is the land of the suburban successful, of lawyers, doctors, airline pilots, corporate managers, and stay-at-home soccer moms. The homes on Columns Drive are just the tip of a very valuable real estate iceberg. West Cobb, especially to the south, is becoming more diverse; Hispanics are moving in, and the older neighborhoods that surround Marietta west of U.S. 41 pale in comparison to those in the east. Cobb had become a place where aspirant, hardworking people with conservative views congregated, far from the "urban" problems and high property taxes that plague Fulton County, just on the other side of the Chattahoochie River. It was, truly, Ronald Reagan's America, with towering white spires above huge red brick Baptist churches, "rim cities" with office towers that rival the main skyline of Atlanta, and Republican majorities of a magnitude that made that old bastion of Republicanism—Orange County, California—pale by comparison. While Democrats continued to represent Cobb in the legislature and Congress, they were a dying breed in the county by the 1990s. The county voted overwhelmingly for Ronald Reagan, George H. and George W. Bush, and Bob Dole, and Cobb was carried by every gubernatorial Republican who ran since 1990.

It was also a community with challenges, and it could not isolate itself entirely from them. Cobb developed beyond its capacity, the roads constantly clogged with traffic. The public schools are good, and while problems like methamphetamine are not rampant, there are other challenges. This community of hardworking hard-chargers had children who were four to five times more likely to be diagnosed with attention deficit/hyperactivity disorder (ADHD) and placed on Ritalin; when news of the "prescription epidemic" attracted national media attention in the 1990s, north side Atlanta and Cobb County were indicated as prime examples of a growing national phenomenon. Because of the affluence of the community, local kids were often unwilling to work in retail and service jobs, so employers had to bus in labor (Cobb refused to join the regional MARTA train and bus service in the 1970s and now finds itself largely isolated from Atlanta mass transit). Nonetheless, Cobb County was still a suburb of dreams.

District 31 took in most of east Cobb between Johnson's Ferry Road and I-75, and it was, without question, one of the most conservative legislative districts in the United States. Despite the wealth of the community and the sprawling, suburban nature of his district, Dollar got here the old-fashioned way: sweat and hard work.

## Dollar Signs

The campaign was built around family, mainly Dollar's parents and two brothers, and also friends of the family and from church. "It really was a simple campaign," he said. "We wore out the grass, doing doors, waving at cars, getting out the signs . . . campaigning a district like this is all contacting and name recognition." Matt elaborated on his activities: "You ID the likely voters and then go and ask for their votes. . . . Direct mail is also good, but the problem in a district like this is that people get so much mail, it probably just ends up getting tossed. . . . With doors, maybe you get to talk to someone, or you get to leave a little note—'Sorry I missed you, Matt'—and that means a lot around here."

By the week of the primary election, Dollar had cultivated a powerful grassroots presence. Everywhere in District 31 there were big, green Dollar signs. "I handled the signs myself, and they went up a little late, because I was trying to run under radar. I worked the doors, trying to make all the contacts I could, and then put out the signs. One day, I put up the big ones at some strategic corners we had scouted out. Then, overnight, we put out three hundred signs. They were everywhere."

Dollar was one of three young candidates from Cobb County to run for the state house in 2002.[2] In profiling these candidates, the Associated Press (AP) struck on the "fresh" theme of Dollar's campaign: " 'We have energy, insight, and fresh ideas,' said 23-year-old Democrat Alisha Thomas, who hopes to represent district 33. 'We're not just leaders of tomorrow, we're leaders of today.' . . . Dollar is running for the 31st District Seat . . . 'a lot of people think my youth, my energy is exactly what makes me qualified . . . what we're doing is bridging generations.' " The coverage is about being young, about making the young responsible, rather than about the themes and issues of the particular campaigns. As the AP noted, "The candidates are using their youth to raise voting awareness among their peers. Dollar said he made a tour of Cobb County high schools just before graduation to help about 300 seniors register to vote."[3]

Dollar received some favorable media coverage in an environment where it was tough to get covered. But that coverage was not nearly enough to win. It would be up to the candidates to make the case directly to the voters, because the media were not going to act as a vehicle for meaningful discussion of their campaigns, especially in such a huge media market. For Matt Dollar, he had to take the case to the streets.

"This campaign was all about name recognition," he said. "There are just too many races in this area to get any real ink . . . every candidate had some form of equity to run on—money, connections, experience. My equity was time."

## *Runoff Campaign*

Matt Dollar's election is the product of hard work. But, to hear him describe it, despite his hard work and determination, the victory was nonetheless surprising. Dollar readily conceded his steep learning curve as a candidate. "To be honest, I had no idea what I was doing, no idea what I was getting into. . . . In the primary, I was going on my gut . . . what I should do. In the runoff, there was more advice and guidance" from some of the back-running primary candidates and also from some other current and former politicians.

In the August Republican primary, Dollar finished second in a four-candidate field, twenty-five votes behind the front-runner, Pat Wilder. Georgia uses a majority-vote requirement to win party nominations, so Dollar and the front-runner proceeded to a runoff election in September. Dollar's strategy during the first round—building his name recognition, contacting voters, waging a campaign that emphasized his background and character rather than particular issues—resonated well with local politicos and also the eliminated candidates. "We got to the runoff with no plans and no funds. All we could do was keep going, contacting, calling. . . . We had no money left after the primary. Nothing." Help was not long in coming, however. "Immediately after the primary, I started getting calls from other candidates and people, saying, 'We want to help.' "

The front-runner, Wilder, was a fifty-one-year-old transplant from Phoenix who had lived in the metro Atlanta area for less than eight years. She had been in local government in Arizona, served in the Arizona legislature, and challenged the previous incumbent, Mitchell Kaye, in the 2000 GOP primary. In her effort to attain a legislative seat in a second state, she crafted a campaign rhetoric that set up a stark contrast to her youthful opponent. The goal was to communicate to voters that her "more than five decades of life experience, which includes . . . serving in the Arizona legislature, makes her more qualified for the job. [As she would explain while campaigning,] 'I think to serve you need to pay taxes and be involved in the community and have done something.' "[4]

With an opponent old enough to be his mother, it would be hard to keep the age issue out of the race. Wilder was out the gate running against Dollar's youth, so he in turn played his youth to his advantage. "Matt Dollar, the 24-year-old, says many of the people he's met on the campaign trail are inspired to vote for him because of his youth. He uses words like 'fresh' and 'energetic' to describe himself." In response to the criticism from his opponent that he basically had seen nothing and done nothing, he responded, " 'It's not just age. It's being able to take information and do the best with it . . . if you have to have been personally involved with every issue to be qualified, then no one is qualified for government.' "[5]

Was trashing Dollar's limited life experience sufficient in Cobb? This was a fast-growing suburb, and most people who lived here were not born here. However, many were transplants from other parts of Georgia or the South, and Matt Dollar was a local boy in an area where, despite high growth, being from there still mattered. At the very least, being from Cobb was closer to most Cobb residents than being from Arizona. Matt Dollar was born in Cobb County; he still lived in east Cobb with his parents, and his campaigning and interviews placed a heavy emphasis on nativity, locality, and community. "I grew up in the area. It's near and dear to my heart. . . . I knew I wanted to do something to serve." As Matt Dollar noted, "I had little life experience, and she tried to make an issue of it. But, her acting like her political experience in Arizona somehow mattered [here in Atlanta] did not help. It didn't matter."

Indeed, much of Wilder's campaign and presentation served to enhance that she was not from Cobb, and it did much to mobilize support for Dollar. Dollar says he previously made a pledge not to go negative and expected Wilder to also honor it, though he believes she did not. Dollar indicated that she accused him of engaging in negative and deceitful campaign practices. "Her and her husband would call me . . . trying to tell me how to campaign. At one point, she was convinced that I was tearing down her signs, and she called here and said, 'I have two big four-by-eights that say MATT DOLLAR IS TEARING DOWN MY SIGNS. Now, I don't want to have to put them up.'" If this was an effort to intimidate the young candidate, it did not work but appears to have only emboldened Matt to prevail.

Former incumbent Mitchell Kaye called and offered to help in the runoff. He gave the young candidate an endorsement and campaign advice, and he also cut an autocall endorsement for Dollar. Back-runner Mark Wortham made calls and helped with fund-raising for the runoff. At least some of the motivation for helping Dollar was driven by the ill will generated by his opponent. "A lot of people were fed up with her . . . she won't play nice," Matt said. It was part of a general mood in Georgia. Dollar, later reflecting on the 2002 campaign, noted that "negative did not work in Georgia in 2002. If you look around, every candidate who went negative—Barr, the McKinneys, Barnes—they all lost."

Age ended up being a campaign asset for Dollar. Georgia is hot and humid during the summer primary season, and Matt Dollar labored under the hot Georgia sun from first light until dark. "Being twenty-four helped a lot. At nine P.M. I can still be running from house to house; these other guys just can't do this, not in a hot Georgia summer." And he persuaded other young volunteers to come out and help his campaign. "Whenever I sent volunteers out to do door, I always tried for a girl-guy combination, a girl to talk to the men, a guy to talk to the moms . . . and, whenever I sent a group out, I always went to the neighborhood with them, so that they could say, 'We're out here with Matt Dollar.'" But doing doors is not just about walking and talking. It is about presentation and mastery of the art of the walking cards, the informative voter profiles that can be developed from voter registration and participation data. "When you do the doors," Matt remarked, "you have to know that card. Who is this person? Who is the wife? Kids? Dog? You have to have a good memory to do this."

The campaign combined energy with persuasion, and he was carrying the weight of his campaign. "I really was the campaign, and I really managed the whole thing. Signs, cash, volunteers . . . it was the last thing I thought about at night and the first thing I thought of in the morning. I have never had that happen with anything before. " He walked the hilly, pine-shaded subdivisions of Cobb County, relentlessly working doors and persuading potential primary voters to look past his age and to hear his argument.

While walking and doors were part of the plan in the runoff, Dollar modified his tactics, deemphasizing door knocking and moving toward phone contacting to turn out voters again. "What we did, is we scrubbed the walking lists real thorough. Then, we set up a phone bank of volunteers over at [a supporter's insurance office] and had fifteen phones working to call people and talk about the campaign. We determined if they were pro-Dollar, pro-Wilder, or undecided. Then, we went to work remobilizing the pros on the night before the election. We must have made two thousand phone calls . . . then, the night before the primary, as the volunteers called, I just roamed around and talked to anybody who asked."

Election night was lonely. As the returns rolled in for Dollar on September 10, his parents were at Bible study, and he was sitting at home eating Chinese food and watching election coverage. The Marietta paper had interviewed him in the afternoon and then left to spend the evening with the Wilders. Dollar's win surprised everyone, especially Pat Wilder. A photograph in the Marietta paper the next day shows a smiling Dollar (shot in the afternoon) and another photograph of an emotional, angry Wilder reacting to the news of her loss late that evening. On hearing of Matt's success, his parents came home, some friends dropped in, and an impromptu champagne party erupted to marked his success.

## But Why Do They Run?

Matt Dollar exerted and exhorted himself to his physical and emotional limits for a seat in the legislature. To do so, he endured criticism and denigration from his opponent, sleepless nights and hyperactive days in the grueling heat of an Atlanta summer. He placed his other professional dreams and ambitions on hold for an opportunity to serve as a decision maker. Was it the money? No. Once a politician gains office, he or she will find that the material rewards of political life are not nearly so great. Matt Dollar will not get rich as a legislator. The job pays $16,200 a year, and, with the budgetary crisis confronted by Georgia, one of his first votes will be on a proposal to cut legislative pay 10 percent. In addition to the pay, there is a per diem of $128 per session day and also a $7,000 office account that covers all expenses other than the secretary shared by sets of four members. For those who have money, politics is made easier by their wealth.

So, why would anyone pursue a life in elective office? The general disdain in which many Americans hold politicians detracts from any prestige motivations; as a people, we are not especially impressed with politicians as a class. Ehrenhalt (1991) says "a political career in America . . . is not easy, lucrative, or a particularly good route to status in life. This places increased importance on one other motive for entering politics: sheer enjoyment. You pretty much have to like the work" (9).

This nation has countless examples of individuals in the public service because of an issue of concern, or a desire to alter the outputs of government to address what they perceive to be social failings, or the belief that they can do the job better, and some notion of public service necessarily precedes the election to office, if only because the nature of the work—social problem solving—and the meager financial returns from legislating cause those with avarice in their hearts to look elsewhere for satisfaction and sustenance. Max Weber (1965) advanced a similar duality of the pursuit of public station, that "one lives off politics, or one lives for politics." Under this definition, either politics as a career is pursued as an ends to sustain one's self, like any other profession; or, alternatively, there is a political animal, a person who engages in civic life because he or she cannot imagine doing anything else and who serves for a variety of motives that defy fiscal security. Politicians who live for politics are like sharks in the sea: if they do not swim, they do not breathe.

If we assume, for the moment, that the pursuit of office is for the purpose of wielding political power, a further distinction can be made in the rationale for the pursuit of political office. In describing the behavior of legislators in office, David Mayhew (1974) advanced three motivations for the service in Congress: policymaking, the pursuit of institutional power, and the pursuit of sustained reelection. To these Richard Fenno (1996) adds a fourth: the pursuit of progressive ambitions. Politicians run to seek higher station, higher office, and to further their ambitions. Are those varying motivations present at the beginning of the career? According to David Canon (1990), they are, and the differences in motivation are related to subsequent political success. Canon observes that, while prior officeholders most often made the jump to Congress, there were sizeable numbers of nonofficeholders who also managed high lateral entry. Some are "ambitious" amateurs, some are "policy" amateurs, and others are "hopeless" amateurs. Ambitious amateurs were more often successful than policy amateurs, indicating that the policy motive was secondary to the larger, personal motives of ambition. To succeed, the passion for the job should go beyond the desire to pursue a particular policy and be rooted in an intensive desire for office that transcends issues.

It is not entirely surprising, then, that Matt Dollar, a smart candidate elected from a well-educated, prosperous district, had a campaign virtually devoid of issues. We expect such candidates and constituencies to be issue driven or at least issue aware. An examination of the campaign record and conversations with Dollar reveal that issues never really came up in the district, in part because it was so homogenous and because there was widespread agreement about major issues of concern. "Pat [Wilder] ran on water . . . and water is going to be an important issue here in the future," Matt told me. "But what everyone in this district is concerned about is good education, low taxes—it helped that we were running right after everyone got their property reassessments—and transit issues." But those issues do not come up on the campaign trail. Dollar emphasized himself and his personal qualities as reasons to vote for him: "It's funny you asked, 'Give me three reasons to vote for you,' because the conventional wisdom is that three reasons is all most voters will listen to before losing attention. When I talked to people, the three reasons to vote for me were (1) I'll work hard, (2) I'm a product of the community, and (3) I'm accessible." With regard to the issues of the community, Dollar was in line with his district. But he sees a limit to strict issue campaigning: "You have to sell yourself. Issues are an accessory to you. These are not your identity."

Matt was down-to-earth about his new status: "I know who are my friends. . . . Johnny Isakson [congressman from Georgia's Sixth District] told me, 'It's not your hand they're kissing—it's the ring.'" The other problem is the speculation, about his political present and about his political future. "You know, the one thing about winning this young is that people figure it must be part of a plan. And they start speculating about what is next. . . . I'm ten days old in this job." Does that mean that Matt Dollar would not accept a seat in Congress, even at zero cost? "No, not now," Dollar observed to me. "I am not qualified, and I would do a disservice to my constituency by going. . . . Maybe, in twenty years, if all the pieces fell into place, if I could be effective and competitive, then I would go." Even then, it is contingent on family. "I wouldn't go if I had a five-year-old . . . family has to come first. Maybe . . . when my family becomes more independent." Even in the context of the 180-member state house, Dollar is modest about his ambitions. "Right now, what I do is strive for the respect of my colleagues . . . I do not need to lead now. Later, when I'm ready, but not now." He quickly adds that "this wasn't part of a plan. I am not trying to jockey for a higher position."

## Careers in Context

To evaluate political events and political actors requires an understanding of not just the actor and event but also the broader circumstances surrounding the actors and events, in space and time. Fenno (1978) observes that "you cannot know what you want to know of [a politician] until you have knowledge of . . . context. By knowledge, I mean to include what you learn by looking at the context yourself and what you learn by seeing the context through the eyes of the individual politician" (quoted in Fowler and McClure 1989: 25). Context is actually a collection of several circumstances, each of which in turn encompass numerous actions and decisions of politicians, in space and time. Fowler and McClure (1989) contend that "every opportunity . . . comes wrapped in a context—those few undeniable realities of time and place that provide a modicum of order to an otherwise topsy-turvy political world" (25). These contexts matter because they affect the decision to seek office, actions in office, and decisions to move on from the current office: "Would-be candidates first assess the risks of a political campaign . . . they begin with the campaign's context not only because of the concrete structure it lends to their decision making but also because the context of a campaign naturally works to the advantage of some politicians and to the disadvantage of others" (Fowler and McClure 1989: 25).

Numerous political scientists have found that campaigns and careers are affected by circumstances. Sandy Maisel and his collaborators (1998) found candidate political decisions were affected by strategic factors that influence winning and losing and also personal factors. Thomas Kazee (1994) cites a broader set of influences that were sufficiently well defined to differentiate the influences on candidate decisions and sufficiently holistic to encompass most influences on career decisions. These several contexts—structural, personal, eligibility, competitive, resource—could all influence the decisions of individual candidates to seek office. If we reflect on Matt Dollar's decision to run, we can see that the act is rife with contextual considerations; furthermore, to understand the origin and development of a political career requires understanding contexts. These contexts also affect legislator behavior and reelection decisions.

The context of *access* determines the extent to which an office allows entry via multiple avenues or whether one group (or a small set of groups) determine who will run. Do parties still have control over the local selection process? Are there local social and political elites who recruit candidates? Is there a "waiting list" to run for a seat, and are there informal sanctions for jumping the queue?

Another influence on the pursuit of ambition is the effect of *structure*. Structure includes the defining characteristics of the constituency, characteristics of the legislative body, the "opportunity structure" for higher office (and the role of *this* office in that opportunity structure), and election laws that concern eligibility and resources or that govern the potential electorate. For the new candidate, the choice of office through which to pursue her aspirations is a product of the level of aspiration at the time of the decision and the benefits to pursuing office at the time (see also Powell, Niemi, and Carey 1998). When Matt Dollar was bitten by the political bug, he saw the opportunity as distant, because of his perception of the structural context and other contexts. Redistricting, and his experience on the inside of the General Assembly, altered his understanding of the structural context and the opportunity structure.

Once in office, the pursuit of further ambition is mitigated by the costs of giving up the current office, the investment in effort and reputation in the current office that makes a run for another office possible, or the perception that further pursuit will advance the power, prestige, or policy goal of the individual. The institution of the legislature can affect these decisions, in part because of the opportunities those institutions afford to politicians (Squire 1988, 1992). Gary Moncrief and Joel Thompson (1992) point out that there are three distinct structural dimensions to state legislatures: recruitment and retention, task specialization and the division of labor, and authority distribution within the chamber and among members. Matt Dollar exists on the first dimension. The legislature as an organization exists between an external environment—the state it governs and the constituents of the members—and as an internal environment, to meet the internal needs of members of the organization. The ability to satisfy members' professional career needs or the needs of their progressive ambition affects who runs for (and serves in) the institution. This second, mediating role is one which candidates will consider when evaluating the value of candidacy and membership.

Gordon Black (1972) found that political structure and the costs and benefits of different options affected the choices of politicians. Politicians with ambition for higher office consider such a move based on the risks associated with such a move, and the political assets of the current office which can be brought to bear in pursuit of higher office. Fenno (1978) describes such politicians as "both goal-seeking and situation-interpreting individuals." The benefits of a higher office must outweigh the benefits of staying put, given the probability of victory.

Ambitions are often curtailed by nonpolitical demands that are part of the *personal* context. These are numerous and varied, and they often find themselves lumped together because they are not structural or political. These influences include family considerations, career demands, health, the will to run, and the ability to handle the pressures and personal barbs which accompany the political campaign. Survey data of over six hundred candidates for state legislative office indicate that, of all the influences on the decision to run, family is singularly important (Hogan 1995). As indicated in table 1.1, family was the most important in affecting the decision to run. Among young candidates, local political organizations influenced the decision of some of them to run, while older candidates were more often influenced by state and legislative party organizations or, sometimes, by interest groups. The party

Table 1.1   Influences on the Candidate's Decision to Run for State Legislature

| Candidate Age | Family (%) | County Party (%) | State Party (%) | Legislative Party (%) | National Party (%) | Interest Group (%) |
|---|---|---|---|---|---|---|
| Under 35 (n = 103) | 68.9 | 19.4 | 12.6 | 13.6 | 3.9 | 5.8 |
| 35–55 (n = 369) | 73.2 | 23.1 | 17.6 | 22.8 | 1.9 | 17.1 |
| Over 55 (n = 136) | 70.6 | 22.1 | 24.3 | 33.1 | 4.4 | 19.9 |

Source: Hogan (1995).
Note: Percentage indicates influence was "very important" or "extremely important."

organizations' roles are nonetheless subordinate to family and personal factors.

What are the personal consequences of running? Are they a factor? Rohde (1979) and Prewitt (1970; see also Prewitt and Nowlin 1969) find that potential officeholders consider changes in personal income or other costs to their career and livelihood in weighing possible runs for office. Black (1972) suggests that time and effort are also costs, a perspective reconfirmed by Maisel et al. (1998). Matt Dollar intuited these same observations and articulated them in describing his candidacy. He had no competing challenges, making time his greatest asset. This freedom made it easy to run. But, as Dollar noted when quizzed about progressive political ambitions, family considerations weigh against the pursuit of progressive political ambition.

Then, there is *eligibility*: Who can really win? Once, governing was the province of white men, and white men still hold most elective posts in most states. Some state legislatures are far more open to female or minority candidacies than others. From state to state, the need of minority candidates to rely on minority populations to win offices varies, though most Hispanic and black legislators represent districts with substantial minority populations. Age can be a factor. States such as Wisconsin or Maine are far more receptive to young legislators than, say, Nebraska. In this case from Georgia, despite the efforts of other politicians to make age a factor in the eligibility context, youth and energy overcame cunning and old age. Pat Wilder surmised that age was a part of the eligibility context in Georgia, while voters indicated otherwise.[6]

Does it help to "be from here" when you run? Prior research says nativity is not a prerequisite to serve, but it does not hurt. Moncrief and Thompson (1992) found that about one-third of state legislators were not native to their state. Nativity and eligibility vary by state, with nativity being lowest in Alaska and highest in Oklahoma. In the Matt Dollar–Pat Wilder campaign, the election occurred in an environment where nativity was relatively low but where localism and nativity were generally viewed favorably.

One cannot seek office without *resources*. This context varies across states, across structural contexts, and among candidates. In modern American politics, money is clearly the most important resource (e.g., Thompson and Moncrief 1998). Even in state legislative contests, expert assistance is increasingly used, and this expertise does not come cheap. Volunteer support and the strength of a candidate organization is another resource, though volunteer-based campaigns are slowly disappearing (Monroe 2001). The evaluation of opposition resources also enters this equation, as does the potential influence of party or other independent, organizational resources. Dollar marshaled financial support and tapped his network of friends, family, and church congregation to field successful challenges under circumstances where he was not expected to win.

The resource context looms large in the formulation of campaigns. Among all candidates surveyed by Robert Hogan (1995), resources clearly were the most important factor in affecting how the campaign was waged. Young candidates were most sensitive to the resource context. Almost 80 percent of all primary and general election candidates indicated that financial resources were very important or extremely important to the development of their campaign strategy. The proportion of young candidates placing such emphasis on resources was only three to six points higher than the proportion among other candidate cohorts (see table 1.2).

Resources are more important to candidates in shaping campaign strategy than the perceived reaction of voters to the strategy, and they are more important than the actions of the opposition in affecting campaign strategy; this is especially so for young candidates. In primaries and general elections, candidates under thirty-five placed less emphasis on voter reactions to their campaign activities and message, though voter reaction was nonetheless an important consideration. Younger candidates were more likely than other candidates to consider the opposition in developing a primary strategy (34.7

**Table 1.2   Age and Development of Campaign Strategy**

| Candidate Age | Opposition (%) | Voter Reaction (%) | Financial Resources (%) |
|---|---|---|---|
| Primary | | | |
| Under 35 (n = 45) | 34.7 | 60.9 | 82.6 |
| 35–55 (n = 147) | 29.9 | 70.7 | 76.2 |
| Over 55 (n = 44) | 22.7 | 70.4 | 79.5 |
| General Election | | | |
| Under 35 (n = 64) | 21.9 | 51.6 | 81.3 |
| 35–55 (n = 270) | 29.3 | 68.5 | 77.0 |
| Over 55 (n = 103) | 31.1 | 69.9 | 78.6 |

Source: Hogan (1995).
Note: Numbers represent percentage of cases answering that the factor was "very important" or "extremely important" to the development of the campaign strategy.

percent vs. 28.2 percent of the older candidates), yet they were less likely to consider the opposition in formulating a general election strategy (21.9 percent vs. 29.8 percent of the older candidates). Ultimately, though, it was money that mattered.

In their description of context, Fowler and McClure (1989) advance a definition reflective of the *competitive* context of the district, stating that "context is fairly objective: it is the product of a district's party registration figures, election results, political geography, and media market. Also part of the political context are the laws and standard practices that govern campaign finance and party nominations" (25). Related to context, in their eyes, was also the broader backdrop of the general political environment for the state or nation, or what are also termed the trends and tides in politics that might affect a campaign.

Potential candidates must consider the prospect of winning. Is the seat open and potentially competitive, or is an incumbent and her advantages looming over the decision (e.g., Maisel and Stone 1997; Stone and Maisel 2003)? Is the district competitive or the province of one-party politics? Are there major media markets and media outlets that need to be accessed to campaign successfully?

Finally, another part of the competitive context is the major, sweeping political forces in the state or nation that could influence competition and voter choices on the basis of party (Campbell 1997). Breaux and Jewell (1992) observe that those contexts differ in state legislative contests when compared to congressional elections, because state legislative candidates usually have less party support, spend far less money, and more often have more homogenous districts than congressional candidates. Their contests, while not immune to national political tides, are more isolated (Campbell 1997). But, much like congressional elections, both reelection seeking and reelection winning increased in state legislatures after the 1960s, and legislative incumbents became competitive, while legislative elections in general became less competitive. The decline of competition is not entirely the fault of incumbents, though. Tucker and Weber (1992) observe that there is "growing electoral stability" in the states (see also Moncrief, Squire, and Kurtz 1998). Again, in the case of Dollar we see the competitive context affecting the decisions to run.

## Plan of the Book

Matt Dollar has given us a glimpse into the beginning of a political career, a glimpse into a successful first campaign. His career in Georgia was entirely prospective. But this was his beginning, the start of a series of events in public life that would shape his personal, professional, and political future. A place like this is where we start to understand the political career, especially the careers of those who will be our future national leaders. The careers that are most often studied by political scientists are congressional careers, to which many might aspire but which few attain. There are benefits for understanding the future political career from starting at the beginning, because of the large number of both recent and historic politicians who started young.

This book is a report from the field, an effort to describe the story of the beginning of the political career. Most of the material in this book was gathered firsthand, through field observation and interviews with politicians. Other materials were collected from the public record, including media coverage and the proceedings of legislative bodies. Still other information was gathered from previous studies of legislators, candidates, and political activists, which helps inform us about those who hold political ambitions.

Studying young politicians requires the effort of going to their politics. There are so few of them. Moncrief et al. (1998) six-state study of state legislative candidate recruitment found that only 3 to 8 percent of nonincumbent candidates were under age thirty. Carey et al. (2000) comprehensive study of state legislators revealed fewer than three hundred legislators nationwide under thirty-five. Only about a sixth of the respondents to Hogan's (1995) survey of state legislative candidates were under thirty-five. A young candidate or a young legislator are rarities. The offices sought by young candidates receive limited press coverage. In addition, these campaigns occur in small constituencies. Despite their limited visibility and small constituencies, however, the young are running, winning, and advancing in politics.

These careers are studied through the lenses of political ambition and the contexts identified by previous scholarship as important to affecting the pursuit of progressive ambition. Where possible, observations on ambition and careers that are made in the cases are supplemented with survey data of activists, officeholders, and state legislative candidates. These analyses reveal that while there is much ambition at the beginning of the political career, there is also much uncertainty. Progressive ambitions diminish quickly in the human life cycle, and young candidates are distinct in many respects from others who seek public office. There is a lot of shaping and development going on in the minds of politicians in their twenties and early thirties, and the events and decisions in their lives at that time shape their political futures.

This book departs from other studies of ambition and careers in that it goes to the beginning, before ambitions crystallize. Studies of political careers and political ambition are usually exercises in backward mapping. One looks at the successful candidates for the highest offices and sees who fails or succeeds in moving up. Most of the scholarship on moving up is about congressmen jumping to the Senate or senators considering the presidency, or about ambitions for Congress or ambitions in Congress. Only recently have political scientists looked into the ambitions within state legislators (e.g., Maestas 2000a, 2000b). In other words, most of the ambition scholarship is about politicians who have established careers and who are in the midst of pursuing crystallized, progressive ambitions. This book is an effort to flip the process on its head and go into the campaigns and careers of young politicians at the dawn of the political career, when their prospects for success are uncertain. We start with ambition, for the political office that most often starts progressive political careers—the state legislature—and use the pursuit of that office and the career by young, relatively noncredentialed individuals as a starting point to observe the creation of the career and the evolution of ambition.

We have visited with Matt Dollar, and we will briefly meet with him again toward the end of the book. The balance of this study is an exploration of the origins and development of the ambitions and political careers of eight other individuals. First, in chapter 2, a variety of data sources are surveyed to establish the distinctive ambitions held by the young persons in politics. Then, in chapter 3, we take a more careful look into the precampaign and campaign of a candidate for the state house of representatives in Oklahoma, Shane Hunt. Chapter 4 examines the long fight by Wisconsin Republican Joe Handrick to achieve state legislative office and then recounts his decision to leave office after three terms due to changing aspects of both his personal life and his life in the legislature.

Chapter 5 explores in greater depth the legislative socialization and emergence of Adrian Smith, a senator in the Nebraska Unicameral, recounting an observation on Smith's careful socialization to the legislature and then examining his emergence as an effective legislator on issues related to legalized gambling. Chapter 6 relates the election of Thad Balkman, a young attorney, over a vulnerable incumbent in Oklahoma; his efforts to legislate as a minority Republican representing a marginal district; and his rematch with the former incumbent he had previously vanquished.

In chapter 7, we meet Stephanie Stuckey-Benfield, a lawyer in the male-dominated Georgia General Assembly. Her story is that of a political legacy, the daughter of a congressman who grew up in a successful political family and is now consolidating her position and developing a reputation as a legislative force. Chapter 8 examines the brief, meteoric legislative career of Mike Saxl, now a former state representative from Maine. Elected at age twenty-seven, Saxl became whip at twenty-nine, floor leader at thirty-one, and speaker of the house at thirty-three, before being forced from office by term limits at age thirty-five. His story is not just of his career but of his influence in shaping policy and politics as a young leader.

Chapter 9 examines the election, legislative career, and political advancement of Kenneth Corn. Corn was elected state representative at twenty-one, became a committee chairman at twenty-three, and advanced to the state senate at twenty-five. Then, in chapter 10, we meet Jon Bruning, a lawyer from Nebraska. Bruning left a six-figure career to run for the Unicameral at twenty-six and then won a landslide election to become attorney general at thirty-two. His career is a study in both his intense personal ambitions and his tireless efforts to reform the death penalty laws of Nebraska. Chapter 11 draws conclusions from the cases and explores the shaping of political careers.

## Notes

1. "Over Half Million Elected Officials in U.S.," *Campaigns and Elections* (May 1996): 54. This figure includes primaries and runoffs.

2. The others were Alisha Thomas (who also won election as the first black representative from Cobb County) and Jeff Fuller, who was making a second effort for a seat.

3. Associated Press, "Three Candidates under 25 Vie for House Seats in Cobb," July 1, 2002.

4. Associated Press, "Three Candidates."

5. Mia Taylor, "Battle of the Ages: Foes in House District 31 Say Differences in Birth Dates Is Important," *Atlanta Journal-Constitution*, August 29 2002, 31F.

6. Wilder's husband was aware that youth could win in Cobb County. He was bested for reelection by a twenty-seven-year-old K-Mart clerk, Steve Clark, in a GOP primary.

# Life Cycles and Ambitions 2

When are you going to get out and give us young fellows a chance?
—Tip O'Neill to Boston mayor James Michael Curley, 1948

THE CONCEPT OF POLITICAL AMBITION and careers permeates the study of legislative politics. Thomas Kazee (1994) notes that three broad theoretic perspectives are typically advanced for examining the involvement of individuals in politics: the sociological perspective, the psychological perspective, and the rationalist-based ambition theory. Sociological theories of candidacies, typified by Donald Matthews's (1954, 1960) studies of candidates and representation, argue that leaders are drawn from certain groups of candidates; such scholarship focused on the attributes of leaders, and in many ways is rooted in defining the eligibility context for public office by answering the question "Who can *really* win?" James David Barber's (1965) *The Lawmakers* is a psychological examination of character development, drawing on early life experiences or the satiation of personal needs to explain politician roles. Then, there is ambition theory. Political ambition theory presumes that all politicians have motivations for office. The question that ambition theory has been a vehicle for answering is "Why do people run?" Then, once people win office, students of ambition theory turn to another question: "How do people use their office to fulfill their ambitions?"

## Ambition's Avenues

The earliest expression of ambition theory in modern political science was Joseph Schlesinger's (1966) *Ambition and Politics.* Schlesinger observed that political ambition manifests in three forms: discrete, static, and progressive. *Discrete* ambition is the most limiting. The politician seeks a particular office for a limited period of time; then, much like Cincinnatus returning to the plow, he or she retires. Discrete ambition embodies in the minds of some the "classic" notions of American politics: duty for the sake of duty, a limited tenure of office, and then a return to private life.

*Static* ambition is demonstrated by candidates who obtain an office and then seek to perpetuate their incumbency. They have reached their level of political competence or satisfaction and do not seek higher office. While this was initially the least studied form of ambition, often treated as a null condition against which to test progressive ambition, position maintenance is the most common form of ambition. The gross assumption of static ambition masks the presence of other ambitions by mistakenly assuming that staying at the same level of office is an indication of a lack of political goals or personal ambitions.[1]

The final form, *progressive* ambition, is the form of ambition that captures the attention of political scientists, especially the students of congressional campaigns (e.g., Kazee 1994; Stone et al. 1998; Stone and Maisel 2003). Who are the politicians who seek higher office? What motivates them? When do they decide to run for higher office, and when do they defer? Then, there is another question, never explicitly answered by this scholarship: When and how do ambitions change?

Few politicians are compelled to serve against their will (Barber 1988, 1965). Individuals in elective office have some rationale—power, policy, or personal matters of ego—that compelled them to pursue the office. Schlesinger summed up this position when he observed that "the most reasonable assumption is that ambition for office, like most other ambitions, develops with a specific situation, that it is a response to the possibilities which lie before the politician" (7). The individual, as politician, must decide that the office and the timing are such that whatever personal, policy, or political goals he seeks are satisfied by a campaign for a specific office. It is about goals and context.

Some candidates come to politics with definite progressive ambitions, with "the plan." When we examine individuals who do not yet hold public office, such as young politicians, we should expect them to exhibit progressive ambition. It is after attaining office that ambition should become more defined, or at the very least it should evolve from the original ambition held in the heart to an ambition defined by the context and opportunities of their political existence. But, they must prove that they can stay in office to pursue their ambitions.

Why do people start out so early in elective politics? It is not easy to get elected. The prestige and financial rewards are limited. And the work is demanding. Why do we find people like Matt Dollar running for office? A commitment to service is certainly one reason, but there are many ways to serve that demand less personal and financial sacrifice. Given the earning potential and the career opportunities for bright people starting in their twenties and the costs to other careers that accompany the pursuit of elective politics, the young person who seeks and wins elective office is making a long-term career choice; there are benefits foregone in other careers and opportunity costs to being in elective office that mitigate against pursuing parallel careers (Eulau and Sprague 1964). Perhaps it is because early-life office holding is important to later political prospects. To have a progressive elective career means starting young, especially if one wants to go "all the way" to the U.S. Senate or governorship, offices that represent the pinnacle of attainable political ambition for most politicians.

## Experience That Matters

Studies of legislative elections repeatedly confirm that previous office holding has value in the pursuit of future office. Or, to put it another way, if you want to see the governors, congresspeople, and senators of the future, go look in the state legislature. Many legislators see themselves as a future something-else:

> "A state legislator is, by definition, a good candidate" . . . [said a New York legislative freshman]. "My friends in the Assembly . . . think of themselves as congressmen-in-waiting." A state senator voices similar sentiments: "it's a logical sequence. I started out thir-teen years ago in the county legislature, and after five terms in the Senate, [Congress] is the next logical step." (Fowler and McClure 1989: 75)

State legislators have such innate value as higher-level candidates because there is direct value of prior office. Campaign experience, the ability to claim political and governing skill, name recognition, and the existence of previous campaign organizations or support networks all have direct value in seeking higher office. There is also indirect value in terms of the ability to parlay these skills and attributes into fund-raising and the discouraging of potential opponents. There experiences are "valuable to those who aspire to national office, because lawmakers in the state capital learn to deal with complex issues, bargain, and tend a constituency" (Fowler and McClure 1989: 74), and they are also indicators of future performance in congressional office (Canon 1990). For these various reasons, state legislatures are presumed to be the cradle of careers, where politicians with ambitions go to learn the trade.

History is replete with examples of the use of the legislature as a stepping-stone by both obscure and prominent lawmakers. The obscure are too numerous to name. Among the prominent, Franklin Delano Roosevelt, four times elected president, sought his first political office as state senator in New York, running in his twenties for a legislative seat. As Arthur Schlesinger (1957) penned in the FDR biography, *Crisis of the Old Order*:

> One day in 1907, as the clerks were chatting about their ambitions, Roosevelt explained with "engaging frankness" that he planned to run for political office at the first opportunity and that he wanted to be President . . . first the state Assembly, then Assistant Secretary

of the Navy, then Governor of New York. "Anyone who is Governor of New York," [Grenville] Clark recalls Roosevelt saying, "has a good chance to be president with any luck." (330)

Either his ambitions became known or his innate qualities caught the attention of others in politics, for Roosevelt found himself sought out. He consulted with family and friends, including his cousin Teddy (the former president) before finally deciding, at a Democratic beer and clam picnic in Poughkeepsie, to make the run (Schlesinger 1957: 330–31). Roosevelt subsequently became assistant secretary of the navy, governor of New York in 1928, and president in 1932.

The FDR example is exceptional, if only because most state legislators do not run for higher office or harbor progressive ambitions. In their 1957 survey of state legislator behavior, Eulau and Walke found that few state legislators harbored ambitions for higher office. Carey et al. (2000) surveyed the progressive ambitions of state legislators four decades later and found that among state legislators in the 1990s, many of whom confront term limits, similarly few state legislators expressed progressive ambitions. Most state legislators do not see themselves as performing on a larger political stage. Nonetheless, though few aspire to run, a significant proportion of the members of Congress have state legislative experience, and many representatives, senators, and governors in the United States were not only state legislators but also party floor leaders and presiding officers in their state legislatures (Squire 1992). The path to institutional power in states can also be the path of progressive ambition.

When one looks at young candidacies for the legislature, the first thing one observes is that most of these candidates will lose. Many will not seek office again. Many of those who win will not progress to other offices. But if we look to the future, it is from among these young entrepreneurs that we will draw the leadership of the future. Joseph Schlesinger observed that two windows of opportunity existed to enter public office: one point of entry was in the late twenties and early thirties, the other in the late forties and early fifties. In table 2.1, summaries are presented of the ages at which the U.S. senators and governors initially won their first public office, for 1977 and 1995. Major statewide officeholders had incredibly early starts to their elective careers.

Of the 150 senators and governors in office in 1995, over half were elected to public office before age thirty-five, and fully a third were in office before age thirty. A sizeable number (12 percent) were elected to office before age twenty-seven. Many of these individuals won office as early as age twenty-one. Two decades earlier, in 1977, over 60 percent of senators and governors were under thirty-five when initially elected to public office, and, again, a third were under age thirty and 16 percent were under age twenty-

Table 2.1    The Youthful Origins of American Governors and Senators

| Age of First Electoral Win | 1977 Cohort | | 1995 Cohort | |
|---|---|---|---|---|
| | n | % | n | % |
| 20–27 | 24 | 16.0 | 18 | 12.0 |
| 28–30 | 26 | 17.3 | 32 | 21.3 |
| 31–34 | 42 | 28.0 | 29 | 19.3 |
| 35–45 | 40 | 26.7 | 40 | 26.7 |
| 45-plus | 17 | 11.3 | 31 | 20.8 |
| Under 35 | 93 | 61.3 | 79 | 52.6 |

Source: Compiled by author.

seven. For individuals who were seeking to "go all the way," the early assumption of a political career and the massive amount of political experience related to that career choice were reflected in success in achieving major elective office, especially the U.S. Senate.

Part of the decline from 1977 to 1995 in the number of politicians who started their electoral careers before age thirty-five can be attributed to the continued opening of the structure of political opportunities. It is easier to attain high elective office without previously holding low elective office. According to David Canon (1990), the political process has become more open to "amateurs," especially ambitious amateurs who have the resources or celebrity to achieve initial success in pursuit of high office. Prior political office holding is less of a prerequisite for high office than in the past. Political amateurs are especially advantaged in high-stimulus, high-profile elections that favor one party over the other. The large number of such elections in recent years, in which the balance of new members favored one party, means that many individuals who wanted political careers but who did not have early career experience were nonetheless able to gain eventual election to high office. This pattern has received tremendous attention in recent years, as superrich candidates such as Jon Corzine, Michael Huffington, and Michael Bloomberg have spent tremendous personal fortunes in pursuit of high-profile public offices. Despite the declining frequency of the low office as an avenue of entry for those who aspire to high office, most high officials had prior office-holding experience, and, at the very highest levels, a majority of officeholders initially held office before age thirty-five.

## Life Cycles and Ambitions

What we know about young candidates is rather limited and comes largely from the study of congressional campaigns. Young candidates are attracted to competitive races. Robert Huckshorn and Robert Spencer (1971), in their study of congressional candidacies in the 1960s, observe that younger candidates more often emerge when the odds of victory are good, such as when there is an open seat or a vulnerable incumbent, and they run more effective campaigns than older candidates. So why are younger candidates attracted to serve, and why do they do well? Fowler and McClure (1989: 142–43) conclude that the physical demands of campaigning are less tasking for young candidates and that the prospect of relocation is less daunting for an individual or couple in their thirties than a more established person or couple in their fifties. Presumably, thirty-somethings who make the jump in office also have made previous lifestyle choices that indicated progressive political careers. It is also possible that the ambitions of those in their twenties and early thirties are different from the ambitions of the middle-aged.

Is there a life cycle to ambition? Life cycle effects in career ambitions were observed in state executive officers several decades ago (Swinerton 1968). Interviews with fifty subgubernatorial-level state executives in states with strong governors' offices revealed that younger executives possessed greater progressive ambition and engaged in strategic behavior associated with progressive ambition.

There are also distinct life cycle differences in holding progressive ambitions. Swinerton observes that officeholders over fifty-five were far less likely to see themselves as governor and far less likely to engage in activities associated with networking, building a following, and in advancing one's self. Observations of congressional candidates indicated that politicians in their thirties made better congressional challengers (Huckshorn and Spencer 1971). Taken together, these two findings framed a conventional wisdom that the window of opportunity for advancement to major office was somewhere between the midthirties and early fifties. Furthermore, it was also reasonable to assume that during this time period, both progressive ambitions and the ability to wage an intensive challenge for major office reach an apex.

One can see, in a variety of original data sources, evidence of a life cycle effect on the holding of progressive ambitions. For instance, in table 2.2, data on Democratic and Republican Party activists are presented from the Southern Party Grassroots Activist project. This survey of over eleven thousand activists in the South revealed that both prior experience and future political ambition varied across the life cycle, with experience being the province of

Table 2.2   Experiences and Ambitions in the South among Grassroots Activists

| Age | Prior Office | Future Run |
|-----|------------|-----------|
| Under 35 (n = 1,473) | 14.3 | 31.7 |
| 35–55 (n = 4,588) | 19.5 | 21.6 |
| Over 55 (n = 5,410) | 21.4 | 8.7 |

*Source:* Hadley et al. (1992).

older activists and ambition being held mainly by younger ones. Among those respondents under the age of thirty-five, only one in seven held office at the time of the study, but almost one in three—31.7 percent—viewed him- or herself as a future candidate for public office. The opposite was the case among activists over fifty-five, where over 20 percent of activists held or had held office, but only 8.7 percent saw themselves making a future run for some other political office.

Looking elsewhere, Herrera and Miller's (1995) study of national political convention delegates inquired as to both the office-holding status of delegates and the ambitions for state, national, and local office. In table 2.3, the responses are broken into office-holding delegates and non-office-holding delegates. Progressive political ambition was widely held in the delegate population, but it was mainly concentrated among officeholders and those under thirty-five. Among the office-holding delegates under thirty-five, only 17 percent reported no ambition for other political office, and most indicated either state or national political ambitions. While ambitions for national office (congressional or senatorial) did not fall off appreciably among those between thirty-five and fifty-five—it actually increased slightly—static ambition was higher among the older cohort of delegates, while ambition for state office was seventeen points lower. Among those officeholders over fifty-five, static ambition is most prevalent, with 63 percent of officeholders reporting no progressive ambition and with respondents more likely to have state office ambitions than national ambitions.

Nonofficeholders display different patterns of ambition holding, though

**Table 2.3   Future Political Ambitions: 1992 Political Convention Delegates**

| Age | Level of Office | | | |
| --- | --- | --- | --- | --- |
| | National | State | Local | None |
| Officeholders | | | | |
| Under 35 (n = 70) | 30.0 | 45.7 | 7.1 | 17.1 |
| 35–55 (n = 438) | 31.9 | 28.5 | 8.6 | 30.8 |
| Over 55 (n = 341) | 10.9 | 18.2 | 7.9 | 63.0 |
| Not in Office | | | | |
| Under 35 (n = 275) | 23.2 | 24.7 | 17.1 | 34.9 |
| 35–55 (n = 1,052) | 9.6 | 16.9 | 13.9 | 59.6 |
| Over 55 (n = 627) | 2.2 | 7.5 | 8.1 | 82.1 |
| All Delegates | | | | |
| Under 35 (n = 345) | 24.6 | 28.9 | 15.1 | 31.3 |
| 35–55 (n = 1,490) | 16.2 | 20.3 | 12.3 | 51.1 |
| Over 55 (n = 968) | 5.3 | 11.3 | 8.1 | 75.4 |
| Total (n = 2,803) | 13.4 | 18.3 | 7.6 | 57.1 |

Source: Herrera and Miller (1995).

the life cycle differences in ambition for political office were present. Delegates over fifty-five who do not hold office were largely without ambitions for political office (over 80 percent reported no ambitions), while just about 35 percent of such delegates under thirty-five have no office-holding ambitions. Delegates over thirty-five were far more modest about the heights of their ambitions, with fewer than one in four expressing a desire for national or state office. Nonofficeholders in this group had greater ambitions for local office than their office-holding counterparts. The same patterns are evident among non-office-holders in the sample. The frequency of ambition for national office falls from 23.2 percent among those under thirty-five, to 9.6 percent among those between thirty-five and fifty-five, to just 2.2 percent among those over fifty-five. A similar pattern is observed with state office ambitions. Overall, delegates under the age of thirty-five were twice as likely as other delegates to harbor ambitions for state or national office, and the rate was almost three times as great as the rest of the delegate population among young officeholders.

What about state legislators? Surely state legislators have ambitions! If we examine the Carey et al. (2000) survey of state legislators, the age pattern of ambition again emerges (table 2.4). Among current incumbents who returned the survey, nearly half of the state legislators under thirty-five said they might run for Congress in the future, just under 40 percent might run for statewide office, and over 46 percent said they might run for the other legislative chamber in the state. Only one in seven showed indications of "downward" ambition to local office.

Legislators between thirty-five and fifty-five in the Carey et al. study had generally lower levels of future political ambition. One in five indicated a desire to run for Congress, one in four indicated a possible run for statewide office, and just over one in five said they might run for the other legislative

**Table 2.4   Future Ambitions and the Life Cycle**

| Age | Congress | Statewide | Local | Other Chamber |
|---|---|---|---|---|
| | *Level of Office* | | | |
| Incumbent State Legislators | | | | |
| Under 35 (*n* = 239) | 49.8 | 38.9 | 14.6 | 46.4 |
| 35–55 (*n* = 1666) | 20.6 | 26.0 | 12.8 | 21.7 |
| Over 55 (*n* = 1068) | 3.8 | 5.4 | 8.8 | 8.7 |
| Former State Legislators | | | | |
| Under 35 (*n* = 25) | 48.0 | 44.0 | 16.0 | — |
| 35–55 (*n* = 294) | 17.0 | 22.8 | 16.7 | — |
| Over 55 (*n* = 250) | 3.6 | 4.8 | 11.2 | — |

*Source:* Carey et al. (2000).

body. These rates are consistently and significantly lower than the rates of ambition for other offices held by younger legislators.

Among legislators over fifty-five, progressive ambitions are generally absent, and the ambitions expressed by those respondents skew away from the national stage and instead tend toward the local arena. Ambitions for statewide, congressional, and state legislative office run five to twelve times higher among younger politicians compared to their more venerable colleagues. Among former state legislators, a remarkably similar pattern emerges; the distribution of future ambitions for Congress and statewide office is consistent with that observed among current legislators.[2]

## Why They Participate

The southern party activist study included questions that delved into the motivations for participation and the scope of political action among respondents. When we examine these respondents, life cycle differences again were present in the motivations of individuals for participation in public life. To what extent do people attempt to further their quest for economic security or political position by their actions? When respondents from the Southern Party Grassroots Project are divided by age group and the percentage of respondents is indicated who said they were involved in party politics to "build political position" or "create business contacts"—questions that tap political and economic ambition—the breakout of responses shows the life cycle structure of ambition and, to a lesser extent, the promotion of the private sector career. Respondents under the age of thirty-five were most likely to participate in the party to build their personal political position (42.4 percent) and to make business contacts (24.5 percent). The building of political position falls to less than one in three respondents among those between thirty-five and fifty-five and to one in eight respondents over fifty-five. The creation of business contacts falls off in a similar fashion.

## Conclusion

What can we conclude from all of these data, from these different samples of different groups in the population? First, the life cycle is related to holding and pursuing political ambition. In the general population, respondents are more likely to indicate that they engage in civic activities to further a possible political career than are older respondents. Young activists are more interested in the pursuit of progressive political ambitions through future office holding, and the desire to pursue progressive ambitions is more pronounced among the youngest officeholders. The greater desire for higher office among the young is no doubt in part a product of their current political status, especially among state legislators. They are young, they have ambitions, and they have acted on those ambitions and succeeded in getting a rung up on the political ladder. And, because they are so young and successful, they are doubtless the topic of conversation and inquiry about their future ambitions.

The analysis of political ambitions among southern activists by Robert Steed, Laurence Moreland, and Tod Baker (1998) indicates differences in political ambitions that reflect our general assumptions about the ambitious young. Ambitions are not just disproportionately concentrated among the young but appear especially among the Republican activists with political ambition. Ambitious activists are more often self-starters, like Matt Dollar, and they are also more likely to try to create networks of contacts, patterns of communication, and the basis for a potential political infrastructure. To put it another way, they are amassing the beginnings of a core constituency (see, e.g., Fenno 1978). The ambitious are engaged in behavior that is consistent with Schlesinger's (1991) observation that "most goals are inadequate to lead individuals to pay the costs of creating and maintaining political parties . . . only ambition for political office is sufficient to warrant the effort" (482–83). Indeed, according to Steed et al., "where ambition does make a difference is in the recruitment patterns, activities, and communications patterns exhibited by party leaders in both parties. The ambitious activists are more likely to have been [contacted by] elected officials and other candidates" (79) or to be self-starters.[3]

The ambitions of youth are fleeting. A precipitous falloff in progressive ambition occurred in every group surveyed. Events in life and the passage of time temper political ambitions. Whether among officeholders, nonofficeholders, or former officeholders, progressive political ambitions are less widespread among respondents between thirty-five and fifty-five. In this age cohort, the settling-in effects of life are taking hold (Huckshorn and Spencer 1971). People become more rooted; have increased family responsibilities or strong local family ties; have spouses with established, geographically rooted careers; and may be generally less able to disrupt their lives with a run for another office. If those ambitions for higher office that are so broadly held in youth are not highly focused early on, they likely dissipate into the other events of life. Fowler and McClure (1989) indicate that the loss of political ambitions we observe in the empirical data reflect the redirection or pacification of vaguely held ambitions by other events and accomplishments, as well as a growing reluctance to start over again:

> Given these diverse routes to political power, some people who enter politics with the vague thought of going to Congress may be sidetracked along the way. After investing several years in public office, they may find that a seat in the U.S. House of Representatives offers no more influence or opportunity . . . intense ambition

alone is not sufficient to propel individuals to Washington; equally necessary is a highly-focused desire for the distinctive life. (3)

At the point where progressive ambitions fade is where the potency of individual political careers is peaking. This is the window of maximum opportunity for seeking major office that Huckshorn and Spencer observed, and their conclusions were verified by Fowler and McClure (1989) a generation later. At the time of life where politicians have the greatest potential as candidates for major office, most eschew progressive ambition.[4]

Political ambition, especially progressive political ambition, is most prevalent among the young, especially the activists. It is especially intense among young officeholders. And, it is among those youngest officeholders, the early starters who get into office before they reach thirty-five, that we find the politicians who go farthest in American politics. Most political activists surveyed do not possess or pursue progressive political ambitions. Most officeholders do not possess or pursue progressive ambitions beyond their current office. But, among those who do possess and attain progressive ambitions, they are disproportionately from the younger end of those surveyed. Progressive ambition and the events that alter ambition are the province of youth and the experiences of the early political career.

# Notes

1. Contemporary observers of politics recognize limits to this typology. Hall and Houweling (1995) are especially critical of the concept of static ambition when applied to those who make institutional careers: "The assumption that one runs simply to run again (two years hence) is suitable only for a behavioral theory of pet gerbils on a cage-wheel. . . . Lest ambition be somehow purged from a legislator's political heart, the expected value of his or her position in terms of its intrachamber benefits will affect the decision to run again or retire from office" (124). They contend that ambition in the current office can be measured by intrainstitutional ambition—the imputed value of retained or potential leadership positions. Herrick and Moore (1993) observe that the pursuit of those ambitions depends on where you sit—majority members in leadership are less likely to retire, though financial opportunities or changes in electoral conditions can motivate retirement. Kenneth Shepsle (1978) argues that the institutional design of a legislature, especially the committee system, can create opportunity "queues" that have a subjective value to members.

2. When state legislators give up their seat before their term is up, it is generally to pursue a realized, progressive ambition. Hamm and Olsen (1992) observe that only about 3 percent of state legislators vacate a seat before their term is up; furthermore, of those who vacate, less than one-third do so involuntarily. The most common exit is to pursue other elective office.

3. See also Soule (1969), Engstrom (1971), and Loomis (1988).

4. Why do we observe the precipitous decline in political ambitions? Schlesinger (1966), writing almost four decades ago, casts light on the multiple and different cycles that are in play in American electoral politics, observing that in American politics "a man can fail to advance in politics as much because he is the wrong age at the wrong time as because he is in the wrong office" (174). The structure of the American political system erects powerful constraints to the pursuit of political ambitions. Incumbency is such a powerful force in affecting not just voter perceptions and evaluations (Mann and Wolfinger 1980) but also the decisions of potential quality candidates to seek political office; indeed, it is so powerful that entire careers are stagnated because there are minimal opportunities for vertical advancement without challenging an incumbent. The insufferable waiting for an opportunity can stifle ambitions and snuff out even the brightest political lights.

# A Campaign (and a Precampaign)

> Politics is perhaps the one profession where no preparation is thought
> necessary.
>
> —Robert Louis Stevenson

N O UNDERTAKING IS LESS CERTAIN than politics. For the young
politician who initiates a political career, there are many challenges,
including lining up support, raising money and acquiring other
campaign resources, and making the constant effort to introduce, reintro-
duce, and legitimate oneself to the electorate. Students of politics dissect
campaigns, refight campaigns, and look for the indicators of success.

To look at most research on politics, it all starts with the campaign. However, Richard Fenno (1996) reminds us that there are prepolitical careers
before there are political careers. So, too, there is more to the election than
the campaign. There is what happens before the campaign, the precampaign,
when incumbents assess the merits of staying in office, and challengers weigh
the prospects of challenging for a seat. Ambition exists in every constituency,
and, as a result, an invisible campaign takes place before the actual campaign,
wherein potential challengers attempt to line up support, feel out potential
opposition, and attempt to clear the field for their own ambitions. The precampaign affects strategy, planning, and the conduct of the general campaign. Such a precampaign was evident in the unleashing of political ambition
in south Oklahoma City.

South Oklahoma City contains a growing expanse of middle-class subdivisions. This area is a typical bedroom community, and District 91 is in the
middle of the suburban sprawl. The northern precincts in the district are in
older neighborhoods; the residents are more elderly and Democratic. The
southern half of the district is decidedly more Republican. The incumbent in
1998, Republican Dan Webb, was initially elected in 1990. He won handily
in 1992 and 1994 and was unopposed for reelection in 1996. The ambitious
challenger, Shane Hunt, was a twenty-two-year-old graduate of the University of Oklahoma, employed in his family's steel fabrication business. A graduate of the neighborhood high school, he spent his entire life living in this

suburban enclave. Schoolmates and friends describe him as earnest, honest, and enthusiastic.

Most individuals who have political ambitions will act in strategic fashion and therefore avoid running against incumbents (Jacobson and Kernell 1981). Incumbent legislators are too familiar to the constituency, too well funded, and too intimidating to individuals who value their political career. In the ninety-first House district, there was reason to believe that the incumbent would be familiar to most people. The district is not very populous—thirty thousand residents—and it is only about ten square miles in size. But Dan Webb was not that well known. Many legislators are surprised to learn that most of their own constituents have virtually no idea who they are. In their study of descriptive and substantive representation in state legislatures, Charles Bullock and Michael Scicchitano (2001) found that in a variety of Florida, Mississippi, and Georgia state legislative districts, most voters were unaware of the incumbent's identity, race, ethnicity, or almost anything else about the incumbent. A telephone poll commissioned for House District 91, taken six months before the general election, produced similar results (Blocker et al. 1998). A poll taken by the state Democratic Party two weeks before the election revealed a recognition number for the GOP incumbent in the high 60s. People knew Webb's name in the context of the reelection campaign, but it is not certain that they knew him as the incumbent.

State legislators have low recognition of incumbents, and even statewide officeholders and members of Congress have middling recognition numbers (see, e.g., Mann and Wolfinger 1980). Presidential nomination candidates most often have name recognition numbers in the low 20 percents, even in the midst of the nomination campaign and after months of active effort and national media coverage (Lenart 1997). Survey data from state legislative candidates in seven states nonetheless indicate the belief among candidates that, *before the campaign*, most persons know something about them (see table 3.1). An examination of survey data collected by Robert Hogan (1995) reveals that primary and general election *candidates* generally believe that voters know either something or a great deal about their experiences, their party, their community service, their issue positions, and, in general, their politics.

The belief that one is well known is not a conceit confined to incumbents or elder candidates. Young candidates are less likely to think they are known, but even then at least 60 percent of young primary candidates and at least 70 percent of young general election candidates thought they were known in advance of the campaign for their issue positions, their personal qualities, their community service, and their partisanship. Young candidates concede that they were less known for their past political activities, when compared to older candidates. Older candidates, especially those over fifty-five and in general elections, almost universally believed that voters knew either something

Table 3.1   Candidate-Perceived Voter Knowledge of the Candidate

| Candidate Age | Issues | Personal Qualities | Community Service | Prior Political Involvement | Party Identification |
|---|---|---|---|---|---|
| Primary | | | | | |
| Under 35 (n = 47) | 63.8% | 61.7% | 66.0% | 46.8% | 72.3% |
| 35–55 (n = 150) | 68.0% | 76.0% | 75.3% | 60.7% | 82.7% |
| Over 55 (n = 43) | 86.0% | 88.4% | 83.7% | 79.1% | 95.3% |
| | | | | | |
| General Election | | | | | |
| Under 35 (n = 65) | 80.0% | 78.5% | 72.3% | 61.5% | 87.7% |
| 35–55 (n = 271) | 83.7% | 84.1% | 82.7% | 74.5% | 88.8% |
| Over 55 (n = 108) | 85.2% | 92.6% | 91.7% | 85.2% | 93.5% |

*Source:* Hogan (1995).
*Note:* Respondent answered that voters "knew something" about them or "knew a great deal" about them before the election because of their issues; their personal qualities; their community service; their prior political involvement; or their party identification.

or a great deal about them on almost all dimensions of their public existence. One explanation for this disconnect came from a successful former legislator who told me that the biggest surprise for both challengers and incumbents is just how few people know them at all. "They tell me, 'I don't need to get out; everywhere I go, people know me.' And, I tell them, 'That's because you're only going where you know people.' You can't win without campaigning, because no one knows who you are."

Shane Hunt claimed Webb was not prone to campaigning. His last election was unopposed, and the two prior to that had been against underfinanced, unknown challengers. An Oklahoma county legislator observed that the incumbent's inactivity would cost him, were he to confront a serious opponent. "Dan Webb doesn't get out and work. And he can't do that with that district of his. Those new suburbs down there turnover about 20 percent of their residents every two years. That means in the five terms since he last had a serious contest, the whole district has turned over; it is new, and they don't really know him, and he doesn't know them. That's Shane's opening."

Despite the intimate nature of the district and the perceived invulnerability of the incumbent, there was an avenue to beat that incumbent. The effort would require the challenger to neutralize the issue and name recognition advantages enjoyed by the incumbent. Hunt believed the effort would be facilitated by the incumbent's reluctance to campaign and his disconnection from the district. In the month before the general election, Democratic Party internal polls indicated that Shane Hunt had a recognition number of almost 60 percent and that his positive perception was almost 80 percent among those who recognized his name. The key was to complete the disconnection of the voter from the incumbent and create a connection with the challenger.

Disconnecting voters from the incumbent meant overcoming a substantial hurdle: age. A telephone poll of the district conducted the previous April indicated that the age issue would be a factor to overcome. Over half of voters indicated that age and experience were "important considerations" when choosing a representative. Shane readily acknowledged the obstacles he had to overcome. "When people look at me, they know I'm young; that can't be changed. I have to impress them with maturity, honesty, and energy. No one ever sees the incumbent down here, and he won't get out and campaign. So I have to make the most of that opportunity."

## Political Context

Joseph Schlesinger (1966) characterized Oklahoma politics at midcentury as a wide-open politics, where aspirants to high office did not follow a rigid, established opportunity structure. The politics of Oklahoma have changed dramatically since then. If one looks at the movement of politicians up the political ladder to the House of Representatives, the governorship, and the U.S. Senate, a distinct opportunity structure had emerged in Oklahoma during the 1960s and 1970s: Aspirants to higher office generally came from the state legislature. At the same time, a series of young politicians entered the legislature, and many moved on to higher office. The rigidity of this opportunity structure was especially apparent in the U.S. Senate elections: Of the six men elected to the U.S. Senate since the 1970s, four were previously governor, one was a congressman, and all six had served in the state legislature. Of the eleven individuals elected governor, senator, or both, over half were elected to the legislature before age thirty.[1] Governors come to office with an apprenticeship in the General Assembly: Seven of the last eight governors served in the legislature. The receptiveness of modern Oklahoma politics to young officeholders made it easier for young candidates to run and be viewed as legitimate candidates. The emergence of a legitimate ladder of political ascension meant that most individuals who harbor political ambitions would realize that the avenue to high political office starts in a local constituency.

Oklahoma requires residents to be twenty-one in order to run for the state House of Representatives, twenty-five to run for state senate, and thirty to run for governor.[2] Legislative elections are held in single-member districts. The typical district will have about thirty-two thousand residents and between twelve thousand and twenty thousand registered voters. Election costs are low by contemporary standards. Thompson and Moncrief (1998) observe that there is a definite disjuncture between citizen legislatures with small constituencies and professional legislatures with larger constituencies in terms of the costs of campaigns. The smaller, citizen-oriented legislatures are easier for candidates to access because the costs of running a successful challenge are low. Even in the late 1990s, it was possible to run a successful campaign for less than $30,000, and expensive campaigns for the state senate rarely cost more than $120,000. Oklahoma legislators are among the best paid in the United States, receiving about $37,000 per year, plus per diem during session. The legislature is a remarkably amateur operation in other respects, however, having only thirty-seven full-time staff and minimal personal staff for members. Individual representatives often share staff. Legislators are term limited and can serve up to twelve years in the legislature. House members serve two-year terms, while senators serve four-year terms.

## Precampaign

Shane formally decided to run in the summer of 1997. After graduating from the University of Oklahoma, he opened his campaign account and filed paperwork to organize a campaign committee. To hear Shane tell it, he had planned this campaign since high school. In the spring of 1998, he came by my office at the University of Oklahoma, popped his head in the door, and said, "I'm running for the legislature." I asked him to come in and sit down, and we had a conversation about the district and his decision to run. For being only twenty-two, Shane had given a great deal of thought to how to conduct this campaign: "The last few years, Andy [Hicks, Shane's campaign coordinator and college roommate] and I have talked about this district, and we think we might be able to pull it off. Dan [Webb] doesn't get out and work the district. No one ever sees him, and we're banking on being able to outhustle him."

Shane started campaigning early. Every day and evening, throughout the spring and summer, he rang doorbells and shook hands, trying to make contact with voters and get his name out. As an employee of the family business, he was able to take leave and dedicate his efforts to campaigning. The economic uncertainty of a full-time candidacy was not a threat to him or his lifestyle. That same economic security made his campaign possible; his start-up costs and other campaign expenses were paid for with family money. Shane readily admitted before the election that there was "no way" he could have run a campaign without his family's support.

Hunt ran a direct market campaign that reflected the transient nature of the constituency. His effort to create a core of support came less out his political activism than from his social connections through family, church, and school. Hunt engaged in substantial groundwork when planning his campaign. He and his campaign manager, his college roommate Andy Hicks, spent weeks analyzing the district traffic patterns before purchasing billboards. They made use of reliable political data to target neighborhoods, blocks, and houses for door-to-door efforts. He has also relied heavily on traffic analysis, precinct voting analysis, and voter walking cards to plan his campaign technique.

A large part of Shane's motive to run was his desire to see the Democratic

Party revitalized. During our first conversation, he observed, "I'm a Democrat. I love the Democratic Party, because I think government can do things right, that government is important to people." There are problems with the Democrats, however, in Shane's opinion. "What the Democrats need to do is realize that they can't win without families, without churchgoing people. I think you can be a Christian and a Democrat. We let the Republicans take that position out from under us, and we need it back." In his campaign, he sought to build bridges between the traditional, older Democrats and the churchgoing families. The balance of voter registration in the district is closely divided between Democrats and Republicans, which meant that Shane Hunt would have to convince some Republican voters not to vote for a Republican incumbent and convince most Democrats to vote for a Democrat. His literature and campaign strategy reflected the need to pull crossover voters. "It doesn't say Democrat on my literature or signs; I run as a candidate."

Shane's case is illustrative of the benefits derived from early organization and contacting in the preprimary stage. Sandy Maisel (1982) argues that the key to defeating incumbents is to get them in a contest one-on-one. By doing so, the challenger presents himself as the only viable alternative to the incumbent, and the campaign focuses entirely on the incumbent–challenger matchup. If other opponents emerge, a party primary will be necessary to determine the eventual nominee, and money, reputation, and effort will be expended to get the nomination. Hunt's campaign exemplified how early contacting, organizing, and demonstrating a willingness to spend money clears the primary field. It was an exercise in the politics of deterrence. During an October campaign visit, Shane stated that the only reason he was doing as well as he was against the incumbent was because he had no primary: "No matter what people say, any time you have a contested primary, even if you get 70 percent of the vote, some voters will walk away mad, they won't back you. A primary divides the party. If any of the other challengers had emerged, it would have meant a costly primary . . . $10,000 or so, just to get the nomination. Those are resources we can use [against the incumbent]."

Cost and divisiveness were not the only factors. Shane's campaign strategy, to surprise the incumbent with a four-week blitz, would have been rendered ineffective by a costly, visible primary. "The incumbent would have been alert to our campaign theme, and we couldn't use the campaign strategy we have . . . we are not flying under radar anymore, and Dan has increased his activity. A primary would have tipped him immediately [to what an opponent could do]." So Shane Hunt's first goal was to act to ensure that the primary field was cleared, enabling him to concentrate on the incumbent.

Shane indicated two potential candidates who had loomed in the background. One, Ed Cox, was "not an especially dangerous opponent." Cox had run against Webb in 1994, garnering 34 percent of the vote. The other possible challenger, Paul Heath, brought both celebrity and financial assets to a possible challenge. Heath was the spokesman for a group of survivors of the 1995 Oklahoma City bombing. Heath proved instrumental to the survivors movement, serving as a strong, sympathetic voice for victims and survivors. Heath considered running after Webb appeared on a program for a bombing conspiracy theory group.

Hunt made his decision to enter this race over a year before the primary. In August 1997, he opened his campaign account and filed his paperwork with the ethics commission. Upon returning from vacation, a friend of his father indicated that Shane should meet with one of the incumbent senators from Oklahoma City, Keith Leftwich, and the then-speaker of the Oklahoma House, Loyd Benson. In the initial meeting with the speaker, Shane outlined his intentions. "I told the speaker that I was in this race, that I would be running. If I lost a primary, I would endorse and work enthusiastically for whoever was the party nominee." That conversation impressed the speaker, who put money into Shane's campaign. It was a strong indication of party support in a year when the state Democratic committees were strapped. Meetings and conversations with Senator Leftwich were similarly positive; Leftwich served as a mentor and adviser to Shane throughout this campaign.

Potential Democrats who were interested in the nomination quickly became aware that, were they to run, they would have to fight for the nomination against a candidate who had financial resources. Shane visited with Dr. Heath, who came away "most impressed" with Shane and supported the young candidate's campaign. Shane's intention to run, his decisiveness, convinced potential opponents to forego the primary. Similar conversations with Ed Cox convinced him not to run. Early efforts at contacting and developing relationships paid off by the July filing deadline; Shane Hunt was the only Democrat to file. He passed the first critical test, deterring potential opponents for the nomination.

## Campaign

About two weeks before the general election, Shane took me out to make the rounds of political meetings in the district. After a cup of coffee and a morning of sign waving in front of a Carl's Junior, we headed over to a barbeque restaurant on the eastern edge of his district, to talk politics with Keith Leftwich. Leftwich once represented District 91 for several years, before moving up to the state senate in the 1980s. His grassroots campaign style is local legend. One fellow legislator observed that "Keith Leftwich walks those neighborhoods, knocks doors, and gets more mileage out of not just knocking doors, but then telling people about [the door knocking]." Leftwich was most forthcoming with advice for Shane's campaign, despite being involved in a tough primary and reelection fight.[3] Over a lunch of beef barbeque, I listened to Leftwich coach Hunt on the traffic flows and the campaign ethic of south Oklahoma City: "You need to be out there knocking doors and campaigning every day, every night from now until election day. This is the stretch run, just a few days [left in the campaign]. Now, up in the northern part of the district, it isn't unusual to door-knock up there on Sunday; you don't do that [in the Cleveland County precincts]. . . . Every morning, you get out there with your signs, and wave the [heavy traffic] intersections. Then, you go to [these other intersections] at night and let them see you there."

During the campaign, Shane perceived his political success as tied to the success or failure of Leftwich. He consistently argued that, if he could just run at 52 percent in the precincts where Leftwich expected to run at 63 percent, it would offset a weaker performance in the more Republican part of the district. The senator served as a tutor, mentor, and, as described earlier, opportunity broker. Seeing them huddled in conversation, I saw plainly that the senator had an interest in Shane's success.

Hunt's campaign plan reflects the strategy often pursued by successful challengers: He sought to equate his name recognition with the incumbent and, wherever possible, create the perception that he is the incumbent. This meant getting his literature out through multiple-wave targeted mailings, stumping the district, and using billboards to cover the high-traffic streets that run into the district. As he observed seven months before election day, "for the people of the Ninety-first District, I need to create the perception that Shane Hunt *is* their representative."

Related to the goal of creating a positive tie to the constituency was the need to disconnect the voters from the incumbent. Disconnections are rarely the product of pleasant campaigning, and they require negative campaigning. Hunt perceived a very real downside to engaging in a negative campaign. "First, bringing up my age is not negative campaigning. I am young! But a young candidate can't go negative, because you end up looking desperate and immature. I cannot afford that; I cannot do that." In a later conversation, a week before the general election, his opinion was largely unchanged. As we drove through a brick-home subdivision, Shane brought up the negative card again: "We have one more piece of mail to go out on the day before the election. It'll be in the form of a personal letter from me. We haven't decided what to put in it yet; it depends on how we are doing and what Representative Webb does. If Dan goes negative, we have some negative stuff we can dump on him . . . otherwise, it's a positive piece. On Monday we'll have about forty-five people who will spend all day stuffing envelopes. We'll run ten thousand copies and stick them in the door of every house in the district."

He spoke of going negative with regret. "The one thing I know is that it helps to be positive. No one wants to be around someone negative or who is always dishing that kind of stuff." He clearly wanted to win on the ground, through effort, and based on what he said and what he represented.

The negative campaign by Shane Hunt was clearly issue oriented.[4] The content of his comparison flyer responded to assertions by the incumbent regarding both Shane's campaign and the incumbent's record. It was, by the standards of negative campaigning, restrained; his differences with the incumbent were aired on issues, questions about public policy, public priorities, and discrepancies between what the incumbent says and what he does. The key for Hunt was to take back the family values label from the GOP, especially from this incumbent. The trick for a Democratic challenger was a daunting one: Steal away the cloak of family and Christian values and economic frugality from the GOP, and demonstrate that those values are consistent with liberal government. The last mailing sent out by the Hunt campaign was a personal appeal, over campaign letterhead, distributed to four thousand Democratic-leaning households in an overnight dead-drop. The mailer traced distinctions between the incumbent and the challenger on family values and taxes, emphasizing taxes and fees that Webb supported that were not beneficial to families, all in an effort to show the disconnect between the incumbent's actions and his words.

If Shane Hunt lost the general election, it would not be for lack of trying. Between his expenditures and in-kind receipts (i.e., organized labor–printed yard signs and literature, and party get-out-the-vote [GOTV] flyers), he estimated costs at $22,000. Every voter in the district had between four and seven contacts with his name and his campaign between October 4 and November 3. Ten days before the election, we drove from a political meeting, and he recounted the mail campaign by the numbers.

"We sent four mailings out, one a week for four straight weeks, to twelve thousand households. We have people out making door drops, and I've been knocking doors for weeks . . . I figure I have visited about four thousand houses. . . . The last day of the campaign we'll make one last door drop, and there is a GOTV mailer that goes to Democrats. We're phone banking, got about forty-five volunteers to stuff envelopes . . . when someone goes to vote on November 3, they will have encountered my name between five and seven times."

Shane Hunt had access to basically unlimited resources. One afternoon, just before the election, I stood for two hours on a street corner with him as he waved at cars and greeted passersby at a busy south Oklahoma City intersection. I asked him about the financing of his campaign. His response was direct: "I couldn't have run this campaign without my family. I can take off from work, and the family has been very supportive of the campaign. We could spend more if we needed to, but I can't imagine what else we could spend it on. . . . Other money is coming in; [Oklahoma House of Representatives] speaker Loyd Benson has been calling to raise funds; he even sent $1,000 [from his PAC]."

Shane attracted leadership money in a year where the state Democratic Party was financially strapped. He had recently attended a party meeting for state legislative candidates, where leadership had presented polling data and briefed nominees on the ability of the party to support the campaigns. "They said not to expect much [money] from the party. The PAC is broke, and they're targeting money into really tight races to hold incumbent seats . . . this Clinton thing [the impeachment] isn't helping [fund-raising], but in terms of votes it shouldn't affect us down-ticket." Any party money was a pleasant surprise.

## Outcome

In the end, Shane's campaign effort would prove to be for naught. He failed to carry a single precinct in the Ninety-first District, and districtwide the incumbent carried 66 percent of the vote to Hunt's 34 percent, a two-point improvement over the underfinanced opponents who faced the incumbent in 1992 and 1994. Shane took his decisive loss in stride. The election result was not as good as he had hoped for, but it was not a total disappointment: in District 91, Shane ran nine points ahead of the Democratic candidate for governor. So what happened?

"We had enough money," Shane remarked, "we just didn't turn out our vote the way we thought we would. I figured, at a minimum, we would have nine thousand votes, minimum, cast in this district . . . they cast ten thousand here in 1994. The turnout was only eight thousand, which was way lower than our baseline, bottom-line lowest guess."

The falloff was not evenly distributed; the voters stayed home in large numbers in the predominantly Democratic precincts where Shane had hoped to run at about 53 percent. He ran at about 40 percent of the vote in those precincts and at about 31 percent elsewhere.

Shane Hunt was disappointed in his election performance. However, disappointment is also far more common than surprise when candidates evaluate their performance in legislative elections. Table 3.2 shows the perception of electoral performance by primary and general election candidates surveyed by Hogan (1995). Hogan asked, "Generally speaking, did you run about as well as you expected, worse than you expected, or better than you expected?" of primary and general election candidates. There are life cycle differences in candidate evaluations. Young candidates generally split evenly between those who thought they ran ahead of expectations in primaries and those who ran behind their expectations. Older candidates were generally skeptical about the evaluation of their performance, with twice as many indicating they ran worse than expected than those who indicated better than expected. In the

**Table 3.2   How Candidate Ran versus Own Expectations**

| Candidate Age | Ran Better | Ran Worse |
|---|---|---|
| Primary | | |
| Under 35 (*n* = 47) | 34.0% | 36.2% |
| 35–55 (*n* = 153) | 23.5% | 48.4% |
| Over 55 (*n* = 45) | 24.4% | 40.0% |
| | | |
| General Election | | |
| Under 35 (*n* = 67) | 20.9% | 41.8% |
| 35–55 (*n* = 281) | 25.2% | 43.7% |
| Over 55 (*n* = 110) | 25.5% | 50.0% |

*Source:* Hogan (1995).

general election, the perception of a disappointing performance did increase with age, but also negative evaluation outweighed positive evaluations across age cohorts. Hunt's disappointment was not uncommon.

Part of Shane's assessment of his campaign failure is based on what he sees as a misplaced strategy that overemphasized door-to-door campaigning, especially in the more affluent subdivisions in the southern part of the district. "People up [in the Oklahoma County part of the district], they want you to come out and knock on the doors; they're used to seeing Keith Leftwich out doing this all the time. But down in the rich subdivisions, they don't want you to come to the door . . . they don't want to see you. The problem is that there is no way to get to those conservatives, especially those Christian conservatives, if you're a Democrat."

This barrier arises from the absence of any meaningful civic institutions or community identity in the district. There were no community traditions, events, or organizations to structure the campaign; "you just won't see Rotary Club functions or candidate forums," Shane related. "I probably won't even meet Dan Webb during the campaign." A postcampaign conversation, two months after the general election, reiterated these observations.

"I'm at my best with groups," Shane told me, "and when we can use visual media . . . going door-to-door didn't make the best use of my campaign skills; I want to run a campaign where we can use media. . . . The other thing I learned is, as much as we thought we did all the GOTV and mailings that we could, we should have done that much again—do fourteen mailings instead of seven. . . . The fact is, I am not sure what else we could have done to get those people out to vote."

The lack of highly visible civic institutions was frustrating for Shane, and he noted the impact of a lack of such institutions on his ability to compete. He also pointed out both before and after the election the advantages that are derived by incumbents under those circumstances. Without civic institutions and a viable community identity, it is difficult for a candidate to build an independent political base or a political core constituency, creating advantages for incumbents.

## Conclusion

In the end, Shane Hunt's loss was probably less about age than about the constituency and the shape of his campaign. The constituency was a tough one for any Democrat, under most any circumstance, and the convergence of circumstances that usually lead such districts to oust an incumbent—a string of legislative votes against the constituency, an unexpected national or state political tide up-ticket, or an incumbent scandal—were absent in this campaign. The brevity of Hunt's active campaign and the very late decision to engage in comparative politics left too little time to disconnect the constituency from the incumbent and insert Shane Hunt in the minds of voters as an alternative.

There are lessons to be learned from Shane Hunt. First, the presence of a strong, enthusiastic, and well-funded core constituency of friends and family made the candidacy possible, and without such support, Shane would have been reduced to a candidacy of spray-painted signs, pitiful-looking literature, and no prospects in the eyes of his party and his district. Second, his early preparation and planning resulted in a political presentation of self in the months before the filing deadline that effectively cleared the field. Shane attained credibility through a successful exercise in the politics of deterrence, by persuading other potential challengers within his party that they would be certain to have a contested primary if they ran. Those aspects of his preparation and personality that persuaded older, credible candidates to forego the race also endeared him to experienced politicians who had counsel and resources to offer. Finally, the third lesson, and a hard one for all politicians to learn, is that even if you have a good plan, a good candidate, and ample resources, it is still possible to lose an election to an incumbent. Without a very compelling reason to abandon the incumbent, neither Shane Hunt nor any other challenger can move a majority of voters into their camp. This last lesson, while valuable, must often be learned firsthand and then applied again. A lost campaign is only a true loss if the experiences of the campaign are abandoned and not utilized in the future.

Shane indicated he would run for office again, probably for this district, but not in 2000. For the time being, he was focused on completing his M.B.A. and entering the family business; he was also getting married, and he wouldn't enter another campaign without the full support of his spouse. The personal context, which had been such a plus in his campaign, now weighed heavily in Shane's discussion of the future and in his expression of his political ambitions. When I asked him, "If offered a seat in Congress at no cost, would you take it?" his response was a qualified yes, "but if I have a family and kids by then, I wouldn't take it. . . . I think I would rather be in the legislature and maybe take on a statewide, state office . . . Congress? Probably not." Whatever Shane's ambitions, they do not advance to Washington.

# Notes

1. Such a change is in line with Prewitt's observation about opportunity structures: when the opportunity structure shifts, the context of candidate decisions also changes.

2. The past president tempore of the state senate, Stratton Taylor, was actually below the constitutional minimum of twenty-one when elected, but he did make the age of majority before the beginning of the legislative session.

3. Hunt's effort to move up to the Oklahoma House of Representatives at age twenty-two echoes Leftwich's own entry into politics. When Keith was twenty-four, he made an unsuccessful effort to unseat an incumbent in the Democratic primary. He left politics for four years, married, and returned in 1982 to run successfully for the same legislative seat at age twenty-eight.

4. Political communication research shows that negative, attack advertising is more effective when the emphasis of the advertising is placed on issues rather than personality (Roddy and Garramone 1988).

# The Life and Times of Joe from Minocqua 4

> I know the price of success: Dedication, hard work, and the unremitting devotion to the things you want to see happen.
>
> —Frank Lloyd Wright

N OT EVERYONE WHO RUNS for the legislature wins their first effort. Shane Hunt made his first run, and despite his best efforts he failed to prevail over an incumbent legislator. For those with the desire to serve, it may take repeated efforts to gain election, and this phenomenon has given rise to one of the great old wives' tales of legislative politics: "Run once to get known, and twice to win." For individuals with the insatiable desire to serve, the lessons of losing are instructive and acted on. Shane Hunt has not returned to politics, but he is also not the only candidate whom I visited with who lost in their first effort. Joe Handrick, Republican from Minocqua, Wisconsin, traveled the longest road to the legislature of anyone in this book, spending more time pursuing the legislature than in the legislature. As a twenty-year-old sophomore at the University of Wisconsin (UW), he was recruited to challenge the incumbent in his hometown district. It would be another eight years before he finally made it to the Wisconsin General Assembly.

Joe Handrick's case is interesting for a variety of reasons. He became a conservative Republican because of a strong socialization during the late 1970s and early 1980s, when Jimmy Carter's Democratic Party wrecked on the shores of a bad economy and foreign policy failures, and Ronald Reagan articulated a very different vision for America that resonated with young Handrick. His initial campaign against an incumbent assembly member was surprising in its strength, and it taught the young politician lessons that were incorporated into his subsequent electoral efforts. As a legislator, he was an active member of the majority party, but he soured on legislative life when he realized the institutional limits on his ability to affect public policy as an independent force. His personal context also changed, as he married, had two children, and confronted the challenges of full-time representation of a district 250 miles from the capitol. Joe's story is of several changing contexts within the career, of changes in the competitive context in the district, of changes in the institutional context of his incumbency, and, most important, of changes in the personal context that mitigated against continuing in the assembly.

## Political Context: Wisconsin

The Badger State is known for its powerful liberal political tradition, especially in Madison and Milwaukee. It is also a state with a powerful Republican heritage dating back to the 1850s, though that heritage can be viewed as part of a strident liberal political tradition that finds its roots in the abolition movement. The state legislature has a tradition of access for young politicians. UW students have run for districts not just in liberal Madison but also in hometown districts around the state. In 1993, the Democratic speaker of the assembly, Wally Kunicki, was just thirty-four. Tommy Thompson (a four-term governor) was elected to the state assembly almost immediately out of law school in 1966. Thompson served twenty years in the assembly, all the while consolidating his position in the GOP caucus, first as assistant floor leader, then as floor leader before being elected governor four times.

In Wisconsin, advancement to higher office is predicated by prior office holding. Of the nineteen major officeholders in Wisconsin in the 1990s, ten were first elected to public office before age thirty, and fifteen were in public office before age thirty-five. The path to power runs through the assembly. Thirteen of nineteen major officeholders came through the assembly, and all of the assemblypersons who made the jump to major office were in the assembly in their twenties or early thirties. Assembly members with progressive ambitions do not necessarily act immediately on their ambitions, but they do not stand still. Every U.S. House member who came out of the legislature spent ten years or less in the state House. Three moved from the assembly to the state senate, and two had prior local office experience before going to the legislature. The average tenure in the legislature before seeking higher office was just over nine years.

Wisconsin requires residents to be eighteen in order to serve in the state House of Representatives and senate. Members-elect have forty-five days to take up residency in their district. Party nominations are determined by primary. Wisconsin legislative elections are held in single-member districts. The typical assembly district has about fifty-four thousand residents. Senate districts are created by combining three entire assembly districts, resulting in the nesting of three assembly members and their constituency entirely in senate districts. The assembly has been generally Republican and the senate generally Democratic for the past decade, and in 2002 Republicans won control of both the assembly and senate.

# Meet Joe Handrick

Joe Handrick came from the North Woods, a region of lakes and tall trees not far from the Upper Peninsula of Michigan. Summer cabins have long dotted the chain lakes, and communities grow by a factor of ten in the summer. His hometown, Minocqua, is classic small-town Wisconsin, a place where everyone knows everyone else. Social touch points in these communities include the high school football game and a trip through the market. Groups of men still gather for coffee the same way they have every day for forty years, playing pinochle and swapping tales over coffee. A Friday evening out can still consist of a trip to a tavern for a boilermaker or a fish fry at a local supper club that has not changed since 1958.

As the youngest of five children of a local propane dealer, Joe grew up immersed in the culture of snowmobiling, fishing, and the small-town social swirl that is the North Woods. Gifted neither as an athlete nor as an academic standout, Joe Handrick did one thing especially well: politicking.

"My attraction to elected office began in high school. . . . Although I was smart, I was far from the top tier of students . . . at everything else—music, band, art, athletics, et cetera—I was just average. The one thing I was good at was student council, in terms of both getting elected and being a leader on the council."

The way he made student council was that he had friends everywhere, across groups, and he kept winning because he was everyone's second choice in a system that allowed second choices. These innate political abilities translated into an opportunity that would lead to an intensive socialization to the Reagan revolution and the Republican Party. Joe's student council adviser, Dave Anderson, first interested Joe in Republican politics. As Joe related, "At the end of my freshman year . . . Dave Anderson, my student council adviser, invited me to go to the Republican State Convention with him. Although my upbringing and basic outlook on life were dictating that I become a conservative, I had no party identity at fifteen. I did after the convention; [it] allowed the dots to connect."

Anderson would subsequently run for the local assembly seat, losing to Democrat Jim Holperin by eighteen points. Watching Anderson lose that election made an impression on Joe. "You have to take a stand," he said. "In the debate, Anderson kept saying he would 'have to look into [whatever subject] more' before he could give an opinion. . . . It is better to take a stand and please somebody than to take no stand and please nobody." As Handrick recalled, his mentor's tentative debate style bespoke a fundamental problem with his candidacy: Either Anderson either did not have a clear message, or, if he possessed a clear message, it was not being communicated.

## First Run: Assembly, Age Twenty

After the 1984 election, Joe Handrick was absolutely certain what he wanted to do. "Beginning in 1984, every big decision in my life was made with the backdrop of wanting to run for the state assembly." As a college student, he structured his life and his time to build, quietly but deliberately, toward that goal.

"Summer was spent in Minocqua working at a grocery store. Every morning I sat with the coffee klatch at the Parkway restaurant. I stayed active with the local party and regularly expressed my opinion in a letter to the editor. . . . [In 1986,] I approached Don Walker [publisher of the *Lakeland Times,* a local newspaper] about working there for the summer . . . experience at the newspaper would be good. It would provide the opportunity to make contacts with the business community and local civic leaders."

At the end of June 1986, Joe was approached by Dave Anderson about running against Holperin. Joe's father, Glenn Handrick, recalled over coffee at Tula's, "You should have seen it. Here he is eighteen or twenty, and these guys, local Republicans and businessmen, they all come to him trying to get him run. And he sits there and hedges a little, kind of drawing them out like he had never really considered running. He looks at them and says, 'Well, you know, I haven't really thought about it' . . . after they've 'talked him into it' and Joe commits, he whips out a complete campaign plan, and says, 'This is what we're going to do.' Ha!"

An examination of that plan reveals an impressive degree of research and sophistication on the part of a twenty-year-old with no prior training or experience. Handrick had conducted an extensive study of the patterns of electoral support in every precinct in the districts across several elections. He identified precincts where the Democratic incumbent had run ahead of expectations, and then he sought explanations for that surge, such as a friends-and-neighbors effect. Joe developed a budget, an issue strategy, and plans for advertising, door knocking, and dead-dropping to create the exposure and visibility necessary to take on the incumbent and mute his advantages.

Prior planning is common among state legislative candidates, though evidence shows that the emphasis of such planning varies by candidate age cohort. As indicated by the data in Hogan's (1995) survey (see table 4.1), most candidates suggested that they engaged in precampaign activities such as the construction of voter databases, precinct analysis of past elections, and voter targeting. There are no great differences across candidate age groups in the creation of voter databases; most candidates do it, regardless of age. However, the conduct of precinct analysis by candidates under thirty-five was seven points lower that candidates between thirty-five and fifty-five and seven points higher than among candidates over fifty-five. The other difference that

Table 4.1    Precampaign Analysis and Targeting by Candidates

| Candidate Age | Precampaign Analysis | | Voter Targeting | |
|---|---|---|---|---|
| | Voter Data | Precinct Analysis | Primary | General |
| Under 35 | 82.8% | 70.5% | 83.0% | 69.1% |
| | ($n = 105$) | | ($n = 47$) | ($n = 68$) |
| 35–55 | 82.5% | 77.7% | 80.5% | 72.4% |
| | ($n = 372$) | | ($n = 154$) | ($n = 283$) |
| Over 55 | 79.4% | 63.1% | 57.7% | 62.1% |
| | ($n = 141$) | | ($n = 45$) | ($n = 111$) |

Source: Hogan (1995).

emerges is in the targeting of voters. Candidates under thirty-five and candidates between thirty-five and fifty-five are far more likely than older candidates to target voters in primaries, and they are somewhat more likely to target voters in general elections. All age cohorts had solid majority responses engaged in targeting, though younger candidates are more prone to convert prior planning into efforts to target voters.

Even with this degree of preparation and planning, taking on an incumbent is a daunting task. The incumbent had been in the assembly for some time and had followed the classic playbook for an incumbent in a competitive district. Handrick describes the district as "leaning Republican," which is also borne out by empirical analysis of statewide elections in the area. The incumbent overcame this partisan disadvantage because of a friends-and-neighbors benefit in his home community of Eagle River and an ability to do lots of constituency service. In sum, given his personal incumbency advantage, "Jim Holperin simply could not be beat." Handrick had planned to wait for the incumbent to retire and then to run. So why the change in plans?

"I was easily talked into running . . . for a number of reasons that allowed us to conclude I had little to lose. The bar had been set quite low, and if I just avoided doing anything stupid, I would be fine. . . . I knew I could perform better than the candidate in 1984 who received only 34 percent of the vote."

So Joe Handrick, a junior at the UW–Madison, ran for the assembly. His evaluation of the district revealed a political context in which an active, Republican candidate might be successful. "I looked at the district, which is conservative and 55 percent Republican but has been going 65 percent for Holperin. I had to find some way to get those voters back to where they were supposed to be, and that meant running on issues."

This evaluation would create a mind-set that framed Joe's career behavior and that emerged in his first campaign as a hallmark of all of Handrick's political campaigns up in the North Woods: using aggressive ideology to polarize the contest. His entry into the controversy over Native American fishing rights—specifically, the rights afforded to the Chippewa to spearfish for wall-eye and muskie—was an example of the application of the tactic. The incumbent was vulnerable with sportsmen for his lukewarm opposition to the special fishing rights for the tribes. Combined with the growing unpopularity of Democratic governor Tony Earl, an opportunity existed to take advantage of an issue of interest in the constituency, while also capitalizing on the failed incumbency of Earl. As Joe recalls, "Our three big issues were treaty rights [spearfishing], insurance liability crisis, and taxes. On all three issues Tony Earl was vulnerable, so our task was to connect Earl and Holperin at the hip."

The first campaign was run pretty much on the weekends. Handrick was a full-time student at UW–Madison; he took the fall term off to avoid making the more than 250-mile drive home to campaign. The age issue never really took hold, and Joe had a ready answer: "My youth is not important to the voters. Eleven of Wisconsin's assemblymen were elected when they were under thirty years old." Joe Handrick would not be unique if he won.

Handrick's first campaign was visible and relatively effective. Joe made a strategic decision "to try and win as many towns as I could. . . . I knew that a candidate can create the impression that they ran a close race if they win a lot of real estate." The Democratic stronghold of Rhinelander was out of reach, and in the estimation of Joe and all those around him, it would be won by the incumbent with impressive margins. "We spent a relatively small amount of resources there. . . . I focused on Vilas [the Republican county] . . . this is where the Republican voters are who had supported Holperin. . . . It worked well. I received 41 percent of the vote [and] won Minocqua, Hazelhurst, Woodruff, Arbor Vitae, Plum Lake, St. Germain, Manitowish Waters, Boulder Junction, and Phelps. In [the previous election,] Holperin had lost only three towns . . . around Minocqua, Holperin's huge margins were gone as we won back much of the conservative base."

Handrick campaigned the entire district, and he had the attention and support of major Republicans. Tommy Thompson, challenging Tony Earl for governor, made a strong and public endorsement of Joe and campaigned for him in Rhinelander. Handrick's campaign left an impression on the incumbent, who said in reflecting on the race that "he would counter attacks from his opponent." If anything, the lesson was that while negative campaigning doesn't work, assertiveness doesn't hurt. The result, nonetheless, was an electoral loss to a strong incumbent.

Joe's own campaign postmortem includes geographic analysis of the last three campaigns versus the incumbent, including his own, by township. There was a definite east-west division of the electorate, with Republicans running strongest in Minocqua, Hazelhurst, and northwestern Vilas Counties, and the Democratic incumbents running strongest in the eastern parts of both Vilas and Oneida Counties, especially near his home bailiwick of

Eagle River. This contrasted dramatically with the Republican performance in presidential and gubernatorial contests, where Republicans were strong throughout Vilas County and, on average, ran about ten points better. Holperin had an incumbency advantage throughout the district and a friends-and-neighbors advantage in the townships around East Eagle River. But Handrick did better than any other challenger to Holperin.

In this first campaign, Handrick entered the race with the mind-set that is presumed to be common among first-time challengers to incumbents: Run once to get known, beat expectations, and wait for the open seat. Joe Handrick had beaten expectations and established his name as a viable candidate for representative in the future. He was "back to plan A—wait for Holperin to retire."

## Senate Campaign, Age Twenty-two

Fighting the good fight at twenty brought Joe Handrick what many aspiring young political activists crave: attention, recognition, and legitimacy. He returned to school in Madison and also made his way into "big-time" Wisconsin politics, serving as a staffer in the administration of the new Republican governor, Tommy Thompson. It was a part-time position at first and allowed Joe to pursue his degree while also getting networked with the Republican in-crowd in Madison. The plan was to finish college, build stronger ties in GOP circles, and wait for the shot when the seat came open. What happened, though, was another campaign in a bigger constituency.

In 1988, Joe Handrick was again approached to run, this time for the state senate. This would be a bigger, more expensive, more challenging campaign. The Wisconsin legislature has ninety-nine assembly members and thirty-three senators. Each senate district wholly encompasses three state assembly districts. Handrick would be running not just in the two counties of the assembly seat but also in two other constituencies. Again the fight would be against an incumbent Democrat, Senator Lloyd Kincaid. The best account of the decision and the lessons of the campaign come from Handrick's own words, which acknowledge a bad case of youthful hubris:

"Unfortunately, 'me ego' started to believe all the people in Madison who said what a great candidate I was and that I should run against [Kincaid] in 1988. I was working in the governor's office . . . and allowed myself to get talked into something that was probably not in my interest. I began planning a senate run in the spring. The party pledged to make this the number one target in the state."

Joe had resources, expertise, and high-profile backing from one of the most powerful Republicans in Wisconsin history. The campaign was polished and professional; but, of all the campaigns that Joe Handrick waged, this was probably the most painful and least favorably recalled. It was also, like many of life's experiences when young, one of the most valuable in shaping him.

"[It] was unenjoyable, but I probably learned more in this loss than in any other campaign. . . . Kincaid had never been beaten, so getting 47 percent against him kept my image as a good candidate intact back home. . . . Senate Republicans viewed me as only a marginal candidate. [Political people in] Madison began to view me as a much better strategist and manager than candidate."

This is often the painful juncture for aspiring candidates. While many possess the technical knowledge and political skills to analyze political environments and ascertain successful strategies, candidates and those around them begin to question their quality as standard-bearers. Was Joe Handrick meant to be a political leader or one of those who made leaders? Clearly Handrick relishes in the role of strategist and kingmaker.

"What I like about campaigns more than anything is the planning of strategy and development of the game plan. I especially like doing so in a primary [that is more candidate centered]. In a general election, much of the outcome is decided by the makeup of the district. In a primary, it is much more up to the candidate whether they win or lose. A hardworking, well-organized candidate with a solid plan can outsmart and outwork the opposition."

This perspective on the ability of a candidate to influence elections is widely held by legislative candidates. Returning to the data from the Hogan survey, candidates of all ages are convinced of the ability of a candidate and their campaign to influence the election outcome. This belief if more intense among candidates in primaries (see table 4.2).

Handrick faced admittedly "weak opposition" in the primary and tried to use it as an opportunity to build momentum to the general election. The press portrayed Handrick as "a former aide to Governor Tommy Thompson." Joe tried to parlay that tie and his maturation since his first campaign into greater legitimacy, arguing that "I have the background and experience to be an intelligent, articulate, and effective voice for the North [in Madison]." The campaign focused on three broad issues: economic development, environmental protection, and property tax relief.

Table 4.2   Extent the Candidate's Campaign Influences Election Outcomes

| Candidate Age | Primary | Candidate Age | General Election |
|---|---|---|---|
| Under 35 (n = 47) | 70.23 | Under 35 (n = 67) | 66.60 |
| 35–55 (n = 153) | 75.24 | 35–55 (n = 281) | 64.77 |
| Over 55 (n = 45) | 73.63 | Over 55 (n = 110) | 65.13 |

Source: Hogan (1995).
Note: Mean for category, based on 100-point scale where 0 = no influence and 100 = total influence.

Things were going well for Joe coming out of the primary, which he won handily. They used the primary to push contacting and practice their voter targeting for the general election. Then, as Joe described in his own words, "things went downhill." He was in over his head and could not keep control of the campaign.

"The campaign was the state's number one target race, and [it was] simply too big of a campaign for me to keep a handle on. In the end we set a new state record by spending over $100,000. During the race, they made me go out and do what a candidate is supposed to do and kept my involvement in strategy and implementation of the plan to a minimum. That took all the fun out of it. I [was] simply not motivated. I was running because others wanted me to—I never had that fire in my belly."

The campaign handlers from Madison were "very good and ran the campaign very well." But it was not how Joe would have run the contest.

Out of the campaign came lessons of maturity and character that stayed with Joe throughout his political career. "Our attacks on Kincaid were not just negative—they were downright mean." In no subsequent campaign that Handrick ran in or managed for another candidate would he go negative, other than engaging in comparative advertising on specific issues. His conscience could not live with it. A note Joe sent me summed up his own thoughts on the effect of that campaign on his reputation:

> The attacks on Lloyd Kincaid led people to believe I was mean. I vowed to never again let others set the tone and tenor of my campaign. I know that candidates are not supposed to run their own campaigns but I would have it no other way in the future . . . candidates can and should control their own campaigns and that this can be done without the candidate getting tied down in deciding what color balloons to have at a fundraiser.

Second, he learned the relative value of types of media and also the limits of media in running for office. "We spent a lot of money and ran a media campaign but never had a network put together in much of the district. In three counties, we had no ground troops, no coordinators, no nothing." The one constant of legislative candidates is the value of doing doors. "I knew door-to-door worked, but [with the failure in the general election,] I saw exactly how. When looking at the primary vote results, we could see which wards we had done doors prior to the primary."

Joe Handrick recognized that part of the failure of the campaign was a product of the same failing as his mentor's challenge to Jim Holperin, in that "we had no overall theme." The campaign was out of his control, run from the top-down; it was run using a generic, impersonal strategy without an appreciation of the particular context of the district; and there was no central

focus to the campaign. The theme of national conservative politics was insufficient to displace a known incumbent in a down-ticket race, because the national forces were insufficient to allow candidates to make a meaningful connection to them.

## Hiatus

Two consecutive losses to two different incumbents in two years left Joe Handrick wondering whether he had pushed too hard, too fast, to get to the legislature. As he observed to me, "It was *definitely* back to plan A: Wait for Holperin to retire." He went back to Madison and enrolled at UW to pursue a degree in occupational therapy. "It was time to think about getting through school . . . the plan was to get through school and get home."

Handrick still managed to dabble in some politics at UW. In 1989, he and some College Republicans engineered a takeover of student government. The low-turnout campus elections turned into a laboratory for voter targeting and mobilization. His time in the student senate offered the chance to develop rhetorical devices he would later use in the assembly. And, while working a half-time position for the Republican assembly floor leader, Handrick would grow his relationship with his future wife, whom he met during the 1988 senate campaign (she worked for Bob Kasten). Joe dropped out of college for two years to work full-time for the assembly. As he described it, "the pay was so good," he now was a family man with a spouse, and he had ambitions beyond stocking shelves at Wal-Mart. As he put it during our drive north to Minocqua, "Now I was married and poor instead of just poor."

Other political opportunities would beckon, too. Handrick was passed over for the chance to run in a special election in the senate seat he contested in 1988 (the party candidate ultimately lost in the primary to an unknown twenty-four-year-old), but he did get back into campaigning, managing an open seat race in another North Woods district adjacent to his own home district.

On returning to Madison, Joe found that his boss in the assembly, Randy Radtke, was the Republican chair for redistricting. Randy brought Joe in to work on what would be Joe's legacy in Wisconsin: the crafting of legislative maps. In the 1990s, states across the nation were making extensive use of new geographic information system (GIS) technology to craft legislative maps. Handrick was not initially a principal in the crafting of maps, but, when exposed to the technology and asked to participate, his spatial analytic abilities became evident to Republican mapmakers. "When they sat me down at the terminal, I just had a knack for being able to see how to craft the kind of districts they wanted, with the right political skew and in a fashion that would be attractive to a court."

Wisconsin would end up going to federal court to have its state legislative maps, and Joe would ultimately craft the legislative map proposal Republicans forwarded to the federal courts. While the court did not formally adopt those maps, the map that the court produced was sufficiently similar to Handrick's map that the convergence of his map and the logic of a court-drafted plan were evident; it was a de facto adoption, and in the Milwaukee area the Handrick map was directly adopted, including its proposed minority-majority districts. After redistricting, Radtke retired, and Handrick returned to occupational therapy school. Plan A would be put into motion in short order.

## Prior Planning Ensures Performance: Success at Age Twenty-eight

In 1992, as redistricting was winding down and Joe was getting back to school, rumors started to circulate that Jim Holperin was casting about for a full-time job and would retire from the legislature. When the rumors started, Handrick established a fund raising operation, in order to have money on hand should the seat come open. Soon there was a few thousand dollars in the account.

It was time to go back to the district. Periodically, during the summers, Joe had worked at the local supermarket—Trigs—as a supervisor. In early 1993, he started spending weekends back in the district, bagging groceries and "seeing literally hundreds of locals." There was a tremendous rationale for making the lengthy trip, up and back, every weekend for Joe: "I feared that I would be accused of being a carpetbagger. It was five years since I had run for the senate." He also became more active in the local GOP organizations in Oneida and Vilas Counties, and he started helping local candidates with campaigns. "I built some nice IOUs in the process," Joe recollected, "and the fact that I built a voter list for the Thirty-fourth District and shared it with other candidates didn't hurt, and I helped design their ads." Handrick set himself up as the volunteer consultant of choice for like-minded candidates, while crafting an organization for his assembly run.

The opportunity to capture District 34 very nearly slipped through Handrick's hands. In late 1993, word leaked from the governor's office that Tommy Thompson was going to appoint Jim Holperin to a full-time state job. This would not have fit Joe's window of opportunity as "there would be a special election. . . . I could finish school by early 1994, but not in time for 1993." Handrick inoculated against losing his place in the order of succession by sending an announcement to the state capitol that he was moving back to Minocqua to "prepare for a special election." The goal of the move was to scare Democrats into talking Holperin into deferring his retirement, for fear that Handrick would win any special election. Democrats at the time held a narrow 52–47 majority in the assembly and did not want to cede a seat. Holperin delayed his departure by nearly a year.[1]

The announcement of Holperin's retirement was accompanied in local papers by a story announcing Handrick's filing of candidacy papers with the State Elections Board. Included in the story was the notation that, in his last race for the Senate, Handrick had a thousand-vote plurality over the Democratic incumbent inside the borders of assembly District 34 and a 76 percent vote margin in the 1988 GOP primary inside the district. Front-runner status was not conferred, but his viability was readily noted by the local press. Before Holperin's retirement announcement, Handrick had filed for a position on the County Board. Joe recollects that he "used the race as a dress rehearsal for the upcoming state assembly primary." Joe Handrick won over incumbent Robert Wendt by a margin of 318 to 138. Now the real campaign would start: running for assembly District 34.

## Winning in 1994

Unlike Joe's previous efforts, this time he confronted a broad field of similarly ambitious competitors. The open seat had loosened political ambitions in both parties, as nine candidates filed. The challenge for Handrick was to stand out, first in the Republican primary, and then in the general election. As Handrick saw it, "whoever was the winner of the GOP primary would win the district. . . . The district was trending more conservative, and the Democrats would be hard-pressed to find another Jim Holperin." Winning the primary would propel him toward general election success, especially if Handrick used the primary to build up his name recognition and create a feeling of momentum. While still young, he was a veteran campaigner, a known political operative, and far more mature and seasoned at twenty-eight than he had been at twenty.

At the very least, Handrick needed to win his hometown. His perspective on primaries in rural Wisconsin was that they were friends-and-neighbors events: "In a primary a candidate should win their home town. Our strategy was to . . . win Minocqua by more than the [other candidates] win their hometowns by doing a better job of getting out the vote, and to come in second in all the other candidates' hometowns by having a better network, working harder, and [having] a better-delivered mass media plan." It was not unlike the previous circumstances of running for student council. Handrick had to be better at home than everyone else and then be everyone's second choice.

The big break came through a campaign stunt, designed to separate Handrick from the rest of the pack. "The challenge was standing out among nine candidates. Our vehicle for doing this can be summed up in two words: *the dog*." Joe is a dachshund enthusiast and has a large Dachs by the name of Molitor.[2] "In parades, we pulled a trailer with a kiddy pool on it filled with water. My fifteen-pound dachshund would splash around in the pool and try to kick out the water. Our sign said, 'Joe Handrick will make a splash in Madison.' The response was unbelievable. Everyone was talking about the 'guy with the dog' . . . we had our TV people film a parade in July knowing this would be our TV ad come August and September."

Doing TV in a Wisconsin assembly primary was "almost unheard of," but TV in the North Woods is cheap and can drive up name recognition rapidly for a candidate. "If others were to do TV, it would be in the last five or six days before the primary. . . . Our TV started twenty-one days out . . . the opposition went into panic mode." Joe from Minocqua was all over the TV, by himself, for over a week.

Party people in Madison thought that the dog was a singularly bad idea; it "didn't fit" the campaign mold that the assembly leadership likes to see. Voters had a very different reaction. "We were," Handrick said, "the highlight of every little parade we went to. People just went crazy when they saw Molly splashing around in that pool. And when we put it on TV," he continued, "it caught everyone's attention. Two days after the dog ad began, volunteers from Madison were doing a literature drop, and they reported that nearly every person they saw said, . . . 'Yep, that's the guy with the dog.'" Handrick admits that he stole the idea of the dog from Senator Russ Feingold, whose offbeat 1992 campaign ads helped fell Republican Bob Kasten. The catch line of Handrick's dog ad was "Joe Handrick doesn't care if his dog gets soaked, but taxpayers have been getting soaked long enough." As Joe noted to me recently, "the dog stuff was also a reflection of my desire to avoid the 'mean' label that I got in 1988."

Handrick had other advantages. He was an experienced candidate, one who had built a political résumé from the experiences of electoral defeat. Unlike his previous campaigns, he had a legitimate background in public service, and he was the only candidate with experience in state government. On the other hand, he also tried to run on the "outsider" track, and, like many Republicans who ran in the 1994 elections, he challenged the status quo. He won the Republican primary, carrying his hometown and coming in second everywhere else.

With the primary behind him, Joe turned to the general election. Party help came from Madison, and, with the memories of his Senate campaign, Joe worked hard to keep control of method, message, and strategy. The decision to use TV early and intensely accrued benefits going into the general election. His best estimate is that, based on the strong primary showing, they came into the general election campaign with a twenty-point lead. This suited Handrick, because "it put us in the position of being able to stay positive and let the other side be the negative campaign. When attacked we hit back, but . . . in a way that tried to portray the opposition as mean and our side as victims"—again, the opposite of his 1988 senate campaign.

Handrick's general election opponent was a U.S. Army reserve lawyer from Rhinelander, Jenny Owen. Owen was in line with the constituency and Handrick on many issues. The issues that differentiated them were partisan, ideological wedge issues that favored Handrick in this conservative constituency. Owens was an advocate of government-sponsored universal health care and prochoice on abortion.

The campaign was not without problems or setbacks, and Handrick observed that he has never been involved in a campaign where "the people in Madison did not screw up on at least one issue. Usually it is a technical thing, like where they claim that an incumbent voted one way" when in fact the opposite was the case. In Joe's 1994 campaign, the "screw-up [was] that Scott Jensen wrote our TV scripts after the primary, and in the crime spot I said, 'No more cable TV in prisons.'" After the spot aired, a staffer informed Joe that there was a "problem—'we don't have cable TV in prisons in Wisconsin' . . . normally I would have panicked, but . . .I was aware that some counties had cable in their county jails, and that is a form of prison." There was really no downside, in Joe's mind, because "I dare the opposition to raise this as an issue—I'd have made them look like they're defending prisoners."

In the closing week, his opponent depicted Handrick as a professional politician, and she used push-polling to paint Handrick as a right-wing radical.[3] He inoculated against these efforts on two dimensions. Joe's campaign ran a prepared TV spot, showing Joe in his white hospital coat as an occupational therapist, walking around a hospital and talking about how, as a therapist, helping people lead more independent lives was also part of his qualification to legislate and also consistent with his political philosophy, that government should help people live independent lives. They flipped the effect of the push-poll in the media. Joe prevailed on one of the local TV affiliates to break the story, and a grievance was filed against the Owens campaign (Democrats were later chastised and fined for the use of this campaign tactic).

Handrick won 56 percent over Owens's 44 percent, a fifteen-point swing from his first effort in District 34. The election in 1994 was a watershed in American politics, and Wisconsin Republicans garnered substantial gains. According to Handrick, his win and others were not necessarily part of any broad-based national tide; rather, he attributes the gains to opportunities that were cashed in by the GOP. "Republicans took the assembly because three Democrats retired from GOP seats in Districts 1, 2, and 34. The gains coincided with '94, but the national tides of '94 didn't matter. Wisconsin just does its own thing. It doesn't follow national trends." A look at Vilas County (the northern county in District 34) lends credence to this observation. Running in an open seat, Handrick carried the county by a margin of 1,345 ballots and 58 percent of the vote. Republican governor Tommy Thompson carried the county by a margin of 4,088 votes and 73 percent of the vote. Democrat Jim Doyle, who won the attorney general race statewide, lost Vilas County by seven ballots, while Democratic secretary of state candidate Doug

LaFollette carried the county by 628 ballots. In 1986, Thompson carried Vilas with 67 percent of the vote as a challenger, while challenger Joe Handrick lost the county by 362 votes. Some of the surge in Republican ballots can be attributed to national tides, though an equally valid explanation is the elimination of Holperin's incumbency advantage. The notable swings in ballots from candidate to candidate substantiate Handrick's mirthful observation that in Wisconsin, "ticket-splitting is our favorite pastime."

Now Joe confronted a question that had never occurred to him before: "What do you do when you're twenty-eight and you've accomplished everything you set out to do?"

## Outgrowing an Old Dream

Joe Handrick attained a seat in the Wisconsin General Assembly on his third try. He had pursued the assembly all of his adult life and had delayed his formal education and the initiation of his professional career to work in politics. Along the way he picked up skills and abilities in campaign management and media relations, and he proved adept in the application of new technologies, particularly the use and application of geographic information systems to the problem of crafting legislative districts.

By 1999, he was in his third term in the legislature. He was a member of a close majority in the chamber, led by an energetic speaker, Scott Jensen, and was chair of the assembly committee that was preparing for the coming legislative redistricting. He had several legislative accomplishments and a reputation as a serious legislator with a strong independent streak. However, he was also restless and dissatisfied with the legislative life and was tiring of his role. As he described it to me as we left a fund-raiser in the Fox River Valley, "a trained monkey could do my job." He was tired of sitting on the floor, hitting a button with the party line, and not having substantive input into legislation or strategy. "There was no challenge. . . . When it was evident that I could not exercise power in the institution, I decided it was time to move on. But I wanted to do the redistricting."

Joe left the assembly in 2000. But, as he was headed out the door, he laid the foundation for his transition to a postlegislative career as a consultant and lobbyist that will prove far more lucrative than his position in the legislature. Postlegislative politics is being good to Joe Handrick, and he is still young and energetic enough to enjoy his new role.

### Legislator

Joe Handrick had a good legislative career. As a freshman, he asserted his intention to follow his conservative principles but also to consider what his constituency wanted. First and foremost, he saw himself embodying the inde-

pendence of the rural North Woods. In a piece of correspondence, he laid
out for me his perception of the role of the legislator:

> There are some lawmakers who always vote their conscience no
> matter what their constituents believe. Others always put their fin-
> ger in the air and side with the majority. On issues of personal
> moral or religious issues I vote my conscience—abortion, for exam-
> ple. I'm pro-life and that's how I vote. If a poll showed my district
> was pro-choice, I would still be pro-life. As it works out, this prob-
> lem never arose for me because on issues like abortion and the
> death penalty, the majority of my constituents share my views.

Sometimes, the need to reconcile his informed perspective on an issue
with the less informed perspectives of his constituents would rear its head. In
those situations, Joe said, "I try to vote the way my constituents would if
they had the same information I did," which allowed him latitude in going
against his conservative constituency. He noted, though, that "this can be
tricky."

"Take the gas tax. . . . If you asked voters if they supported a penny
increase in the gas tax, they would say no. If you asked voters if they supported making Highways 29 and 51 into four-lanes, they would say yes. In
1997, I had to decide whether to support a one-cent increase in the gas tax.
Without it, the Highway 29 and 51 projects would have been delayed. . . . I
had to use my judgment, and in my judgment, the majority of residents in
my district would have supported the one-cent increase if the question were
not asked in a vacuum but was coupled with the question relating to Highways 29 and 51."

Joe Handrick was a voice that represented the perspectives and priorities
of his constituency, though he would temper the delegate role. He asserted
the independence of representing this last frontier of Wisconsin and, implic-
itly, also his independence as representative of the North Woods.

As a freshman legislator, his prior experience working with the assembly
inculcated in him an immediate appreciation of the need to follow the norms
of the chamber, especially in terms of cultivating allies and forging coopera-
tion with other players. "One of the first things you learn is that you can
accomplish nothing on your own. An effective legislator must work with colleagues, members of the senate, the governor, the press, the lobbying community. Passing laws truly is a team sport." A failure to recognize the need
for cooperative behavior in the chamber would only further frustrate a legislator's ambitions, because "a legislator who never compromises is a legislator
who will never accomplish anything."

Handrick was not above being forceful in pressing home his views or in
challenging the core tenets of his opponents. At the time he was in the Wis-

consin assembly, he was the only occupational therapist in the United States to serve as a legislator. As such, he did bring a unique perspective to issues relating to persons with disabilities. One of his hallmark moments on the floor of the legislature was when he made "rather strongly-worded statements aimed at Democratic lawmakers on disability issues . . . liberals have a very condescending view of persons with disabilities. They view them as helpless citizens who need their big government 'compassion' and care. In my view there is nothing compassionate about a political party that seeks to do things for people rather than giving people the tools they need in order to do things for themselves."

Handrick was in the legislature when sweeping changes were made in the social welfare system. He credited this as the top "team" accomplishment of his three terms, as it fit his philosophy of government as a helper. "[Before reform,] if parents on welfare became employed they would lose their benefits and receive no help in obtaining health care and child care. We said, 'This is wrong.' Instead of paying people not to work, let us help them obtain employment and use the money we were using to pay them to stay home and use it to help with child care and health care. . . . Because of our work . . . thousands of people are going to live better lives, more independent lives . . . that is a very rewarding feeling [to break the cycle of dependency]."

He was also hard at work on specific legislation related to constituency issues. Northern Wisconsin has long been a vacation spot for people from Milwaukee and Chicago. The cool breeze of the lake country and the outdoor recreation opportunities grow some of these communities by a factor of ten in the summer, and, more recently, many retirees created permanent homes in District 34. One consequence of this historic vacation trade is the existence of old, historic structures in close proximity to lakes, rivers, and streams. Many of these structures violate newer state laws regarding construction near water sources and in wetlands. But, because these structures predate the creation of these laws, they cannot be arbitrarily pulled down for nonconformity.

The other side of the issue that concerned Joe was the fate of such structures if they were damaged or destroyed by accident. The boathouses, small vacation cottages, and dinner clubs that nestle up to the bodies of water are part of the character of this region. On occasion, a boathouse might collapse or a restaurant might burn, and issues of reconstruction of facilities versus environmental preservation would come into conflict. The preservation and protection of these structures was important to Handrick, and he sought as a legislator to deal with the problem of nonconforming structures.

"If you drive around the North, you notice there are hundreds of small cottages and homes that could never be built today. They are on property that is not large enough on which to construct a home given current zoning laws. The change [in the law] we made says that if you own [a nonconforming property that is damaged or destroyed] by fire, wind, or vandalism and if your property does not allow you to relocate the structure to make it conforming, you can rebuild in the existing 'footprint.' "

This was one of several examples of Handrick acting to find practical compromises to problems confronted by his constituency. In some other areas—equalizing the fishing rights of other residents with the rights of the Native Americans, or limiting legalized gambling—he was less successful.

## Strategic Reelections

Reelection campaigns for the young incumbent in District 34 were uneventful but never taken for granted. Handrick ran two reelection campaigns, in 1996 and 1998, and won each by large margins. However, he never got past the observation that "paranoia is why incumbents survive." Much like other legislators we meet in this book, Handrick waged constant politics in order to deter potential strong challengers and obliterate others who might run. His specialty was working to take out potential challengers before they could run against him. Most typically this meant trying to knock local Democratic officeholders off balance or out of office. During a conference with me and a legislative staffer in Madison, Joe recalled one such effort.

"We went to this kid—he looked to be about twelve—who was running against this Democratic mayor, and we said, 'Hey, we're here to help you beat [the incumbent].' He couldn't believe that we wanted to come in, do GOTV for him, help him with money and advertising and door drops. Well, we did, and this kid, he becomes mayor of Rhinelander."

Strategic campaigns were run against county board members, school board members, and other local officials. Such practices served three purposes. First, it tried to eliminate potential rivals for Joe's seat in the assembly; a vanquished challenger is less formidable. Second, in addition to the removal of immediate threats, Handrick built up a reservoir of goodwill with other local GOP officials and the local party by building grassroots strength. Finally, he kept his campaign organization and get-out-the-vote data in top shape by constantly exercising it in various off-year local contests. In both 1996 and 1998, Handrick was reelected by substantial margins.

As a campaigner, Handrick was not easily pigeonholed with a variety of national consultants who advocate a top-down, electronic campaign or a one-size-fits all strategy. Despite his evaluation that there was too little grassroots and too much media in his failed senate campaign, Joe sees subtle distinctions of the value of both approaches. As he noted earlier, working doors works. But, at the same time, the other, more visible symbol of grassroots campaigning—yard signs—hold no value to Joe Handrick. "Signs don't vote. If they did, I would be a senator." Handrick recently managed an incumbent campaign where they used no signs, "just to test the hypothesis. Well, we might put *one* out on election day."⁴

While Joe sees media as having limited value by itself, it is highly valuable when used well. "Look, TV is more powerful than any other medium. You can run newspaper ads and put up signs all summer, and no one knows who you are. One week of TV and everybody knows you." Even in small-town Wisconsin, the encroachment of professional political techniques was becoming evident.

This perspective is indicative of an evolution in the politics of the United States. Even in relatively small, local constituencies, the political campaigns are becoming slicker, more media oriented and are increasingly influenced by political professionals. Johnson (2001) observes that this change both affects the opportunities for volunteer participation and is also a product of decreasing campaign volunteerism. When nonprofessionals take part in campaigns, they are driven by numerous motives. The main commonality across them is that they "have personal interests in the candidate, the office, and the issues." In many instances they are continuing a long-standing relationship with the candidate, because they worked for them in the past. Some are looking for entrée into professional politics or government. And, they will work across campaigns when asked, because they are part of a class of amateur political activists who "can usually be relied upon to help other candidates [though their efforts] are almost always limited to their city, county, or state . . . election work is not their principal source of income" (xv).

At the end of the twentieth century, the political landscape of the United States became increasingly professionalized:

> The 1990s witnessed another transformation. Candidates for office below the statewide level were beginning to seek the advice of political consultants. For many candidates, the dividing line was the $50,000: those who could not raise that kind of money had to rely solely on volunteer services . . . professional consulting services, such as phone banks, telemarketing, direct mail, were supplanting the efforts once provided by volunteers. (Johnson 2001: 7)

State legislative campaigns are becoming increasingly costly, even in states with small districts. There has been a decline of engagement in a variety of community activities that undermines the maintenance of small-scale politics on the backs of volunteers. Also, the evolution of communication technologies have changed how even small-scale campaigns are run:

> There is a dwindling number of people who devote free time to helping candidates . . . veteran Republican strategist Stuart Spencer observed that the combination of money and television was leading

to the disappearance of volunteers. "Because of the new technology, few campaigns are 'people campaigns' any more. You don't need a bunch of little old ladies stamping envelopes to send out a direct mail piece." (18)

It is into this new realm of small-scale political consulting that Joe Handrick had been moving, slowly, deliberately, for a number of years, as he planned, coordinated, and executed campaigns for Republican assembly candidates. His future in politics would come from the part of the game he liked best, planning and executing campaign strategies and allocating campaign resources in order to do the most good.

Why is such professionalization increasing? Well, to look at Joe Handrick, his campaigns, and his postelective career, it is because of the increased access to sophisticated production and analytic technologies—video production, layout software, and computerization—and also because active, intelligent campaign technicians like him take an interest in the art of designing campaign materials and messages. "When you look at my commercials," Joe recalled, "you can see the influence of other campaigns, other advertisements in the ads. What I would do in scripting and planning my own ads is look to national and major-race examples of effective ads—you know, like the 'Morning in America' ad, and find a way to adapt it to my own campaign" or a client's campaign. The production values on Handrick's early TV are about what one would expect in a local campaign, at the high end of the cable advertising food chain, but the content and delivery are very professional. His product improved through time.

## Getting Out

Joe from Minocqua was getting tired. The assembly in Wisconsin paid a decent salary by state legislative standards—midthirties—but that pay was not substantial when one considers that a member was constantly gone from home or maintaining two households. The round trip from Minocqua to Madison was five hundred miles, and the drive became tiring after a while. In the spring of 1999, Joe Handrick was into his third term. He had sponsored important legislation for his constituency, completely dominated all comers in his reelection campaigns, and risen to a position of significance on the Reapportionment Committee. Yet, by the end of spring, he was informing the leadership and his constituents that he would not seek another term. At age thirty-three, Joe Handrick was moving on. But to what? And why?

"It first hit me after I won reelection in '98," he told me in the living room of his parents' bed and breakfast, "that I wasn't sure what was next. I mean, here you are, you've accomplished the one goal you had in your life at twenty-eight, and you've risen steadily and done all you can with a job. You start to ask yourself, 'Should I have set my goals higher?' or 'Is this all there is?' " Joe wasn't necessarily bored with politics; instead, his current position posed no challenges. Handrick is very open and specific about the constraints that existed on members to affect public policy design in the majority caucus.

"It got to the point where I realized that a monkey could do my job. I just sat in a chair and pushed green or red depending on where the party was on the issue. Anyone can do that, and you don't have to be very smart to be a legislator if you don't mind having no independence.

"The speaker has total control of everything in the majority caucus," he continued. "If you are not on the inside, completely in line with the leadership, then you are outside." The majority caucus was tightly controlled by a small group of legislators who were close to the speaker and who were completely in agreement with his agenda and would defer to his decisions. Historically, the assembly speaker enjoys substantial power and control, though not always to the extent that Speaker Jensen exercised. "Jensen is brilliant but had to be in control of everything. If you wanted power, you had to be willing to give up your power and your discretion."

A good government advocate, Handrick expressed early and public concerns regarding the party caucus system in the state legislature, and on several occasions he sponsored legislation to defund the caucuses and move their activities out of the capitol. This early recognition of the potential ethical problems in the caucuses was borne out in 2002, when majority leadership in both the assembly and senate were indicted on charges of extortion, ethics violations, and abuse of public office for political activities involving caucus employees. "People now come to me and say, 'Joe, what did you see going on back when you sponsored those bills?' " Joe recalled, with no small amount of regret, that the whole problem might have been avoided.

Ultimately, though, politics and power were not the only reason for Joe Handrick to hang up his spurs. His life had changed dramatically from 1994 to 2000, and he saw other, more important demands on his time. Married in 1990 and elected in 1994, he and his wife were expecting during the 1996 campaign, and Joe campaigned with his new daughter during the 1998 campaign. Another child would arrive in 1999. Handrick put it quite simply to the press: "Many people are qualified to serve in the assembly, but only one person in the world can be my kids' dad." Later, he also commented, "I am leaving for the right reasons. Conservatives talk about family values, and I want to do more than talk about them. Holding this job with two small children is simply not in their best interest."

There were other, powerful ethical reasons for Joe's decision to move on. In 1994, he had run for the assembly as an advocate of term limits. In a press release timed to coincide with his retirement announcement, Joe stated that

> there are a lot of big egos in politics. Candidates need to have a certain amount of ego. You need to believe that you can do the job,

you need the self-confidence that you can make a difference. Where some politicians go wrong is in thinking that the office is about them and forgetting what is really important. . . . [T]his is why I support term limits. People who serve too long simply get too wrapped up in themselves and in getting reelected. They forget who sent them there and what they sent them there to do.

In the end, Joe from Minocqua was confronting the dilemma of many in public service. His personal context had changed; he had children and a spouse, and therefore variety of personal life demands that competed with legislating. He was also professionally frustrated. The situation he described with the leadership and the process by which power was allocated and policy was crafted also frustrated him; he could no longer tolerate the limitations on his ability to affect policy in the legislature. Handrick was going to phase out of his role as assemblyman and phase into the role of campaign consultant and redistricting consultant for the assembly Republicans.

## Postlegislative Career

After leaving the assembly, Joe Handrick started slowly, deliberately to build a clientele in Wisconsin politics. While he was no longer in the legislature, he was still in Madison, housed across the street from the capitol building in an office tower full of government relations law firms and lobbying groups. He was starting small, doing work for two groups, the Bear Hunters and the organization that represents the seven hundred anesthesiologists in Wisconsin. His major contribution over the past two years, though, was a reprise of his 1992 role as the creative master of the Republican legislative redistricting proposals for the assembly and senate.

Handrick was a master of electoral analysis. He knew where to find information and how to glean useable knowledge from numbers that is implicit and based on understanding the totality of issues and messages associated with particular candidates and their circumstances. In 1992, he demonstrated his marriage of technical and political skills in crafting a set of maps for the assembly Republicans that, while not entirely adopted by the federal court panel, were sufficiently close to court-applied standards that they anticipated the map crafted by Judge Posner and his colleagues. In 2001, Handrick would confront a similar challenge, as redistricting bogged down into a stalemate between Republican assembly speaker Scott Jensen and Democratic senate majority leader Chuck Chvala. Again a federal court would craft the maps, and, again, Handrick demonstrated remarkable skill in crafting a set of map proposals that, while not adopted by the court, again reflected the priorities of the court and anticipated the design of the map created by a three-judge panel.

Handrick, together with former Republican caucus staff from the assembly, was contracted as an independent consultant, working through the law firm representing the assembly in redistricting, to develop legislative maps that would stand up to a high degree of scrutiny by the courts and that would also be favorable to Republicans.

Legislative district plans are evaluated on a variety of dimensions, some of which are legal, constitutional, political, or aesthetic. It is expected that state legislative plans will be designed so that all legislative districts have approximately the same number of residents. Legislative district plans cannot violate the racial provisions of equal protection under the Fourteenth Amendment, and they must also comply with the Voting Rights Act while navigating the restrictions against race-based redistricting that arise from Supreme Court cases in the 1990s. State-specific legal standards must also be considered, such as the Wisconsin requirement that senate districts be composed of three whole assembly districts.

Then, a variety of political and aesthetic factors are typical of the "good government" mentality of fair legislative maps. Superior legislative plans under the assumptions of the good government perspective are expected not to divide towns or counties needlessly; not to create needlessly oddly shaped legislative districts and to pursue overall compactness as a virtue of the map as a whole; to avoid needless incumbent pairings from one party over the other party but also not to consider incumbent placement over other criteria; and to have no more political impact than necessary of the balance in the chamber, in order to accommodate population changes since the last census. All Joe Handrick had to do was to craft a set of potential legislative maps that would incorporate all of these features, in a map that was superior to an alternative that Democrats or some intervening party might propose, and that the Court would accept.

As Joe recalled to me, "Our conversations and initial planning indicated that, if we just drew a fair map, we could get a map that would advantage us in the coming decade. . . . I recalled our work with Professor Bibby [John Bibby, of UW–Milwaukee] in the previous redistricting and set about trying to find a measure of partisan fairness that would allow me to baseline changes in the map. We tried to avoid splitting up towns and cities needlessly and worked to draw compact districts."

Just because Joe Handrick produced a fairly neutral map (his best map had very low population deviations, compact districts, competitive districts, very few town divisions, and a very low rate of senate voter disfranchisement) did not mean that he could not craft a better map for Republicans. "Oh, I could have crafted a map that would have allowed us tremendous advantages . . . we could have really done the Democrats." But that map would not have been as good on other, neutral factors that courts might consider when evaluating maps. And, to assist the lawyers and political leaders in the assembly in convincing those with more partisan motivations of the wisdom of the "fair" map, Handrick crafted a "doomsday map. It was the worst-case scenario of what the Democrats could do to us if we were not careful." That map was helpful in convincing those with highly partisan motivations to pursue a strategy of minimizing harm.

The trial established the basic soundness of this strategy, which was advocated by the Republican legal team and implemented by Handrick's electoral artistry. Experts for the various maps on all sides attempted to debunk opposition maps and to advocate for the principles of their client maps. Issues of electoral fairness were interspersed with questions about equal protection and the implementation of the Voting Rights Act vis-à-vis the Wisconsin maps. But, for the federal court, the goal was to collect information, assess the validity of the claims of the various parties, and then take action based on the principles of neutrality and fairness that are the hallmark of court-drawn maps. The court would undertake to remedy what it identified as legal and constitutional defects under the old legislative map, while making no more changes than necessary.

The Handrick map ended up being not far off the mark. The map produced by the three-judge panel remedied the constitutional and legal defects in the old legislative map, and, while it did not come as close as Handrick's maps in terms of population deviations, there was remarkable similarity to the Handrick maps in terms of the neutral "good government" elements of the map. The placement of new districts ensured that Republicans would not only retain control of the assembly but might also win the senate. For his efforts, Joe Handrick was well compensated.

## Running the Conduit

Working in redistricting can be interesting and lucrative. However, redistricting and reapportionment are "seasonal" work; most states will only craft legislative boundaries once per decade, in the wake of the census. Joe Handrick was a talented artisan of electoral maps, and he planned to develop future consulting opportunities for the next reapportionment and redistricting after 2010. In the meantime, he had to find other work.

Handrick's primary role since the end of the redistricting litigation was to run a campaign finance "conduit" for the organization representing anesthesiologists in Wisconsin. This entailed examining legislator voting and behavior, networking, and making recommendations regarding the targeting of donations that channel through the conduit.

He was approached by the organization to come to work for them directly as an executive director. While Joe clearly wanted to work with the organization, given his own professional ties to the health care industry, he did not especially want to be tied down to one client, one job, and acting as

Table 4.3    Candidate Use of a Political Consulting Firm (%)

| Candidate Age | Strategy | Ads | Direct Mail | Polls | Voter Info | Phone Banks | Management | Fund Raising |
|---|---|---|---|---|---|---|---|---|
| **Primary** | | | | | | | | |
| Under 35 (n = 47) | 17.0 | 19.1 | 19.1 | 10.6 | 10.6 | 10.6 | 8.5 | 6.4 |
| 35–55 (n = 155) | 15.5 | 18.1 | 25.2 | 14.2 | 9.0% | 8.4 | 6.5 | 5.8 |
| Over 55 (n = 46) | 10.9 | 6.5 | 17.4 | 10.9 | 8.6 | 8.6 | 6.5 | 4.3 |
| **General Election** | | | | | | | | |
| Under 35 (n = 68) | 11.8 | 8.8 | 16.2 | 20.6 | 11.8 | 5.9 | 5.9 | 5.9 |
| 35–55 (n = 284) | 15.5 | 14.1 | 21.8 | 15.5 | 12.0 | 9.2 | 12.3 | 5.3 |
| Over 55 (n = 114) | 14.0 | 15.8 | 25.4 | 13.2 | 7.9 | 10.5 | 4.4 | 4.4 |

Source: Hogan (1995).

an association executive director might limit his ability to pursue other options. Instead, he suggested that the organization contract him to perform political action on their behalf. The cost was actually somewhat less to the anesthesiologists than if he had come to work for them directly, because the organization did not have to pay payroll taxes or provide benefits to Handrick. For Joe, it meant higher pay and more autonomy, though he would be carrying the tax burden of self-employment.

In addition, Handrick continues to be active in local campaigns, developing mailers for candidates and interest groups, and also occasionally managing a candidate and developing strategy for assembly candidates. This career has potential for growth, especially in a state where the professional legislature and a competitive two-party environment ensures a stream of money for competitive campaigns. Most state legislative campaigns have not used consultants extensively, but the areas where expertise is most often retained dovetails with Handrick's interests. Hogan's survey indicates that consultants were often retained to perform direct mail and, in primaries, to develop advertising (see table 4.3). Handrick has tapped a professional niche, though it is a boutique industry at present.[5]

# Conclusion

Joe Handrick had an early, clear vision of his political ambitions. Those ambitions resided in Madison, as a representative of his neighbors. It was a burning desire, and it was never expressed as a function of any one overarching policy concern or as a part of a larger ambition to attain statewide or national office. Handrick wanted to do government, to act as a conservative voice in a legislature that was, for him, often too liberal. He wanted to represent the values of his neighbors and promote what he describes as the core of the conservative creed: helping people help themselves.

The road to public office for Joe Handrick was not easy. The close calls of his initial campaigns also contained tough lessons about winning and losing that shaped his campaign philosophy and that also caused him to confront both self-doubt and the ego that accompanies the attention paid young, effective politicians. He deferred other goals, including his education and his professional career in occupational therapy, in order to pursue politics. However, it was not until the political context of the constituency changed and Handrick found closure on parts of his life, most notably his education and the initiation of his professional career, that he attained political success.

The Joe Handrick that ran at age twenty was bright, hardworking, and ideologically defined. He did exceptionally well when his performance is compared to expectations, and he was identified as a comer, a rising candidate with promise. But he was also very young, he made mistakes, and there was a limit to his ability to portray himself as a candidate beyond the scope of ideology and energy. The Joe Handrick who ran and won at twenty-eight was a more fully realized candidate. He had a career, a campaign theme that went beyond ideology, and a campaign style that fit his constituency. His win would not have been possible without the person who had lost twice previously. Handrick was considered a serious contender for an open seat because he had worked so hard in his previous campaigns, defying expectations and pressing hard two different incumbent Democratic legislators. He paid his dues, taking the hard lessons of defeat and incorporating them into a campaign plan that would propel him to his personal goals.

Once he achieved his political goal of election to the assembly and had legislated for five years, he discovered that the environment of the legislature did not allow him the scope of participation he sought. His forms of independence and empowerment were not consistent with the power structure of the Republican-controlled assembly; he was unwilling to cede independence to achieve power. Joe moved on from elective office.

If we return to the contexts described in chapter 1, we see that Joe's career is shaped by a variety of changing contexts. The access context held constant. The structural context changed, especially with regard to the continuing value of the legislative seat. In Handrick's first three legislative campaigns, he existed on the first dimension of the legislature's structure, as a recruit, and continued on that dimension as a retained member. He found areas of specialization within the institutional structure. But, ultimately, the existence of a seat that was safe for him and the desire of the leadership to retain him were insufficient to offset the third prong of the legislature's structuring role—authority distribution within the chamber. His needs were not met by the internal organization of the legislature, and therefore the value of his seat was diminished in his eyes.

The context that was most altered was the personal context. Joe Handrick at twenty had one purpose: to run for office. Joe Handrick at twenty-eight was married. Joe Handrick at thirty-three was a father, with a daughter and a son on the way, and, in his mind, legislating and parenting were not consistent pursuits. For Joe, the question he asked of himself in 1994 was irrelevant; it was no longer a matter of what to do after he had accomplished everything he set out to do. In 2000, it was a matter of whether the ambitions of his early youth were consistent with his personal and professional needs. And they were not.

# Notes

1. Holperin had his share of constituency challenges in his last few years in office. In 1990, he was the subject of a recall election because of the spearfishing issue. Holperin opposed special spearfishing privileges for Native Americans, but because he wasn't an active voice against the spearfishing treaty, the most virulent opponents came after him.

2. This is the obligatory baseball reference in this book. Paul Molitor played for the Milwaukee Brewers for fifteen seasons, hitting .306 with over two hundred home runs.

3. A *push poll* is a technique where biased question design, under the guise of polling, is used to persuade a voter by emphasizing candidate negatives.

4. Joe called me before the book went to press and indicated that the incumbent in the experiment was reelected by exactly the same margin as before, when he put out five hundred signs.

5. As an aside, in primaries and general elections, consultant use was typically lowest among younger candidates. Young candidates in general elections most often used professional consultants to develop and implement polls, while other candidates most often used firms to handle direct mail.

# Learning to Legislate 5

> Political society exists for the sake of noble living.
>
> —Aristotle

THE NEW LEGISLATOR faces numerous challenges upon assuming office. These challenges come from multiple directions and can create competing pressures on the new lawmaker. The process of learning legislative procedure, dealing with new colleagues, recognizing and adapting to the power structure of the legislative body, and responding to constituency needs all make demands on the new legislators as great or greater than their campaign experience. The new members have to transition into the role of representative. How do they transition into that role? What do they do? What mistakes do they make?

This chapter focuses on the initial term of Senator Adrian Smith of the Nebraska Unicameral. Senator Smith was initially elected in 1998 and moved quietly, efficiently to create a position for himself in a legislature where he was not only the youngest member, but less than half the average age of members of the chamber. His story is one of careful socialization to the norms of an institution and the creation, incrementally, of a notable legislative agenda.

## Representing

If we start with Hannah Pitkin's (1967) assumption that representation is an activity, then the actions of legislators are part of a larger representing role. There is also, within this context, a general framework for evaluating the process of learning to represent that will inform and affect the pursuit of ambition. All politicians require motivations to run. To take on the onerous task of campaigning requires commitment and some sense of purpose that will be fulfilled by winning. Returning to the work of David Mayhew (1974), those priorities are winning reelection, crafting good public policy, and wielding institutional power.

For the new legislator, the first of these—winning reelection—is the most important. Most legislative bodies possess norms of behavior that limit the ability of new legislators to affect the legislative process. Institutional perks and leadership positions are determined, in most chambers, by some application of a seniority rule, and new members are often bound by a loose body of norms yet a widely prevalent expectation that they will learn the process of the chamber before trying to make their legislative mark (Patterson 1962). Because freshman members rarely enjoy institutional perks out of proportion to their place in the chamber, and because their responsibilities are often procedural rather than substantial, young members will place their first priority on reelection because it is the one activity they can pursue without the direct constraint of institutional norms. It is also the surest activity to guarantee future opportunities for affecting the legislative process or for pursuing political ambitions. Reelection frames and consumes their other political and legislative pursuits.

Reelection is not guaranteed, but state legislators enjoy high levels of electoral security. For the state legislator, then, the activities that pay off in terms of reelection are likely the same ones that benefit members of Congress: cultivation of the constituency, favorable position taking with regard to concerns of the district, and claiming credit for tangible benefits to the district (Cain, Ferejohn, and Fiorina 1987; Mayhew 1974). Another legislative behavior that pays benefits is constituency service and representing constituency values (Fiorina 1977; Mann and Wolfinger 1980). Crane and Watts (1968) indicate that constituency influences are *especially* evident for state legislators, because "the strong parochial bias in state legislative recruitment suggests that, for many matters, the representative will be a 'walking input' of constituency demands to the legislative system" (16).

Within the chamber, new legislators identify and follow norms of behavior in order to establish themselves, pursue their legislative goals, and advance their future ambitions. On the campaign trail, the experience of winning an election feeds the ego and creates a sense of centrality in the candidate; once in the legislature, the new member is just one among a large group of peers and often less than equal, depending on the norms and rules of the body. Norms vary from institution to institution, but prior research has consistently reinforced the findings of John Wahlke and his colleagues (1962) that most legislatures in the United States have some form of norms that dictate the performance of obligations, respect for other members, impersonality of decision making, self-restraint in debate, and courtesy to peers and the institution. Members who fail to adhere to norms may find themselves cut off from future avenues of influence or dismissed from potential opportunities to increase their stature.[1]

So what behavior should we expect of the new legislator? The member should be engaged in efforts to build her reputation within the chamber, within the bounds of accepted norms and rules of behavior. The member should set out to make some legislative accomplishment for the purpose of credit claiming, but not necessarily be so active that she violates the expectations of junior members. The member should cultivate the constituency and make efforts to deter possible challengers, in order to help ensure reelection. The member should transition from the role of candidate—the political loner—to the role of legislator—the colleague.

New members develop their initial representative style. Richard Fenno (1991) points out that this adjustment is made by every legislator. In his observation of Arlen Specter, Fenno notes that "in their earliest stages of adjustment, Senate newcomers sort, by trial and error, the elements of prior experience that are usable in the new environment from those that are not" (30–31). Wahlke et al. argue that this idea of the representative role is in fact the organizing concept that integrates behavioral and institutional aspects of legislating. For the young, new legislator, those experiences are limited and may be based more on historical knowledge and education rather than life experience or campaign experiences; institutional aspects can overwhelm prior experiences, because the institutional influences come during the behavioral formation of the politician.

## Political Context: Nebraska

The chamber of the Nebraska Unicameral Legislature resembles a cathedral. The walls are stone, and the balconies and entrances are supported by pillars cut from the marble of the state. The ceiling is vaulted, supported by heavy beams. This chamber, the Norris Chamber, was originally the state House chamber when Nebraska had a bicameral legislature. The state changed to a unicameral legislature ("the Unicam") during the Great Depression, thanks to the prodding and active support of liberal Republican senator George Norris. The body is technically nonpartisan, so there are no formal party caucuses or floor leadership, and the rules of debate allow individual legislators substantial influence in the legislative process. The chamber makes all committee assignments and elects all of the leadership, including the speaker and committee chairs. Actual committee membership is determined by an executive committee, which has administrative control of the chamber.

This nonpartisan orientation formally extends to the state's legislative elections. In Nebraska, all legislative candidates appear in a nonpartisan primary in May. The top two vote getters then proceed to a general election the subsequent November. In fact, the parties recruit and slate candidates, and campaign literature and advertisements will often carry a party affiliation. Most campaigns for the legislature are waged against incumbents. A conventional wisdom of Nebraska legislative elections is that an incumbent who does not lead the May primary vote is in trouble for the November general election. Term limits have recently been enacted in Nebraska and will take hold in 2004. Members will be limited to two four-year terms in the legislature. While incumbents are generally retained, it is not unheard of for incumbents to lose reelection (three Democratic incumbents were felled in 2002).

The Unicam is unique for the amount of access that it affords to both individual members and the public. All meetings are public, and executive sessions of legislative committees are open to the press. The floor of the legislature is bracketed by a pair of porches, the press galleries, which are at the same level as the floor and have tables and chairs for the press. Senators can move to these "porches" to give impromptu interviews or discuss business with reporters and legislative staff. Staffers and reporters can go onto the floor during session, except when a vote is being taken, and red-jacketed sergeants-at-arms staff deliver messages from the informative people who congregate in the lobby.

This is a very old, "citizen" legislator. Remuneration for service is only $12,000 per year, plus per diem during session, which lasts for almost five months. Most legislators are retired, independently wealthy, or married to an individual with a notable income. The average age of the Unicam is fifty-eight, and the average age of the executive committee that administers the chamber is sixty-six. There is a very clear generational divide in the legislature between the middle-aged to elderly majority and the small yet assertive under-thirty-five minority.

The opportunity structure for political advancement is constrained. Nebraska has few major offices to contest—governor, U.S. Senate seats, three U.S. House seats, a few cabinet posts, and the forty-nine seats in the legislature. In this state of 1.9 million residents, few avenues exist for pursuing progressive political ambition. Of the four Nebraskans who served in the U.S. Senate in the 1990s, three—Bob Kerrey, Ben Nelson, and James Exon—were immediate, past governors of the state, while Chuck Hagel came from a broadcasting background. Of the six U.S. representatives elected in the last decade, four had prior elective experience, three in the Unicameral and one on the Omaha City Council. The remaining two frame the span of amateur options, with Jon Christenson winning office at thirty-one without prior office-holding experience, while Tom Osborne, a former national champion football coach, is a classic celebrity.

Nebraska politics allow for both high-level, lateral entry to major office and also vertical advancement by the ambitious who choose the route through state and local politics. One need not start young, however. Of the eleven people who served in high office (Congress, Senate, governor), only one was in public office before age thirty, and just three held elective office before age thirty-five.

## Mr. Smith Goes to Lincoln

In 1999, Adrian Smith was a freshman legislator from the far western Nebraska city of Gering, part of an island of population in Scotts Bluff County. His district was four hundred miles from the state capitol. It is easier to get from Gering to Denver, Colorado, than to Lincoln. Business often deals with the two Rocky Mountain states, and the public sector often looks to the western tristate area for interaction in educational and regulatory innovation. Although metropolitan Scotts Bluff is not large by any standards, it is the home of two network affiliated television stations and several newspapers, creating a role for media campaigning in a small community.

A real estate agent by vocation, Adrian came from a comfortable, established family that was active in local politics. (His father, Neal Smith, was the county GOP chair.) Adrian was involved in politics from his earliest opportunities. In 1992, as an undergraduate at the University of Nebraska, he was a page in the Unicameral, and in 1993, he was on staff for Governor Nelson. Returning home to Gering after college, he was elected to the city council and was subsequently recruited to challenge an incumbent senator. He garnered more votes than incumbent Joyce Hillman in the initial May primary and then won handily in the general election. As he relates it, the incumbent had left a paper trail of unpopular votes during her tenure, reflecting Kingdon's (1973) string of votes thesis. Given challenger Smith's good-natured demeanor on the campaign trail, the combination of a tarnished incumbent and an energetic challenger was sufficient to obliterate the advantages of incumbency (Fenno 1990).

Joyce Hillman served two terms in the Unicameral without serious opposition. But, as the local press noted in 1998:

> Hillman is getting her first taste of partisan politics against a young Reaganesque conservative who interned in her legislative office in 1991 and who finished first in the May primary by 800 votes. An anti-abortion, pro-family Republican, Adrian Smith, 27, is putting the abortion-rights, pro-business Democrat's cross-party appeal to the test.[2]

Former mayor Don Overman observed that one should "keep in mind, this area is conservative, and I would not classify her as a conservative." Local Democrats contend that the GOP is decidedly to the right; Democrat Bill Peters opined that "a substantial portion of the local Republican Party is controlled by people who adhere to very fundamentalist ideas." Voter registration reflects the rightward tilt of the district; whereas 50 percent of all Nebraska voters are registered Republicans, the figure for District 48 is 65 percent.

Smith's campaign combined much of the long-term planning we observed earlier in the campaigns by Shane Hunt and Joe Handrick with intensity and political networking. But there is something more. It was an exercise in deliberate, sustained effort and perseverance. Smith started campaigning over a year before the election. A retrospective by the *Omaha*

*World-Herald* declared that "Adrian Smith has been on the campaign trail so long he remembers being the only candidate on the road." Political observers attribute Smith's campaign for his success, noting that his "early campaign blitz" contributed to his overwhelming victory. Smith was outspent but prevailed by ten points.[3] The Republican who recruited him, former lieutenant-governor Bill Nichol, observed, "Adrian Smith, as I understand it, was going door-to-door a lot. That helped. . . . He's also a sincere young man, and he didn't throw mud."

But it was more than hard work; it was also the values Smith carried and his strong, personal ties to the GOP that interacted with hard work to put him over the top. Smith was closer to his constituency than the incumbent on most issues of concern: He was prolife, profamily, in a part of the country where family ties were still strong and where community relationships go back generations. The "early bird assault" together with the grassroots organization and intensive contacting created a strong challenge.

Local banker Hod Kosman had helped Smith in assembling a grassroots organization for the May primary. According to Kosman, "[Smith] had an organization in place that neutralized the incumbent status [of Joyce Hillman]." His campaign organization was able to tap latent Republican strength that had not been realized in previous elections, including support from the Nebraska Christian Coalition. Dennis Johnson (2001: 19) observes that "Christian-based organizations were very successful at local organization in the 1990s," and Smith's campaign was an example of how the combination of candidate, organization, and message can be very effective at the grass-roots. Newspaperman Jack Lewis echoed the sentiment expressed by others, saying that Smith combined his energy, message, and organization with a strong effort to line up GOP support. "The Republican Party got behind Adrian Smith . . . in my mind, that was the difference."

## Senator

Senator Smith was, in 1999, the junior-most senator in the legislature and therefore filled a special role saved for the most junior member: chair of the Enrollment and Review Committee. This position brings high visibility to the junior member, but it is also a position that is largely ceremonial and procedural in nature. Enrollment and Review has no staff, no jurisdiction, and no real authority. The chair makes procedural motions regarding the introduction and dispensation of legislation in the Unicam. On every piece of legislation, the enrollment and review chairman is expected to make a series of procedural motions, to move forward legislative business. The youngest member becomes especially well acquainted with the process of legislating; it also means that, because of this conspicuous role, the youngest freshman cannot be absent from the floor for long or miss a session entirely without disrupting the legislative process. Smith was acutely aware of his role.

Adrian Smith was a serious, workmanlike man who appeared modest and cautious. Subsequent interaction and reflection has not altered this perception. Smith arrives at the office early and makes use of every free moment of his day. Unlike many legislators, he rarely left the capitol, even for lunch. He took his job in the legislature seriously and was especially careful about avoiding making mistakes or needlessly rocking the boat.

*Caution* was the watchword with freshman Smith. He was cautious in entering this study, and this caution is also evident in interactions with others, whether colleagues, lobbyists, or staff. He refused to even dine with his female staffer, not because it is a taboo to interact with staff but because, according to one staffer "he is afraid that someone will get the wrong idea." Despite all of his reserve, Adrian Smith seemed quite at ease and comfortable with kids, and he related well to young people. Field trips by fourth-grade classes were fun for him, and, when there are lulls in the legislative action, Adrian would sometimes visit with the legislative pages, to talk or joke with them. They clearly warm up to him, and he seemed quite animated in dealing with the pages. This interaction stood as a nice contrast to his more serious, legislative persona in debate, and it was doubtlessly a reflection of his campaign persona.

Adrian gives much of the credit for his successful transition into the legislature to Senator Jon Bruning, whom we will examine at length in chapter 10. Bruning had two more years of service in the legislature, and, as I learned in my interactions with both, Smith and Bruning developed a very close professional relationship that also has a personal dimension. Bruning's first two years in the legislature were far more raucous than Smith's initiation; those experiences of his colleague were not lost on Smith, who looked to Bruning for advice and counsel during the early days of his first term. "That is why I am lucky to have Jon [Bruning] here. I can learn from his experiences the last two years."

Smith was carefully feeling out his role in the chamber. The norms of the Unicam are loose, due to the rules of debate that allow virtually any member essentially to halt the progress of legislation through a very liberal amending and debate process. One norm that is generally followed in the institution is that, during their first one or two years in the legislature, new members deal with relatively safe legislation, take care of constituency service, plow through committee work, and attend to procedural duties. Boat rocking and floor participation during debate are limited to fewer, more senior members or members with recognized and highly particular expertise, or to Ernie Chambers (again, a matter taken up at great length with Senator Bruning's case).

As a freshman, Adrian Smith was not anxious to advance a large number of legislative proposals. His agenda was very much tied to representing his district's interests and to tending duties in the chamber. As he saw it, the four-year term was his advantage in getting socialized. "It gives me time to find and develop issues; I am not under pressure to show now, right now, that I can pass a bill. We're only sponsoring one bill, and it is my priority." This is a good strategy for a member operating under the rules of the Unicam. In the Nebraska legislature, every senator can earmark one bill as a "priority" bill and almost guarantee that it will be heard on the floor. For the savvy young legislator, the priority bill becomes the initial legislative accomplishment and a vehicle for demonstrating their parliamentary skill. Others might mark a bill not their own as a priority, in order to advance an issue of importance to leadership or other, more senior members.

The need to balance legislative life and personal life was not as great for Senator Smith as for some legislators, because he did not have a spouse or children. Still, family mattered. He returned home to the district every weekend during session (an eight-hundred-mile round trip) and also had family down to visit during session. On my last day in Lincoln in March 1999, he hosted cousins from out of town, as guests on the chamber floor. The lack of immediate family ties frees Adrian Smith of all but professional obligations.

The structure of the Unicameral would seem to facilitate the pursuit of political ambition. The four-year term is helpful to the new legislator, because it gives that member time to develop legislative expertise, and it shelters him from the pressures of constant campaigning. The longer term also means that senators can take a "free shot" at higher office, such as Congress or a cabinet post. Two factors mitigate against the excessive pursuit of ambition from out of the Unicam. The opportunities for vertical advancement are few, as noted earlier, and most members are not positioned to pursue that ambition. Almost half of members are over age sixty, which means that there is a limited horizon for them seriously to seek higher state office or run for Congress (see, e.g., Schlesinger 1966; Huckshorn and Spencer 1971; Canon 1990). Also, recall from chapter 2 that progressive ambitions are largely purged from the souls of state legislators over fifty-five. For most Nebraska state senators, the Unicam is the pinnacle of their political career.

Smith has speculated about a future in government service. But does he have progressive ambition? The answer is yes, but any ambitions are tempered by an intense disdain for Washington. In response to Thomas Kazee's criterion question "If offered a seat in Congress at no cost, would you take it?" Adrian turned down the free ride. "Congress and Washington do not represent the kind of politics I want to be in. The two-year term means that you are always campaigning. Congress . . . does not embody the best elements of public service." He has ambition for possible higher office within Nebraska, maybe even becoming governor. Or, it is entirely possible that he will just abandon politics at some point, if the emotional, economic, or other personal costs become too great. As he indicated during our first meeting, "how long I do this will depend on how long I can afford to."

Like many young people who grew up in the 1980s, Smith was strongly influenced by the presidency of Ronald Reagan. Reagan's autobiography and a text of Reagan's speeches adorn the shelves of his office, alongside die-cast models of John Deere tractors. "To me, Ronald Reagan brought back pride in America, pride in the military. He made people respect America." Adrian also subscribes to Reagan's less-national-government philosophy—a distinction that is often lost to many casual conservatives. "Coming out of local government [in Gering,] I know what local government can do, . . . I want to do things that put government action back down where people can control it, give it back to the towns and cities, . . . Reagan didn't say 'less government'; he said 'less national government.' Government can do good things."

## Caution in Action

The first morning I spent with Adrian Smith started with a meeting with a consultant from the computing industry who was working with the University of Nebraska on modernizing computer access and support resources for the law school. He dropped in on Smith to discuss a policy matter related to efforts to complete this project, and Adrian sent him off with advice regarding how to deal with the legislature. Later, there was an extended visit by a lobbyist from the health care industry. She offered extensive—and unsolicited—advice to him regarding pending legislation on the reduction of the number of nursing home beds in Nebraska. She urged him to seek instruction from an industry member in his district. At no point during any lobbyist visit did I see Adrian commit to a course of action, and I suspect that, while he found the information brought by some lobbyists to be helpful, he did not fully appreciate the direction to seek instruction from industry. Nonetheless, he exhibited a gentle touch and showed no obvious displeasure.

An example of Smith's gentle touch with the interest group community came in a meeting with a group representing independent trash and refuse haulers. These lobbyists had particular concerns regarding efforts to maintain their market share in the face of national competition. Adrian convinced the three industry lobbyists of the impropriety of their effort to change a pending bill that would affect their clientele. His argument was persuasive and reflected the temporizing approach that is Smith's trademark. The lobbyists, I learned through indirect means, went back to the legislator who initially agreed to carry the amendment and told him to "forget it. Senator Smith said it was a bad idea."

Writing in 1999, I noted to myself, "What does Adrian Smith have to do to establish himself in the legislature and back in his district?" The answer, based on our visits and my observation, was that issues mattered to his reelection. Smith's predecessor was defeated because of her support for a series of measures that were unpopular in her constituency. However, issues matter not because important matters were not addressed but because the member wasted time on issues unimportant to western Nebraska; she put together the classic "string of votes" against the constituency that can doom an incumbent. Smith was careful, moving to establish himself in the legislature without controversy, while slowly building a portfolio of legislative accomplishments that will allow him to continue this legislative career or pursue some other ambition. The role he sought and exhibited was that of a serious man with a definite policymaking orientation to the job of legislator. His initiation as a politician did not come in the legislature but in his campaign for and subsequent tenure as city councilman in his hometown. He brings those experiences to the Unicam and was following a proven course for success: Keep quiet until asked your opinion, learn how the process works, and hone your skills with small accomplishments. Then, take on something bigger.

The press noted Smith's cautious demeanor, observing, "Most of the new senators say they plan on introducing fewer than 10 bills each; they are more interested in learning the ropes than proposing legislation. 'I'd rather ease in and take things at a manageable pace,' Smith said."[4] Adrian Smith introduced one piece of legislation, LB621, which would have allowed the sale of fireworks from December 28, 1999, to January 1, 2000. Twenty-five cosponsors signed on (out of forty-nine senators). Was this a controversial proposal? Not really. In 1998, thirteen known fires were attributed to fireworks at a total cost in damages of under $25,000, total. (Six injuries were reported in the state that were related to fireworks.) The goal of the legislation was to keep fireworks dollars in Nebraska. Neighboring Wyoming had year-round fireworks sales, and if the one-time increase in sales could help Nebraska vendors, it would be good for local business (and also good for state sales tax receipts). Just after our March visit, Smith's fireworks bill made its way to the floor of the Unicameral. The freshman legislator found himself caught up in one of Senator Ernie Chambers's procedural conundrums. Chambers, a legendary African American political independent and self-described "defender of the down-trodden," is known for his ability to halt legislation he objects to, through a combination of delaying tactics and pointed questioning of opponent in debate. Clad in blue jeans and a short-sleeved sweatshirt with cigarettes rolled up in one sleeve, barber-cum-lawyer Chambers clips his opponents with parliamentary skill and a caustic wit. As the Associated Press reported it,

> Freshman Senator Adrian Smith of Gering thought the one bill he introduced this year would sail through the Legislature like a bottle rocket. His proposal allowing fireworks sales . . . soared out of committee with no opposition. The measure came up for debate for the

first time today with no amendments and no controversy. But then, with no warning, Sen. Ernie Chambers of Omaha filed a motion to kill the bill. All eyes were on Smith, who had the option of skipping over the bill (LB621) or debating the kill motion. "Take it up! Take it up!" nearby senators urged. He did. But Chambers immediately withdrew the motion. "I just wanted to call everyone's attention to the fact that it is April 1." . . . Smith breathed a sigh of relief, everyone had a good laugh and the bill went on to advance 35–2. . . . [Speaking of Chambers, Smith said,] "He keeps me on my toes. It's good for me."[5]

The next time Smith had to tangle with Ernie Chambers, it would be no joke.

## Emergence of a Legislative Force

In the second part of his first term, Senator Smith was very active on issues related to legalized gambling and games of chance. Smith, no supporter of gambling, was especially disturbed by practices that misrepresent games or the chances of winning those games or that use actors to portray players. When the AP surveyed the Unicameral in January 2001 and asked, "Should casino-style gaming be allowed on Nebraska Indian reservations?" Smith was one of twenty-three senators who said, "Definitely no." And, when Ernie Chambers introduced legislation to ban the Nebraska State Lottery (LB905) as of July 1, 2001, Smith signed on to cosponsor the legislation, which he admitted had "little chance of passing."

The young senator would not seek the elimination of state-sponsored gaming, but he was trying to minimize the externalities arising from gambling and was dedicated to using the revenues from gaming to treat those who sought help because they were adversely affected by gaming. In the 2000 session, Smith introduced legislation that would link funding for treatment of compulsive gambling to the state's advertising spending on the Nebraska lottery. His proposal would have tripled spending on treatment of compulsive gambling in Nebraska to $1.5 million, and, fitting with Smith's governmental philosophy, the measure was revenue-neutral. He also proposed legislation (LB1174) to compel the publication of the odds of winning the state lottery grand prize and also proposed to ban actors from portraying lottery winners in advertising for the lottery. "I believe [the advertisements] are misleading . . . to me, they're insinuating that all you have to do to win is play." He contrasted the detrimental effects of gambling against two other out-of-favor sins that are taxed by Nebraska: smoking and drinking. "Would the state, to increase revenues, promote the consumption of alcohol and tobacco? Absolutely not. But the state, to increase revenue, seems to disregard any compulsive gambling potential."[6]

Smith's policy initiative was well placed. Gambling was an increasing problem in Nebraska in the late 1990s, and, at a February 2000 public hearing on the compulsive-gambling counseling legislation, information was advanced that indicated the growing magnitude of the problem. According to testimony at the hearing, the number of callers to the Gamblers' Helpline increased from 419 in 1993 to 6,704 in 1999. The number of persons in state-funded treatment programs increased from 79 in 1997 to 164 by 1999. Those seeking help had increased almost 1,500 percent, and the number of persons in treatment facilities had doubled. During the same period, the budget for compulsive gambling counseling actually fell from about $430,000 to $410,000, even though demand for treatment increased and waiting lists for counseling arose in many areas. The decline of funding was a product of decreased lottery revenues; as revenues fell with the introduction of casino gambling across the river in Iowa, table gambling and slots increased in the population while revenues from lottery gaming in Nebraska declined. Smith argued that "the lottery revenues are going down while the need is going up." And, as lottery revenues fall, states typically increase spending on advertising and marketing new games. Smith's bill would tie counseling funds not only to revenues but also to advertising costs to promote the lottery.[7] This move assured that counseling funding would go up with efforts to promote the lottery, rather than fall as the lottery revenues declined in the face of Iowa gambling.

To advance his counseling initiative, Smith ended up making one of those pragmatic choices that often confront legislators: weighing the overall good of a bill against its overall harm. Much of the population of Nebraska lives within driving distance to casinos located in Iowa or on Indian reservations in other states. This gaming, especially electronic gaming, was cutting into legal forms of gambling that the state has benefited from in the past, most notably keno and "pickle" cards—also known as "pulltabs" or "lucky sevens."[8] Legislation was pending that would have allowed for the placing of electronic pickle card machines in Nebraska. The bill had stalled in part because keno game operators opposed the introduction of electronic pickle games unless electronic keno was also allowed. A touch-screen keno amendment failed 16–19,[9] and gaming opponents were forthright in their reasons for opposition. Senator Jim Jensen made a representative argument, stating that "the closer we get to electronic gaming devices, the closer we get to slot machines." Smith, a gaming opponent, had attached an amendment to increase funding for the Compulsive Gamblers Assistance Fund by $500,000, to be paid from gaming profits. His other legislation had been advanced from the General Affairs Committee, but in the labyrinth of procedures in the Unicameral, advancement from committee is no guarantee of success.[10] The AP reported that "one opponent of gambling, however, ended up supporting the bill. Senator Adrian Smith of Gering cast an 'aye' vote after he successfully got one of his bills attached to the pickle-card measure in the form of an amendment. . . . [Smith commented,] 'I think there's a greater good to this bill.' "[11]

Smith's efforts to help fund treatment for compulsive gamblers would languish for another six weeks. Then, in April, with just days left in session, the legislation found new life.

> A bill that would boost the amount of money spent on compulsive gambling programs earned support late Monday in the Nebraska Legislature. The proposal, passed on a 32–1 vote, was salvaged from a dying bill that would have allowed pickle cards and keno games to be computerized. It then advanced to the third and final round of legislative debate on a voice vote. "We're acknowledging there's a problem and we're willing to address that problem at 9:30 P.M.," State Sen. Adrian Smith of Gering said shortly before lawmakers adjourned at 10 P.M.[12]

## Firestorm: 2001 Legislature

For every conservative in the Unicameral, the time seems to come, sooner or later, when he has to tangle with Ernie Chambers. It is almost like sending a young scout into a cave to tangle with a bear. He might wound the bear, he might kill the bear, but the most important thing is to get out of the cave with your head, so you can remember the lessons of how the bear can be fought. Adrian Smith had his moments with the bear, such as the April Fool's joke over his fireworks bill, but his fight in the cave came during the 2001 legislature. The big fight with the bear came during the session, when LB215, a minor measure introduced by Smith, became the center of controversy after Ernie Chambers introduced a rider amendment to "prohibit real estate license holders from discriminating against people based on sexual orientation" when those people are buying or renting property. Smith said the amendment was vague and unenforceable, but the measure advanced by a vote of 26–8. In explaining his opposition to the amendment, Smith stated, "I believe that sex orientation is a chosen lifestyle and should not receive protective status." He was the only senator to speak against the amendment and, as was his prerogative, retained the right to withdraw the bill before final passage. The original bill prohibited discrimination based on "religion, race, color, national origin, sex, family status, or disability."[13]

Chambers's amendment was another example of the parliamentary games he has played with the legislative process in Nebraska for three decades. His amendment was advanced late in the day, after several senators had been excused, including some of Chambers's most steadfast opponents, such as Smith's close ally Jon Bruning. While the measure was passed with solid majority support, Smith might have been able to use other parliamentary devices such as the filibuster had there been more conservative senators on the floor to help sustain him.

As the session entered April, "Smith, a Gering real estate agent, said he has not decided what action to take . . . he said he doesn't want to discriminate against gay people, but he is concerned that the measure as written lacked public comment and would be difficult to enforce."[14] Among his options were to fight to defeat the bill on final passage, which was unlikely, since a majority of senators had already approved the amended form; withdraw the bill, thereby killing it; or letting it pass. As the legislature entered its final week, Smith had decided to scuttle the bill. "State Senator Adrian Smith has decided to let a real-estate bill die rather than have it approved containing a gay-rights amendment." The Nebraska Board of Realtors and the Nebraska Real Estate Commission, "which worked for several years" to get the legislation developed and advanced, disagreed with the decision. Robert Moine, a realtors' lobbyist, said, "I don't think the Realtors see [the amendment] as a problem one way or the other."[15] It was within Smith's rights, as primary sponsor, to withhold the bill. Senator Chambers, after amending the bill, subsequently signed on as cosponsor (proving that you can pick your friends but not your cosponsors) and asked Smith to step aside and allow him to advance the bill. Smith refused. "It is my desire that it not come up this year . . . my desire is that it not pass with that amendment."

In the end, Smith did withdraw from the legislation and allowed it to advance to final passage. He allowed it to go forward because Senators Chambers and Landis threatened to attach it to another piece of legislation as an amendment, potentially clogging the calendar at the end of the session. When the bill did eventually come up, it was passed on a 27–16 vote on May 30. Governor Johanns subsequently vetoed the measure, stating that "the bill goes beyond mere tolerance and clearly creates a legal classification based on sexual choices." It had advanced with the support of the state realtors, but without the support of the original sponsor. Senator Smith "disowned the proposal after Chamber's amendment . . . and fought against it." The Nebraska Family Council, which had previously campaigned for a ban on same-sex marriage, also lobbied against the bill. An effort to override the bill failed on a 26–19 vote; thirty of forty-five votes were needed to override the veto.[16] Smith had come out of the cave scarred, but with his head intact and with Chambers's amendment defeated. And he would be a better and more effective legislator for the experience.

## Conclusion

The career of Adrian Smith is established. As his first term closed, he could point to some legislative successes that were consistent with his political phi-

losophy and that were in line with the preferences of his conservative constituency. He had gone head to head with the most fearsome legislator in the
Unicameral, and while he did not necessarily prevail on the floor of the chamber, his convictions and constituents were satisfied with his efforts to battle
Chambers, and a sympathetic governor vetoed the offending legislation.
And, in 2002 Smith gained successful reelection to the Unicameral without
opposition. He created a reputation as a serious legislator, a force, and had
also made his seat safe. Unfortunately for Adrian Smith, his career and his
ambitions are now circumscribed by term limits. In November 2000,
Nebraska voted in term limits, holding state senators to two four-year terms.

Events have also revealed that Adrian Smith harbors progressive ambitions. When Nebraska secretary of state Scott Moore resigned in 2001, Smith
was a finalist for the balance of the term. Along with Senator Jon Bruning,
he was interviewed by the governor, and both were cited prominently in press
coverage of the selection. He was not selected. In September 2001, after the
resignation of incumbent lieutenant-governor Dave Maurstad, speculation
abounded regarding who incumbent governor Mike Johanns would appoint
as his successor. Adrian Smith's name was frequently mentioned, though
Smith clearly stated at the time that his "first priority is serving in the Legislature." He still has no expressed ambitions for Congress.

It is in this context of progressive ambition that we can evaluate Smith's
brief legislative career. From the start, with modest legislation related to
fireworks sales, the youngest member of the legislature crafted a reputation
for careful, circumspect behavior and demonstrated a strong determination
to fight for those issues he believed in. While he has not advanced in state
politics beyond his current station, those efforts have created a reputation
that invites positive speculation as to his further political ambitions.

## Notes

1. Jewell and Patterson suggest that norms are, indeed, more important than
procedural rules in the state legislatures.

2. *Omaha World-Herald*, October 18, 1998.

3. *Omaha World-Herald*, "Early Start Led to Newcomer's Success in West,"
November 5, 1998, 13.

4. Associated Press, "Nine New Senators Begin Settling into Their New
Jobs," January 19, 1999.

5. Associated Press, "April Fools! Motion to Kill Fireworks Bill Catches
Freshman Off Guard," April 1, 1999.

6. *Omaha World-Herald*, "Anti-Lottery Bill Seeks to Win Points for Cause,"
January 6, 2000. See also *Omaha World-Herald*, "Bill Targets Actors in Lottery
Ads," February 6, 2000, 1B.

7. *Omaha World-Herald*, "State Should Ante Up," February 12, 2000, 10.

8. In Nebraska, part of the proceeds from gaming are dedicated. Pickle card games are used to fund charitable organizations. Keno games are used to fund special projects in municipalities.

9. *Omaha World-Herald*, "Video-Pickle Bill Stalls," February 25, 2000.

10. Associated Press, "Other Gambling News," February 24, 2000.

11. Associated Press, "Other Gambling News."

12. *Omaha World-Herald*, "In the Legislature," April 11, 2000, 15.

13. Associated Press, "Bill Prohibiting Discrimination of Gays Related to Housing Advances," April 3, 2001.

14. *Omaha World-Herald*, "Gay-Rights Measure Advances," April 5, 2001.

15. *Omaha World-Herald*, "Gay-Rights Amendment Sinks Real Estate Bill," May 24, 2001, 23.

16. Associated Press, "Johanns Vetoes Housing Discrimination Protection for Gays," May 31, 2001; Associated Press, "Gays Getting Housing Discrimination Protection," May 31, 2001; *Omaha World-Herald*, "Legislature Races to Finish Line," May 31, 2001, 1; *Omaha World-Herald*, "Gay Housing Veto Stands," June 1, 2001, 13.

# Match and Rematch                                6

> Nice guys always finish last.
>> —Leo Durocher, manager, New York Giants
>
> Leo Durocher was wrong. By 343 votes, it turns out.
>> —Anonymous observer on District 45

INCUMBENTS DO NOT often lose. When incumbents do lose, it is often due to a combination of factors—some vulnerability, a bad chain of votes that were out of line with the constituency, or a scandal. They also lose because of an altered context of the constituency, demographic shifts through time, or a change in the preferences of the voters in the district. Or they confront a strong, well-funded challenger who negates the incumbent's advantages. In a competitive district with a new incumbent who beat the old incumbent, the newcomer will be acutely aware of the need to consolidate political support lest she goes the way of the predecessor.

In 2000, the Oklahoma House Forty-fifth District hosted a contest that featured an incumbent who had vulnerabilities on issues, on scandal, and on his maintenance of the district. His district was in the midst of an ongoing secular political shift away from his party. And he confronted a young, well-funded challenger. The incumbent lost. Two years later they met again, in reversed roles.

Oklahoma 45 is largely the city of Norman, a college town founded on the first day of the land rush in 1889. The district contains numerous working-class suburbs and small industry. Until redistricting, District 45 ran south out of the city limits, south to the town of Noble. Now, after redistricting, the district stops at the Norman city line to the south and extends east to Little Axe, taking in large stretches of rural territory. New housing developments are springing up on the northeast side of Norman, including neighborhoods with expansive, expensive homes. In 1992, this was safe Democratic territory, with reliable majorities for Democrats up and down the ticket. A decade later, the Forty-fifth has developed competitive electoral habits and has elected a young Republican state representative, Thad Balkman.

This is the story of Balkman's challenge to incumbent Democrat Wallace Collins in 2000, his efforts to legislate from the minority side of the aisle during his first term in office, and his rematch with Collins in 2002. Balkman's status changed, but the nature of his campaign technique and presentation were not dramatically altered. What did change was the context in which he presented himself—incumbency—and his ability to present himself as a performer, rather than as a prospect. A strong effort by the new incumbent was necessary, because he faced what was arguably one of the toughest propositions in politics: unseating an incumbent of the opposing party, and then trying to make the district safe for himself.

# A Competitive Constituency

The Forty-fifth District was a traditionally safe Democratic constituency until 1994. Dominated by university employees, union workers, and old-line rural Democrats, the district last sent a Republican to the legislature in 1921, when Ralph Hardie was elected on the coattails of Warren G. Harding. The district subsequently elected a series of Democrats. The incumbent member in 1992, Representative Ed Crocker (Dem.), won election by a sizeable 57 percent, versus 43 percent for his Republican challenger, Steve Byas. Byas challenged Crocker again in 1994. Despite a dramatic increase in spending by Crocker, the Democrat carried the district by just sixty votes. Crocker vacated the seat in 1996 to run for Congress against Republican J. C. Watts. With Crocker's departure, Democrats held onto District 45 with machinist Wallace Collins. Republicans advanced Steve Byas for a third try, and Libertarian Randy Boyd made the race. Collins held the seat for the Democrats by a margin of just seventy-nine votes out of almost twelve thousand cast. It was a vicious election fight. Collins would later be successfully sued by his 1996 primary and general election opponents for libel. The incumbent was reelected in 1998, with a razor-thin margin of just seventy-one ballots. The Forty-fifth District had become one of the battlegrounds of Oklahoma politics, the type of district where control of the legislature would be decided in the next decade.

In 2000, three challengers filed for nomination to run against Collins. The first of these, former Libertarian Randy Boyd, was a nonfactor who spent little time, money, or effort on a campaign. The other two Republicans were young, attractive, and well funded. John English was a former staffer for Governor Frank Keating, a recent alumnus of the University of Oklahoma, and a well-connected candidate. His father was a former Democratic congressman; English was endorsed by Keating and had a substantial war chest.

The other major candidate was twenty-eight-year-old attorney Thad Balkman. A recent graduate of the University of Oklahoma law school, Balkman was with the law firm that successfully pursued the libel suit against Collins. He had strong ties to the local GOP and brought substantial fund-raising and organizational resources to the campaign, and he also possessed tremendous support from his church. The grandson of an expatriate Oklahoman, he grew up in California and Washington state and was raised in the affluent suburbs of southern California, one of the youngest children of a large Mormon family. His father was a successful businessman, and many of his siblings have enjoyed their fair share of economic success and demonstrate a high degree of civic commitment. Despite being spread across the country, his family converged on Norman to help in Thad's challenge for the state legislature.

The campaign for the Republican nomination exposed a division in the state GOP between Governor Keating and Labor Commissioner Brenda Reneau. In advance of the August primary, Balkman was endorsed by Reneau, while English announced support from Keating. The awkward situation was evident to other GOP observers, who saw the division of endorsements in the primary as a violation of Ronald Reagan's Eleventh Commandment.[1] Cleveland County party chair Virginia Clendening observed, "It has been recommended in the past that candidates not seek personal endorsements during any primary. . . . In this case, I would say this is unusual." Democratic party observers viewed the endorsement fight as an indicator of a divisive primary that would benefit Collins.

Balkman did not evaluate Keating's endorsement of his opponent as a negative. An AP report quoted him as saying he had seen the endorsement letter of English from Keating, and he read it as "support of John [but] the Governor is not opposing me. The goal is to get a Republican into office." Keating's letter confirms Balkman's evaluation, noting that he "oppose[d] noone [sic] in the Republican Primary for District 45." With regard to the endorsement from the labor commissioner, Thad said it must have arisen from their conversation at the state GOP convention. Reneau endorsed Balkman as a "leader with conviction" who could "ensure a more prosperous future here in our state." English was equally gracious, observing that "the real story [was that] you have two solid candidates with the support of the state Republican hierarchy who want to oust Wallace Collins." Balkman proved to be the better candidate, winning the primary by a solid margin.

## Challenging an Incumbent

I hooked up with Thad on the campaign trail after his 2000 primary election victory. The southern end of the district was less urban but nonetheless easy to campaign for an energetic candidate. The most effective means of contacting voters in the constituency was to send direct mail and knock on their doors as often as possible. Thad started walking the district not long after his formal announcement in the spring. By the end of October 2000, he had been to the door of every Republican voter in the district at least twice and was now working on swing voters—registered Democrats and independents who might vote for a Republican if contacted.

As we walked the sidewalks of a 1960s-era subdivision development, we talked about his contacting strategy. "We have most of the Republican base activated," Balkman said. "They have been contacted and contacted again, and they know who I am and they will vote for me. What we are doing today is going after swing voters and Democrats . . . they vote for Collins because he is a Democrat, but that doesn't mean we can't get them."

Balkman related his impression that Collins had not cultivated the constituency. "You walk these neighborhoods, and a lot of people feel like the incumbent has taken them for granted." An example of Collins's supposed presumption was his use and placement of yard signs. One piece of the conventional wisdom of politics is that a single sign in a yard is an indicator of a firm supporter, a vote. As we approached a house with a red and white "Wallace Collins—Democrat" sign, Thad looked over at me with grin and said, "You might be wondering why we're doing this house. Well, we'll do all the Collins signs. A lot of these people didn't ask for a sign, and Wally didn't ask a lot of these people if he could put up a sign this time. It seems like he just looked at the list of registered Democrats and the list of people who took signs last time, and started putting them up."

When we got to the door and spoke with the middle-aged man inside, he confirmed exactly what Thad had said. Someone had just planted the Collins sign. "Well, sir," he said to the potential voter, "I hope you'll consider voting for me anyway. Say," he continued, "would you mind if I put up a sign? For equal time?" On at least a dozen occasions that day, Thad ended up posting a sign in a yard that featured a Collins sign, too.

Campaign vandalism had been a problem for Balkman throughout the campaign. His large volunteer organization, primarily local Republicans, some college students, fellow church members, and his family, was very active in door knocking and performing door-drops. But, on occasion door-drops were disappearing, signs were being vandalized, and efforts were made to intimidate his family and volunteers. While we walked a neighborhood on Norman's east side, we were shadowed for hours by two middle-aged men in a Ford pickup.

This was a campaign of intensive personal effort by the candidate and his family, and in the last two weeks numerous members of his family were involved. The day of the election, at about 2:00 A.M., I found myself out on the roads with Thad and his father, the back of my Chevy Suburban filled with campaign signs. We worked the roads of Noble and Norman, putting up signs everywhere near polling places. Balkman had worked very hard and could think of not one thing that should have been done that was not done. It was now a question of turnout.

At dawn I left him off at his car, so he could get his wife Amy and return to wave campaign signs outside their polling place. As we drove back toward Norman, he told me, "Collins has one issue, mental health, and he's real good on that issue. But there is more out there than the mental health issue, and that's where I beat him." Later, when I stopped for coffee at the 7-11, I saw Collins waving a sign by the road, along with other Collins sign wavers; then, on the way home, I passed some Balkman boosters. The contrast was stark: All the Balkman campaigners were young, often beautiful, and often from his family. They were enthusiastic and upbeat, despite the freezing cold of election morning. Collins and his campaigners were bundled up tight, with toboggan caps pulled over their ears and union windbreakers on their backs, mainly old men out on a cold morning. They looked like they didn't want to be out there.

Thad ran a positive campaign, and he concurs that negative campaigning is not the way to win. He is especially sensitive to personalized attack ads. During the 2000 campaign, nonattributed fliers appeared in neighborhoods, capitalizing on anti-Mormon bigotry. These fliers accused Thad of being a member of a "cult" and of being a "high-priest" in the Mormon Church. There is traditional suspicion of the Church of Latter-Day Saints among certain fundamentalist Protestant sects, and claims that the book of Mormon is "devil inspired" are still heard in certain quarters. Oklahoma District 45 had a heavily lay Protestant, fundamentalist constituency, and someone was doubtlessly playing on the presence of such bigotry. Thad did not engage in personal attacks per se, instead relying on issue comparison. When asked, he would comment on Collins's libel problems, to counter assertions of his opponent. The implication was clear: The incumbent was a convicted liar; how can you believe him?

The tireless efforts of Balkman and his volunteers, combined with a sizeable expenditure of campaign cash, paid off. On election evening, when I dropped in on Thad's victory party, he had just been declared the winner by the local media. His volunteers were everywhere, and a feeling of group accomplishment permeated the air. The candidate and those close to him were certain that his grassroots efforts and persistence led to his 343-vote victory. Supporters pointed to his efforts in Noble, a Democratic stronghold in Cleveland County, as critical to his victory. "Thad invested a lot of time and effort down in Noble. It really paid off for him in the general election."

Balkman's win over Collins was one of eight partisan take-aways that night by Republicans and part of the largest single-election gain by the GOP in decades. The win came in a swing constituency, and it came over an incumbent who had been holding the line against the GOP in a suburban district. Editorial commentary the week after the election emphasized the result in District 45 as part of a trend in Oklahoma:

> One state House victory for the Grand Old Party came in Norman's District 45, where Thad Balkman, an optimistic conservative, unseated incumbent Wallace Collins, a puppet of party leaders. . . . Such GOP strength in a traditional hotbed of Democratic strength [Norman] is powerful commentary on the Republican

surge . . . let's give credit where credit is due. Republicans had good legislative candidates who were properly funded and who ran better campaigns than the Democrats they ousted.[2]

It is often important to take to political evaluations of the *Oklahoman* with a grain of salt; it is arguably the most conservative major daily newspaper in the United States. Still, even when accounting for the ideological lens of the editorial board, the paper recognized what political scientist Jim Campbell (1997) has argued for decades: that a general partisan trend is only as good as the candidates who are there to make it happen. All of these factors—the quality of the candidate, the campaign, the money, and a mood in the electorate—came together to place a now twenty-nine-year-old lawyer in the state House.

## Socialization to the Legislature

Thad Balkman was one of a dozen new Republicans elected to the state House in 2000. They were the largest class of freshman Republicans elected to the Oklahoma House in decades. Commenting on the dozen new members of the GOP caucus, GOP floor leader Fred Morgan commented, "They're aggressive. They came to the legislature to make changes and they're ready to go." Not all Republicans were enthusiastic about the energy in the freshman caucus. Recalling times when freshmen were supposed to sit in the back of the chamber and learn the process, one veteran observed, "Some of the [young] ones are kind of brash, like they're out to save the world. They haven't had their ears pinned back yet." Nor would they have those ears pinned. The new class demonstrated a strong, independent streak that reflected their numbers. The AP's Ron Jenkins recalled that before the legislative session began, the freshmen had their own fund-raiser and solicited lobbyist donations. One lobbyist commented that "it was the first time I can remember a group inside the legislature that was not connected with the leadership or a party PAC had their own fund-raiser. . . . I felt a little funny going since I had not met most of them." Jenkins observed that Balkman was among the "most active new House members." That Balkman was involved in this event is not surprising. His was an expensive campaign, and he repeatedly noted that "early fundraiser[s] reflect the reality of modern politics," if only to pay off campaign debts.[3]

Balkman moved quickly to establish a presence on issues of importance to him and his constituents. On most major social issues they are conservative, and Republicans in Oklahoma enjoyed great success dividing these voters from their Democratic roots in the 1990s (Gaddie and Copeland 2002). Part of the key for Thad to convert this very competitive, historically Democratic constituency into one that would be safe for his incumbency would be to stake out issue positions and obtain successes that would resonate with the populist, socially conservative part of his constituency.

## Legislator: Tapping Populist Sentiments

Balkman came out of the blocks fast on a major issue, the taxation of groceries and prescription medications. Within days of the beginning of the legislative session in February 2001, he was capturing attention for this issue. Throughout the legislative session he would set up in front of grocery stores, calculator and pencil in hand, and give people estimates of how much they paid in taxes each year on food. Legislation he cosponsored to eliminate the grocery tax did not succeed, but he garnered substantial publicity, including television coverage.

One of the challenges confronting tax reform proposals is that they eliminate revenue from a source, but those proposing the reform fail to offer alternative sources to make up the revenue. The good fortune for tax reform advocates between 1995 and 2001 is that state and federal revenues expanded at a rate greater than the growth of government spending. When asked about the loss of revenues from eliminating the grocery tax—about $190 million—Balkman was quick to note that the tax cut had to be contrasted against the then $300 million budget surplus and the real need to expand public services. "It's a question of do we want $300 million in more government, or do we want to give people a tax cut?" He could argue for tax reform with the luxury of surplus and therefore did not have to offer either substitute revenues or programmatic cuts to cover the loss of revenue. The high-profile legislative proposal ultimately passed both chambers of the legislature, but in different forms. As part of an omnibus measure, legislators proposed phasing out $180 million in grocery sales taxes over three years. The plan was mired down in conference at the end of the session. Balkman was unrelenting in his arguments for reform, declaring "Oklahomans want grocery tax sales elimination now," but no reform was forthcoming.

Balkman was also out front to get rid of vehicle inspection in the state of Oklahoma. For decades, Oklahomans submitted their vehicles to annual inspections, while most states eliminated this outdated practice. "I am all for public safety," he said. "If I thought it was going to make the roads unsafe, I wouldn't do it. I'm convinced it is not needed." The problem with abolishing the inspection process was that it eliminated about $2.7 million in fees generated for the state and about $11 million in revenues for the private inspection stations. However, even the contractors who conducted inspections conceded that the process lost them money; the policy was financed on the back of the implementing agents, and Thad illuminated these flaws to his colleagues, stating, "It is a system that is broke and needs to be fixed." To offset the revenue loss to the state, he proposed placing a $1 fee on state vehicle registration. The final version of the House bill stripped the $1 add-on fee; Balkman feared the bill "dead on arrival" in the state senate, but HB 1144 passed to become a significant policy achievement for the freshman Republican.

The most singular accomplishment Balkman had in the legislature was probably the passage of legislation authorizing the "Choose Life" automotive car tag in the state of Oklahoma (HB 2193). Novelty car tags are not unique in Oklahoma. Like many states, the Sooner State has allowed for the sale of a variety of automotive tags that, among other things, commemorate the Atlanta Olympics, bear the logos of state colleges and universities, and recognize the status of groups such as POWs or Purple Heart veterans. In all, Oklahoma has about ninety novelty tags that can be ordered through privatized state tag agents.

The cost of the tags in Oklahoma was $25, of which $5 would go to the state and the remaining $20 was directed to organizations that worked with expectant mothers. Typical of the type of organization to benefit from tag revenues was Birthchoice of Oklahoma, a statewide organization that provided pregnancy tests, clothing, and shelter for pregnant women. The legislation moved quickly through the House, and, during the second week of March of the 2001 session, the House passed HB 2193 by a vote of 99–0. The passage of HB 2193 was followed by substantial public criticism from some quarters; indeed, it appeared that the bill would not emerge from the state senate at all, despite the strong show of support for the bill in the House. The *Tulsa World* criticized the tag in an editorial, stating that "auto tags don't need political slogans. . . . Balkman's bill would open the door for all kinds of license tag sloganeering."

On April 10, it appeared that the "Choose Life" tag was dead for the political session. Legislative rules require a bill to be heard in committee by a legislative deadline, and Balkman's bill was not heard in the Senate. Jim Williamson, a Republican from Tulsa, placed Balkman's bill inside another piece of legislation (HB 2278, the "Mustang Car Club" bill) as an amendment, reviving the bill and keeping it alive in the conference committee. Balkman attributed passage of the amendment to "intense lobbying" by the "Choose Life" tag supporters. Over 1,400 petition signatures and e-mails were collected in support of the "Choose Life" tag. Thad anticipated easy passage, though he also expected the 99–0 vote for the original proposal to fall-off; "I can see a few guys switching their votes now that it is a real deal [to make the plate a reality]." The final vote in the House on the bill was 91–6. With a signature from the prolife governor, Oklahoma would become the fifth state to adopt the custom plate.

Governor Keating signed the bill on May 5. Thad Balkman had something relatively rare for a minority party freshman: a legislative victory. Commenting on his success, Thad observed to a reporter, "Getting this bill passed has been a real struggle but definitely worth it. . . . The Choose Life license plate allows Oklahoma motorists to take a stand for life in support of adoption, and more importantly, this will help women and their unborn children who are in crisis situations."[4] It was a success, and one with symbolic value and policy consequences. Was it enough to help propel the young incumbent to reelection?

## Reelection Rematch

When I rejoined Thad on the campaign trail in 2002, the first question I asked was "How is it going?"

"I think it is going good," he replied. "It is a lot harder to find the time to campaign this go around. I'm trying to find time to practice law and take care of the legislative business, and it doesn't seem to leave as much time to go and do the neighborhoods. . . . Two years ago, I was the challenger, and all I had to do was campaign. Now campaigning takes me away from the family more."

As we went from door to door in one of the old subdivisions of east Norman, I asked Thad what it was like to be out campaigning again. "It is a lot easier to do doors as an incumbent, because people are more willing to talk to you and listen to you . . . I think it has more of an impact, because people are impressed to see you out knocking on their doors. More people know who I am this time." The overall campaign strategy was similar to the challenge to Collins two years earlier: working doors of Republicans and potential swing voters.

Balkman campaigned with grave seriousness. The campaign was again intense, more intense than two years prior. In mid-October Balkman and his inner circle were concerned about his reelection.

"We received polls from Tom Cole in October, and the numbers were disturbing," he told me. "In the district, [U.S. senator] Inhofe and [Tom] Cole were running fine, but my numbers were not up there. A lot of the new voters and swing voters were strong for Cole and Inhofe, but undecided on me . . . you could feel the intensity ratchet up."

One might conclude that the concern was misplaced, if only because the campaign had only really just begun. Balkman, in recollecting that part of the campaign, observed, "Of course, I hadn't sent my mail out yet, but we were worried by the undecideds, those conservative Democrats. . . . A lot of the problem was the new parts of the districts. People out there just didn't know me. But, when undecideds knew both me and Collins, they're pro-Balkman."

So the key was to contact the undecideds and get known to them. Then,

Balkman felt he could win. An examination of Thad's campaign literature reveals an effort to construct the classic incumbent claims of endorsement, service, and accomplishment. It also reveals a subtle effort at inoculation on the issue of importance to his opponent, mental health. One of the principal mental health facilities in the state is in the district. Thad's literature included an endorsement of his "zealous" efforts on behalf of the hospital by its superintendent, Don Bowen. "All of the mail was positive. Some of it was aggressive, but always positive." Eight waves of mail went out, not counting the mailers sent by groups like the National Rifle Association (NRA).

There were other challenges. Redistricting resulted in three substantial changes to Thad's seat. First, the precincts in the south Cleveland County town of Noble, where Thad worked so hard in 2000, were shed from his district. Then, his district tripled in geographic size. And, on the western side of the district, a very liberal and Democratic precinct (Faculty Heights) was added to his district, though with his permission. "It was best for the community. Bill [Nations, the Democrat from District 44] and I agreed that it made sense to run the boundary right down the main road." Thad had been given large amounts of new, rural territory that was difficult to campaign. "The houses out there," he observed, "are far apart, few and far between with long driveways. . . . I go all the way out to 120th Street now." The change added about fifty square miles of new territory, though not so many new voters.

Thad was facing a familiar foe in Wallace Collins. The former incumbent was back for a rematch, and he was well funded. Weeks before the August primary, the district was buffeted with the familiar crimson and white "Wallace Collins—Democrat" signs that voters had been seeing on the east side since 1996. Collins himself was doing what he had not done so heavily in 2000: working precincts and knocking doors. If Balkman wanted to stay in the legislature, he would have to fight to keep the job. Rumors of Democratic bankrolling further concerned the first-termer, who had demonstrated two years earlier how sweat and cash could combine to oust an incumbent.

Thad benefited not only from his own efforts, described briefly here, but also from the efforts of other conservative activists. One big factor in the district was the creation of Campaign Against Libel, the CAL-PAC. Bobby Cleveland, Ken Adair, and Steve Byas got together and created an organization to inform voters about Wallace Collins. Their mailings went out to Democrats and new voters in the district . . . it was a slick, professional mailer. On one side it had the definition of libel; then, on the other side, a letter from [the sponsors] explaining Collins' previous record of libeling his opponents. It was five paragraphs long.

Both Adair and Byas had lost to Collins in the past. CAL-PAC also took out a half-page advertisement in the Norman paper, and included a Pinocchio-like caricature of Collins and an accounting of Collins' libelous history. These efforts freed Balkman to pursue his positive advertising track, while forcing Collins onto the rebuttal track, where he was constantly defending his past record and past actions. Reflecting on the campaign, Balkman observed, "They tied him up. He wasn't telling his story. . . . If I go negative, it doesn't look good."

The young incumbent had a particular skill that benefits him in campaigning: He was not a résumé reader. He developed a very thoughtful style of listening, and instead of reciting what he has done in terms of legislation, he takes notes and tries to do constituent service on the spot. Whether it is a laid-off mechanic who needs short-term mortgage assistance or a person with health benefit problems, Thad seems quite at ease in this ombudsman role.

Balkman ran ahead of his 2000 margin. He successfully mobilized the undecideds in the district, as the freshman ran ahead of not only the losing Republican candidate for governor, Steve Largent, but also ahead of successful Republican major office candidates Jim Inhofe Mary Fallin, and Tom Cole. His sophomore surge was small, but no one could argue that he was the beneficiary of anyone's coattails.

## On the Leadership Team

When the legislature convened to organize after the November elections, Thad Balkman emerged with a new role: assistant whip for the House Republicans. During his initial term, Thad had proved to be an able, visible legislator who also did the hard work of legislating and who passed legislation. These factors, along with his energy and social grace, marked him as a potential leader. But a front-line leadership commitment would require far greater demands, without electoral or personal economic benefit.

"Before the election," Thad said, "there was a lot of talk about exploring the leadership. I did have conversations with people and thought about running for whip. But now that I'm in this marginal district, I really can't take time leading the floor. And, if I'm in leadership, I get tied down on issues that might not fly in my district. I'm always having to think, 'How can I win my seat?' "

After the election, the new Republican floor leader, Todd Heitt, called Thad and asked him to join the leadership team. This role allows Thad the access and role he seeks, but without the visibility of a major floor leadership position. "When I was thinking about running for the leadership, I talked to the old floor leader, Fred Morgan, and he told me, 'Don't run for the leadership. There are too many downsides being from a marginal district.' " But, ultimately, he ended up taking a reduced role as an assistant whip.

"Heitt called me and asked me to participate. When leaders ask, you need to try and do it. . . . Being in leadership gives me a seat at the table. When leadership meets, it doesn't matter if you're majority leader or the assistant minority whip—everyone gets to speak and everyone has a voice. . . . It puts me at the table, where I can help set the agenda and make policy. You all sit at the table with an equal voice. Until I hit my term limit, that is where I want to be. I don't need to be speaker or leader; I just want a place at the table where I can affect what is done. . . . I don't have to be the lead dog . . . becoming speaker is not on my goal list."

So, how long could Thad Balkman stay in the legislature? He confronted the prospect of term limits, which means he has four more terms. But there were other challenges. The Oklahoma legislature pays pretty well for a part-time, citizen legislature, but the job has effectively become year-round, with political commitments and committee meetings and interim studies and special sessions making time demands. Thad Balkman is married, with a stay-at-home spouse and young children. Legislating competes with his law practice for time and attention, and both the practice and the legislature compete with his private time. These competing demands weighed heavily on his mind, and he felt that he made sacrifices to serve. The legislative pay pales compared to what he would make practicing law full-time. "The pay makes it tough. I'm not independently wealthy, and I want to stake my claim in the private sector someday. Maybe that's the one downside, that we'd end up with a legislature made up only of the wealthy or those who are on the take from some interest group."

After the election, as he prepared for the 2003 legislative session, it was evident that Thad had established his bona fides as a legislator. Though a member of the minority party, he was given a committee vice chairmanship of the Mental Health Committee. This was an important posting for Balkman, as the principal issue for his two-time opponent was mental health issues and one of the state's major mental health facilities is in the district. The Democratic chair, Al Lindley, while a good campaigner and loyal Democrat, is not a legislative architect. Balkman was asked to carry the state mental health department's legislation.

When I asked Thad the litmus test for progressive ambition, "Would you accept a seat in the U.S. House at zero cost?" Thad was not hesitant with his answer. "No, absolutely not, not today. . . . I love my family too much to put them through that. . . . It is already too hard to spend enough time with my family being at the state capitol. I can't imagine being gone all the time or transplanting us to Virginia or Maryland. . . . I don't know if I ever would want to run [for Congress]. I can't succeed at being a congressman and at being a father."

Indeed, his ambitions did not even extend to the other legislative chamber. With the decision of State Senator Brad Henry to run for governor, some political observers speculated that the young representative would seek the senate. "I thought about running for the senate, but only for a second. The senate is stuffy, compared to the House, but I would have liked the four-year term. . . . It was all moot, because redistricting took me out [of Henry's district]." The representative's ambitions are decidedly not progressive. He indicated he couldn't see running for attorney general or another cabinet office, and while he conceded that being governor was intriguing, both his body language and his response indicated no real interest in taking on even the executive role in state government. "I could see being in the governor's office, as counsel or in some other, related role. But I really do believe that we are best served as a society by having citizen legislators rather than professional politicians."

There are other lessons to be had. Politicians are sensitive to changes in the political and competitive contexts, and they can adapt. Thad Balkman's district was altered in such a fashion that some of his strongest precincts were removed from the district, and large stretches of new territory were added that challenged his campaign style. He confronted the same opponent, though this time the roles were reversed. Balkman devised a campaign strategy that continued his positive campaign approach from 2000 and that once again left it to other actors to address the deficiencies of his opponent. As an incumbent, he found that he had easier access to voters, who were more prone to give time to a legislator who had come to call. There was less time to campaign, but the nature of the campaigning had changed. Balkman's 2000 campaign was reactive to the actions in office of the incumbent and was prospective in terms of the presentation of Thad's self. Now, two years later, he could point to practical legislative successes that would be supported by large numbers of constituents. His campaign was proactive, defined in terms of his incumbency and his accomplishments, which allowed the young incumbent to point retrospectively to recent accomplishments as evidence of future performance. Thad had prevailed in the realm of evolving political and competitive contexts. The district was not quite yet safe, but Thad's surge of support for his sophomore term indicated that his representative and campaigning style had overcome any detrimental alteration of the state political environment or the design of his constituency.

# Notes

1. "Thou shalt not speak ill of any fellow Republican."
2. *Daily Oklahoman*, November 6, 2000.
3. Thad had budgeted for an expensive primary and general election, but fund-raising was a concern. His primary and general election campaign combined ran almost $90,000.
4. Associated Press, May 1, 2001.

# Legacy

# 7

> Sharpen it up and vote right on election day.
>
> —Billy Stuckey

STEPHANIE STUCKEY-BENFIELD was balancing family and career. She and her husband both trained as lawyers (she is in family law, he in torts). But, since July 2002, she was phasing out her active law practice to dedicate her time to her new son, Robert, and to her legislative career. In early 2003, she was entering her third term in the Georgia House of Representatives.

Life had been challenging since the legislature came back into session. Robert, seven months old, was enrolled in a day care across the street from the state capitol building, so that Stephanie could see him during session days. Even with his close proximity, it was still trying for her. "He goes to day care, he gets sick, the poor thing." And, if he became ill, then they would stay home. "It has become a real balancing act, especially during session. I just prioritize what I can do and what I must do."

As parenthood and politics compete, Stephanie relied on her experience and socialization in the chamber to carry her through this demanding time. As she observed to me, "The two terms give me some latitude. I've made my important contacts and become socialized with the power people. . . . This term I'm focused on the district and committee work."

## Legacy of Service

Stuckey comes from a very political family. To see a Stuckey running for office was not news in Georgia. Her grandfather, William Sylvester Stuckey Sr. (see Drinnen 1997), was a state legislator back in the halcyon days of rural conservative control of the General Assembly, when populist-segregationists Gene and Herman Talmadge headed a political machine that polarized the state's politics (see Anderson 1975; Talmadge 1987). Sylvester also built the chain of Stuckey's roadside stores into an American highway institution. There is hardly a person who has traveled south toward Florida who has not encountered the red-and-white script signs adorning the high-pitched roofs of the home of the pecan log. Stephanie's father, Billy, held Georgia congressional District 8, which stretched from Brunswick on the coast to Bleckley County.[1]

Billy Stuckey was thirty-one when he was elected to Congress, and he likely could have held the seat for as long as he wanted; his generally conservative voting record was consistent with south Georgia, though he was a generation removed from the segregationists who had typified Georgia's Democratic Party. Billy flirted with a challenge to the chair of the Senate Agriculture Committee, Herman Talmadge, in 1972 before deciding to run again for the House. He subsequently retired from political life at age forty-one.

Stephanie, like Billy, did not made her early career in corporate life but rather in politics. Born just before her father went into Congress, she grew up between Washington and Georgia. As a young adult, she moved quickly into Democratic Party politics (she was one of the youngest delegates at the 1988 Democratic convention) and continued her activism in law school. Stephanie first realized she wanted to get into public office in college.

"Sure, I grew up around politics, but I was twelve when Dad got out. . . . Mainly I remember the campaigns. . . . My parents were a big reason that I got into politics. . . . When I was growing up, Dad encouraged us to have dialogues, around the dinner table, anywhere, about political issues. I grew up around political activity and political conversation. . . . Mom is also *real* politically astute."

After finishing at the University of Georgia School of Law, she moved to Decatur, outside Atlanta, and put her degree to work. By the mid-1990s, she was working as an aide to neighbor and incumbent senator Mary Margaret Oliver and networking the circles of liberal political and social organizations in metropolitan Atlanta. "It was when I was working for Mary Margaret in the [state] senate that I knew I wanted to run. When she retired and the House seat opened up, then I decided I could take my shot. It is neat how things work out." In late 1997, Senator Oliver left the legislature to try and move up to lieutenant-governor, and the incumbent state representative in Stephanie's district was going to make the move up from the House. Her seat had come open, affording her the opportunity to continue the family tradition of representation in Georgia. The state senate staff attorney and Democratic Party activist stepped out front, as a candidate for the Georgia House of Representatives.

In April 1998, when Stuckey decided to run for the legislature, she was accompanied by her parents to file her papers. Filing in Georgia is something of a coming-out party, and the press prominently reports the quirks, humorous episodes, and drama that can accompany filing, such as a candidate forgetting filing money and panhandling the fee from other candidates or, in the case of Ralph David Abernathy Jr., the subsequent bouncing of his filing check at the bank. When Stuckey filed for office, longtime Georgia politics writer Tom Baxter focused on her: "Former congressman Billy Stuckey was there to beam as his daughter, Stephanie Stuckey, signed up to run as a Democrat for a state Senate seat [*sic*]. When she realized she'd forgotten to bring her qualifying money, however, Stuckey turned to her mother for a check."[2]

Open seats typically attract large crowds of candidates, especially when the party system is poorly developed or the district is in an area that affords numerous opportunities for local office holding, like a district composed of small, rural counties. District 67 was not such a district, being centered on Decatur, a small suburban city in the heart of one of the most populous counties in Georgia. Stuckey confronted just one other opponent, Kay Young. The *Atlanta Journal-Constitution* described the matchup:

> Kay Young, 47, said her experience is the key to change for the district; Stephanie Stuckey, 32, said her age allows her to be committed to the district for the long haul. Young cites her past as a public interest lawyer . . . and registered lobbyist. . . . For Stuckey, public office is part of her family history, with her great-grandfather, grandfather, and father serving in the Georgia Legislature. "Growing up as a part of a family that has a history of public service has given me respect for public servants." . . . Stuckey said the only influence the business has had on her campaign is use of the same logo on her campaign signs. . . . "The name brings back a warm memory for many people, though it is simply an ice-breaker." . . . The issues she is focused on—controlling growth and development, education reform, and more options for senior citizens—are long-term. "We need folks who are willing to roll up their sleeves and stay with this. . . . Have the energy to do that. I'm in this for 20 years, and I think that's my advantage."[3]

The excitement of her candidacy was not lost on her family. Billy, known for his quick wit and the little blue pencils he handed out when campaigning ("Let's keep the Eighth District moving") was quite willing to help in his daughter's campaign. "He had about five hundred T-shirts made up that said 'I'm a happy Stuckey Volunteer.' . . . I had to explain to him about campaign expenditure limits."

Billy was also a wealth of information. A campaigner of no small repute, he advised his daughter, "Never ride in a parade—always walk," and "Always bring candy to give to the kids. Always leave people with something." Retail politics is retail politics, and some things never change, whether you are campaigning in the swamps of Chatham County or in suburban Atlanta.[4]

"Oh, Mom and Dad were great in the campaign. Dad was a tremendous campaigner, and he was my unofficial campaign manager. They opened the door to raise money and line up support . . . we raised about $85,000 for that campaign. It was the most expensive campaign in Atlanta that year. . . . The Stuckey name made a difference," and raising and spending a lot cleared the field both for 1998 and for the foreseeable future. Stephanie Stuckey won the primary in a walk and had no general election opponent.

# Getting Oriented

Stuckey's first political experience as an incumbent was a three-day conference at the University of Georgia's Carl Vinson Institute. The workshop was designed to orient lawmakers to the issues of the General Assembly. It is often a venue where the press gets a feel for the legislative priorities for the coming legislative session and where emergent stars are identified.

Representative-elect Stuckey was ready to go. Kathy Pruitt, who was covering the orientation, observed of Stuckey that the "Decatur Democrat and one of 22 newcomers in the House is so anxious to wade into the thick of legislative issues that she's arrived a day early to talk women's and family issues with a bipartisan group of female lawmakers."[5] However, Stuckey was modest and almost demure to the attention paid to her and her previous experience under the Gold Dome; she understood the precarious balance that confronted a freshman incumbent in the tradition-heavy, parochial Georgia House.

> Even after working the past two years as the Senate Judiciary Committee's staff attorney, Stuckey said she's still got a lot to learn. . . . "Certainly I'm not going to go in there and think I'm going to rewrite the state constitution or anything . . . but the constituents who elected me don't want me to go in and sit quietly on the back row."[6]

Stuckey was quickly socialized into the circles of power. She went for (and captured) a seat on the House Judiciary Committee. This accomplishment clearly marked her as a comer, as Judiciary is one of the busiest, most powerful committees in the legislature.

Stephanie recalls that, going into that first session, "I had good contacts going in. . . . My grandfather served with some of them, and they remembered." And, the good ol' boy environment was not entirely hostile to her. The "little lady" comments did not seem to trouble her. "It was not as difficult as I thought to get socialized into the General Assembly. And, also, having been around Dodge County and growing up in south Georgia, I knew not to be offended by the 'little darlings' and 'sugars' from the older men. The context matters; it was always in light-hearted moments, and it is one thing to hear it from an older, rural man and another thing to get it in a committee hearing or from a young legislator."

By mid-March 1999, when she got up to speak on behalf of her first pieces of legislation, the old boys of the legislature welcomed her to the club in a fashion that is typical of the General Assembly:

> Speaker Tom Murphy likes to call the Georgia House "one of the world's greatest fraternities." If so, that might make freshman Stephanie Stuckey (D-Decatur) a little sister. And when new legislators make an initial visit to the podium—or "well" in capitol parlance—they're often barraged with inane, obscure and irrelevant questions. It's sort of like hazing frat pledges. This week, Stuckey, a lawyer, expected the worst as she explained three bills she sponsored. The first two bills passed without a ripple. On the third, the vote tally board lit up with red lights symbolizing "no" votes next to nearly all the reps' names. She shrank a bit, until the lights turned green and it was clear the class was up to tomfoolery. . . . [A member] asked for reconsideration, meaning the bill would be held for a day. A few minutes later he undid his motion. Just joking.[7]

So, from inside Stephanie's head, what was it like going into the well for the first time? "It is intimidating. You can really get picked apart." Most freshmen go to the well with a noncontroversial bill that has high prospects for success, such as a piece of local legislation. "The bill will probably be noncontroversial, if only because the rules committee won't let a freshman go to the well with a hard bill. . . . Details? Well, that's the problem. You could go to the well and go into every detail of the legislation, and the leadership is standing there saying, 'Hurry up and pass it,' or you could just go down and say, 'Pass this, it is a good bill.' . . . There is a strategy to going to the well; you don't want to talk it to death, but I always want to explain everything. I passed a complex, forty-eight-page statutory revision of the child custody law with two sentences. . . . Most members trust the leadership and the committees to get a bill right before the bill comes to the floor."

By the end of her first legislative session, Stuckey had legislative successes; a reputation for hard work, expertise, and team play; and the growing respect of the old men of the general assembly. In the next legislative session, she would put the good ol' boy reputation of the Georgia General Assembly to the test when, together with a Republican legislator, she took on one of the bedrock institutions of Georgia: high school athletics.

## Tackling Title IX

> I had not realized . . . that athletics is the single most important thing in the United States.
>
> —Casper "Cap the Knife" Weinberger, 1975

If athletics is the most important thing in the United States, then football is the *only* thing in Georgia. It is the source of school pride, community identity, and sometimes a prerequisite for leadership. Since the 1970s, many school athletic programs, especially in the South, have felt the hot breath of federal rules with fear, loathing, and trepidation. Say "Title IX," and folks in high school and college athletics know what you're talking about. And, more than likely, they have a strong opinion.

"Title IX" is Title IX of the 1972 Education Amendments that were passed by Congress and signed by President Richard Nixon. The gender follow-up to the educational provisions of the 1964 Civil Rights Act, Title IX declares, "No person in the United States shall, on the basis of sex, be excluded from participation in, be denied the benefits of, or be subjected to discrimination under any education program or activity receiving federal financial assistance." The sponsor of the legislation, Edith Green, kept a low profile for the amendment by dissuading women's groups from testifying, while debate instead focused on the racial balance provisions of the amendments (Gelb and Palley 1996).

Title IX has been applied to high school and college athletic programs to ensure that equal opportunities exist for men and women to participate in athletics, and, as a consequence, female participation in varsity college athletics has increased dramatically since the 1970s (Sigelman and Wahlbeck 1999). The problem for many institutions, and especially for major colleges, is football. Football programs require large numbers of athletes and resources, and therefore football uses lots of scholarships. Complying with Title IX requires a school to balance the number of men's and women's scholarships, which results in fewer men's than women's sports being offered, in order to maintain scholarship parity when a football program is present.

Stephanie Stuckey stepped into the Title IX issue in late 1999. That fall, the Atlanta papers ran a series of reports on Title IX compliance in Georgia athletics. The results of that study were read by Stuckey, who was concerned about the legal implications of the facts in the story, which indicated that the state high schools were grossly out of compliance with federal law. During December, she went public, along with her colleague Kathy Ashe, with her intention to introduce legislation to rectify the problem. "If we don't deal with the problem legislatively, we're going to have to do it through the courts," Stuckey said. "Georgia is potentially facing some huge legal fees if we don't comply. I'd rather do it through legislation and fix the problem up front, than have expensive and prolonged litigation that is going to be bad press for our state."[8] Ashe's husband was with a large Atlanta law firm, and one of the lawyers from the practice with extensive gender-based litigation experience helped research the bill. And, they did a lot of legwork before they unveiled the legislation.

"There was also lots of behind the scenes legwork," Stuckey recalled.

"We met with legislators, education department people, the GHSA [Georgia High School Association]. . . . We even went to the governor and said, 'Do you want it in your legislative package?' which would have heightened the prospects for passage. . . . He turned it down because it was not a popular issue."

Prompted by the investigative series into the compliance of state public high schools with Title IX requirements in athletics by the *Atlanta Journal-Constitution*, the two urban, female legislators announced their intention to craft legislation to offer incentives and sanctions to ensure school compliance with federal law. The newspaper's investigation revealed no monitoring of Title IX, and "gender inequities [were found] to be commonplace." Among the deficiencies in state high school athletic funding vis-à-vis gender equity, the newspaper discovered that:

- 75 percent of local salary supplements for coaching went to boys' sports;
- 95 percent of extended pay supplements went to coaches of boys' sports (about $12 million/year); and
- 64 percent of high school athletes are boys (but most students are girls).

Such gross sexual discrepancies could provide powerful evidence for a judge considering a challenge to the state's high school athletic system. Such differences would most likely meet standards of statistical significance, and given the clear mandates of Title IX, it would be difficult to defend the male-advantaged bias.

Under Title IX, there existed a three-pronged test that an institution must pass to maintain compliance (these are ordered tests, with failure on the first test being a precondition to applying subsequent tests). First, were opportunities to participate "substantially proportionate" to the school's sex mix? If a school failed that test, then a second test asked whether there was "a history and . . . practice" of programmatic expansion that developed interests and abilities of the underrepresented sex. If this test was also failed, then a program could comply if it "fully and effectively" accommodated the interests and abilities of the underrepresented sex (Sigelman and Wahlbeck 1999: 520–21). Failure of all three tests constituted violation.

A 1996 Clinton administration Office of Civil Rights advisory had further narrowed the test, arguing that achieving the first prong was the only, truly safe circumstance for avoiding a Title IX violation. The odds were that many, if not most, public schools in Georgia would fail the three-pronged test, and most would definitely fail the first prong. Furthermore, noncompliant schools were more likely the numerous rural and small-town schools. What no one was saying, but what everyone knew, was that boys' football was the problem.

Stuckey and Ashe had to find a way to navigate this legislation through a predominantly male legislature that included numerous rural members for whom their football coach was only next to Momma and Jesus in shaping their character. They had to control the debate to make sure that this was not viewed as an antifootball initiative. When the General Assembly convened in January, Stuckey and Ashe (who was, back then, an Atlanta Republican) introduced a bill to allow for state sanctions against schools out of compliance with equity in sporting opportunities.[9] Press coverage of their initiative afforded a degree of inoculation against anticipated reaction to their initiative. Sports reporters for the Atlanta newspapers, in covering the initiative, observed that

> Stuckey . . . is an unabashed football fan. A former season ticket-holder of the Washington Redskins, she and her family passed on a ski vacation to follow the team to California for Super Bowl XVII in 1983. As a cheerleading captain, she cheered on her high school team. She and Rep. Kathy Ashe . . . want to dispel notions about the motivation behind a state gender equity bill they plan to introduce when the Legislature convenes next month. "We're not antifootball," Stuckey said, "we just want to level the playing field to make sure athletic opportunities are available for boys and girls."[10]

Other reports noted Stuckey's long-standing family ties to south Georgia. Politics in Georgia often align on an Atlanta-versus-the-country axis (Key 1949; Bullock 2002), and in rural Georgia, high school football is the focal point of life. Local fans will travel a hundred miles to away games and three hundred miles for state playoffs; some local high schools have stadiums that seat twenty thousand fans and have legendary dynasties that are talked about in hushed tones.

Stuckey, who was raised in a family who comes from such a community, appreciated the challenge before her. "I don't see it as being a male [against] female or Democratic-Republican, but more rural-urban. . . . This is going to be seen as a threat in the more rural communities, where football is king and the community sort of revolves around the football culture."

The Sports Equity Act of 2000 was introduced during the first full week of the regular legislative session. When the press described it as a "sanction" bill, Stuckey and Ashe emphasized that the purpose of the bill was to ensure monitoring to ensure compliance with an existing federal law. No new requirements were placed on schools other than achieving compliance with federal requirements under Title IX. Nor did Stuckey and Ashe make the announcement a quiet one. Alan Judd of the *Atlanta Journal* observed that

> the sponsors . . . wore T-shirts around the state Capitol that declared, in bold blue letters, "Girls Can!" . . . "Federal law

requires that boys' and girls' sports programs in our public schools be treated equally," said Stuckey, "but 27 years after the passage of Title IX, there are still great disparities in the sports programs of the school in our states. For too long we have allowed Georgia's female athletes to be treated as second-class citizens."[11]

The proposal required reporting of expenditures and participation rates by gender to the state department of education, starting in 2003, with rereporting for continued compliance every five years hence. Failure to comply with Title IX would result in possible loss of federal educational assistance funds and bans from postseason play. The proposal, as advanced in December, included a possible reorganization of the state High School Association to ensure monitoring and enforcement of Title IX. The crux of the Stuckey–Ashe bill was to require state public schools to offer sports for which scholarships are awarded at state colleges. Stuckey was quick to remind reporters that "it's not all about scholarships, though . . . the aim is simply to provide opportunities for girls to be involved in athletics."[12]

Stuckey and Ashe anticipated opposition from the Georgia High School Association. A survey by the *Atlanta Journal-Constitution* of members of the executive committee for GHSA (thirty-seven men and two women) revealed that about four in five members saw no need to create a state Title IX law or for the state to monitor the GHSA.[13]

Stuckey described the evolution of the legislation: "The final design of the bill was designed to encourage compliance, rather than to seem punitive. . . . We were able to get it done because I teamed up with a real vet, Kathy Ashe, who knew how to get a bill through. I basically told her, 'Just steer me and I'll do the work.' I brought the energy and she brought the know-how. I credit Kathy with making this law possible. . . . she would always rein me in and say, 'Let's do it slow and right.'"

The rhetoric was eerily similar to arguments used to deny black civil rights in the 1950s and 1960s, wherein the advantaged group in control of the governing authority saw no problems with the biases that gave advantages to people like them. The solution would require a strategy reminiscent of the efforts to integrate Georgia public schools in the 1960s, an act of "coercion to compliance" (see Bullock and Rodgers 1976). The bill provided to withhold not only federal monies but also state monies from noncompliant schools, and it included an exclusion of noncompliant schools from postseason competition. It also explicitly asserted the right of the state to control the Georgia High School Association, the principal governing body for school athletics. This change would not be just symbolic. The state association would become responsible for providing the legislature with an annual report on its activities and would have to comply with state open record and open meeting laws. Failure to comply with the law would result in a prohibition against state public schools from participating in GHSA events. At the grass-roots level, every school would have to designate a "gender equity coordinator" and to adopt and make public a system of pursuing grievances. Girls would be eligible to try out for "noncontact" boys' sports.

The media reported that resistance would be substantial. "Getting a majority of legislators—especially from sports-passionate rural Georgia—to agree is the challenge." Independent research identified particular pockets of resistance. Students at Agnes Scott College, a selective women's college in Atlanta, surveyed Georgia schools to ascertain the degree of knowledge among principals and students about Title IX. Interviews revealed "resistan[ce] to change," especially among rural educators and woeful ignorance about the need to comply with federal law.[14] And, it was among members with these communities, and other areas with strong football traditions, that Stuckey and Ashe had to build support and reassure reluctant members.

"Lots of legislators were concerned about booster clubs, about how the local football coach would react, . . . but the press loved the bill because it all started with their investigative work, because the press inspired it. . . . We started getting all of this good press, and then parents of girls started calling their representatives to complain, saying, 'My daughter plays soccer on this lousy field with no facilities, but my son plays football with the new equipment and the fancy locker rooms and the concession stands.'"

As it was, the stiff resistance anticipated to the legislation did not materialize; instead, the bill took off like a runaway train, and when the sponsors went to enroll the bill "there was not enough room on it for all of the cosponsors who signed on." Three days after the introduction of the legislation, the major papers endorsed the bill. Stuckey and Ashe demonstrated substantial political acumen in lining up support for the legislation. As the papers told it, they "spent months touching all the bases before introducing their legislation, and say they expect the support of the Georgia High School Association, which oversees school sports. . . . GHSA, with only two women on its 39-member boards, has a record of denying gender inequities and of fighting initiatives to fix them."[15]

The final blow to the opposition came in athletic fashion. On February 5, a group of female athletes, including forty high school stars and three former Olympians, came to the capitol to lobby. In image- and Olympics-conscious Atlanta, it is unlikely that any better lobbying strategy could be had. How could these legislators, especially the men, many of whom had daughters, look at these bright, capable athletes and tell them their opportunities didn't matter?[16]

By April, it was all over but the shouting. "The speaker was concerned about getting the bill through Rules; they created a special rules subcommittee, chaired by Jimmy Skipper [the majority whip] to craft the rule for the bill. He sat down with us and worked for about ten hours to groom the bill in order to get rid of the objections."

Skipper's big contribution was to revise the bill in order to create graduated sanctions—reform, competition ban, then funding cuts—and to give the schools time to come into compliance with data collection. The bill passed out of Rules and came to the floor. On the 17th, the House passed out the bill on a unanimous vote, followed soon after by passage in the state senate.[17] Stuckey and Ashe had created zealous allies. On the senate side, the bill's sponsor, Mike Egan, collapsed on the floor. As he was wheeled out of the chamber, he shouted, "Who's going to handle my bills?" Senator David Scott (now a congressman from Atlanta) took up the bill and reflected later, "The fact that it was on his mind as he was being carried out on a stretcher is amazing . . . it was something Mike really believed in." In late April, Governor Roy Barnes, who owed his election to strong support among women, signed the bill into law.[18]

## Careerist

The Title IX legislation is probably the most significant legislative accomplishment of Stuckey's career. She enjoyed a variety of legislative successes as a freshman: Her first three pieces of legislation authored as a freshman passed out of the chamber with nearly unanimous support, and she has been a cosponsor on significant legislation with senior power brokers in the House. But the Sports-Equity Act was a departure, as Stuckey and Ashe challenged one of the most powerful institutions in Georgia and bucked long odds. Of greater importance, though, was that the legislation rectified a problem in policy implementation that was long-standing, and it did so before a greater legal problem occurred that would prove costly to the state.

Such an effort, especially by a freshman female legislator, would not have been possible in the General Assembly a generation ago. But the state of Georgia is changing, and the legislature is changing with it. Where this bill would not have exited committee in the past, it garnered unanimous support because of the changes in the state and the legislature. In the 1980s, blacks and some women moved into the white, male power circle of the House, and the growing GOP caucus in the House led to a leftward-moving Democratic majority. The constituencies that members represented became increasingly suburban and affluent, and the residents progressed with the times; their sons play football, but their daughters play softball and soccer. For a legislature that includes large numbers of new, suburban representatives, a vote against girls sports might have been every bit as suicidal as a vote against football in Valdosta.

The evolution of the legislature and the respect for Stuckey's skills are evident in the aftermath of this legislative triumph. The move to challenge athletics did not cost her at all with the leadership, as indicated by the unanimous support for the initiative; indeed, it probably enhanced her standing as an emergent force. In coming legislative sessions, Stuckey would increasingly be signed on as a cosponsor of significant legislative proposals, with individuals such as the speaker or the Judiciary Committee chair as her cosponsors. In her first term, she defined herself as a shrewd, forward-looking legislator who would tackle difficult issues with great skill.

## Safe Urban Liberal

In 2000, Stephanie Stuckey represented one of the most diverse, liberal constituencies in Georgia. As such, she was out front on a variety of liberal causes in the state, including such controversial topics as removing the Confederate Cross of Saint Andrew from the state flag (she authored an article in law school ten years ago calling for removal of the "battle banner"),[19] formally defining Hispanics as a minority group under state law,[20] advocating laser-based technology to monitor traffic and issue citations by mail, and placing driving restrictions on motorists under age eighteen. She has also been active on legislation that would increase patient access to their physician's medical and criminal history,[21] and, since being named to the Environment and Natural Resources Committee in 2001, she has committed herself to developing expertise on water policy (metropolitan Atlanta is in a state of perpetual water crisis, and it endured five years of drought from 1997 to 2002).

She has also advanced legislation that is relevant to a more sophisticated, urban constituency, such as a measure to increase the alcohol content of beer in Georgia (the state currently has a 6 percent limit) in order to allow for the sale of high-content microbeers; argued for "mile-based" insurance premiums in order to give drivers who drive less discounts on car insurance; and helped advance the international "Yellow Bikes" program in Atlanta. She is also still out front on gender and family issues, such as the child support system.

As a legislator, she is one of the safest Democrats in Georgia. She has not faced an opponent in the primary or general election since 1998. In redistricting, she was confronted with a substantially new, larger constituency. The new state House map that was adopted in 2001 reintroduced the use of multimember districts in the Georgia General Assembly for the first time in a decade (Bullock and Gaddie 1993). Roughly a third of members now shared a constituency with at least one other member. Stuckey found herself in a two-seat multimember district with her law partner, neighbor, and friend, Democrat Mary Margaret Oliver. "I was very skeptical and opposed to being in a multimember district. Now that I'm in one, I'm actually looking forward to it, because it increases the power that my district has."[22] There was another incumbent in the district, Republican Paul Jennings. Jennings went from a competitive single-member district he could win to a Democratic multimember district he could not win. Oliver, a former legislator looking to make a comeback, bested Jennings in the general election.

Stephanie is adapting to a legislative scheme that was designed to maximize Democratic electoral power. Large parts of her Democratic base have been pared with some other Democratic precincts and the remains of Jennings's districts to create a two-member district that the Democrats will carry. Her friend and mentor, Mary Margaret Oliver, won the other seat. The district was generally Democratic, probably about 58 percent. Stephanie had no reelection opponent in 2002 and indeed had no opposition since her first election. The old district was probably 85 percent Democratic, very liberal and affluent, with lots of gays and lesbians and white, liberal, Emory University types. The new part of the district, Tucker, is older, white suburban, and very conservative; as Stephanie observed, "The issues change. . . . My new district is very concerned about predatory lending practices and legal revisions, for example." These new constituency demands are pushing Stuckey in a more conservative direction.

The remap did not alter Stephanie's basic election strategy but rather just intensified what she would have done. In January, four months before filing opened, she was already hard at work holding fund-raisers and introducing herself to the new parts of the district. She noted to me in our last conversation, "It is all about raising money and getting on TV now." In her district, "it is mainly about direct mail, but I still believe in door-to-door. . . . You can't do doors in a multimember district the way I did in my old district, but we still do highly targeted doors. . . . I miss that aspect of [campaigning]."

Early fund-raising was especially important, and Stuckey pulled in the biggest guns, including the governor, for her fund-raisers. "My district doubled in size because of reapportionment. I want to have a show of strength in case of opposition. I don't want to wait until the last minute raising money if I'm opposed. You always prepare for opposition and hope you're not opposed." For the Barnes fund-raiser, the suggested contribution was $250 per person, with an expected turnout of fifty people. In one morning, Stuckey could net 10 percent of the cash needed for a general election.[23] Incumbents cannot raise funds during the legislative session, which was primed to start. It would be the end of April, after filing, before Stuckey could raise money again, which limited the time frame to build a war chest. Still she was eager and excited. And, when filing opened, Stephanie Stuckey-Benfield, now married and eight months and change pregnant, was at the front of the line to file for reelection. "I'm tired and I'm cranky, but I'm here. . . . I wouldn't have missed it unless I was in labor."[24]

Are there any potential challengers? "Yes, without a doubt," Stuckey-Benfield concedes. "The potential challenges usually come from issue-specific candidates. For instance, I have this one man in my district who is a 'mad dad.' He has a problem with my work on child support and says he's going to challenge me. Where's he going to get support? Other deadbeat dads? It'll take a $100,000 to run a challenge."

Part of how Stuckey-Benfield deters challenges is through careful constituency cultivation. "Before every session, I have a consultant who develops and sends out a survey for me. It is highly targeted, to about two thousand likely voters, Democratic and Republican, and covers a variety of issues and session items. They can check off on their opinions and also indicate their e-mail address. Then, I can e-mail them my weekly update and also send them my newsletter at the end of the session." Communication and contacting are part of her established representation style. The rest is classic constituency politics: "I just try to keep my name out there, generating lots of press releases and making sure I get into the community and to their events. . . . These events matter. It is harder with the baby, but I try to make everything in the district."

## On Progressive Ambition

Stephanie Stuckey-Benfield has been closer to the Washington establishment than anyone else we will meet. She grew up in the environment, the child of a member of Congress, and was schooled in Washington. Still, she is amazed by people who try to make the jump to Congress, and she does not miss the lifestyle of D.C. "I am amazed by people who think they can start out running for Congress. . . . They are often very naive. Now, Dad did it, but he had tons of money and a really weak opponent, and that is when the Stuckey stores were at their height." So, would Stuckey-Benfield take a seat in Congress at no cost?

"No . . . the main reason is family, and my husband's business is here in Atlanta. I don't want to go to D.C., even though it is fun and I went to school there, and I don't want to commute. . . . I want to have one or two more children, and the congressional job nowadays takes away from family. . . . State politics is fun! You can do a lot and still have a life. It is real hands-on. . . . D.C. is removed from what is really going on. In state government, it is three months of legislating and then back to reality."

Stephanie is still committed to the career path she chose when she first ran for the legislature. "I'm still dedicated to doing twenty years on the job; I do not want to go national. Right now, I can handle being in the Georgia House and also take care of family. We have forty days to get our business done, so the job only really takes three months a year. . . . Besides, I'm building seniority, and I've got good committees. . . . I would love to be chairman of Judiciary someday [she is currently vice chair]. It might be nice, maybe, to be a floor leader."

Stuckey-Benfield is also one of ten assistant whips. The institutional lad-

der in the Georgia assembly goes through the whip system, then into committee chairmanships, and, for a few select members, eventually the floor
leadership and, remotely, the speaker's chair. If she stays on her twenty-year
career plan, she just might attain those distant positions of institutional
power.

## Conclusion

Freshman legislators can shape policy. Stephanie Stuckey entered one of the
most traditional, "good ol' boy" establishments in American politics and
carved a niche for herself as an effective legislator. Her effectiveness and rapid
success was a product of many features, not the least of which was her powerful socialization to the politics of the state. It was not so much that Stephanie
was the favored daughter of the legislature but instead that her personal
socialization and two years on the state senate staff had prepared her for the
environment of the General Assembly. The institution has a go-slow attitude,
an expectation of adherence to several norms of behavior, and numerous rites
of passage. Stuckey is successfully navigating those norms and passing
through the tests before her.

Stuckey's career would be characterized by the casual observer as being
an example of static ambition: She attained an office and expressed the desire
to stay in that office for the rest of her career. Yet, to examine her career more
closely reveals a set of ambitions that are not static and are not progress
through offices but progress to power in the legislature. Her bid to reform
Title IX in Georgia cemented Stuckey's reputation as a serious legislator, as
someone who could work the inside of the legislative process, learn how
things are done, and produce a broad-based consensus on a policy that most
skeptics would otherwise regard as dead on arrival. Success led to momentum
to undertake new policy challenges of importance to her constituency and
her community. While she may not progress beyond the state legislature, she
is on a track to acquire, through formal and informal means, more power,
more influence, and greater stature in a quickly evolving institution that
nonetheless values longevity.

## Notes

1. Family lineages are not uncommon in the Georgia legislature. No fewer
than a dozen current state lawmakers succeeded to a seat held by another family
member.

2. Tom Baxter, "Qualifying Gives Newcomers Chance to Make First Mark,"
*Atlanta Journal-Constitution*, April 28, 1998, 3B.

3. Nirvi Shah, "Election 98: House District 67: Democrats Cite Youth,
Experience as Appeals," *Atlanta Journal-Constitution*, July 16, 1998, 8JA.

4. James Salazar, "Legislative Ambition a Genetic Trait," *Atlanta Journal-Constitution*, February 3, 2002, 1E.

5. Kathey Pruitt, "Freshman Legislators Learn the Ropes," *Atlanta Journal-Constitution*, December 6, 1998, 5E.

6. Pruitt, "Freshman Legislators Learn the Ropes."

7. Bill Torpy, "Capitol Corridors," *Atlanta Journal-Constitution*, March 13, 1999, 5C.

8. *Atlanta Journal-Constitution*, "The Gender Gap; Equity Backers Stirring," December 19, 1999, 1E.

9. Associated Press, "Lawmakers Push Equal Sports Opportunities for Girls," February 1, 2000.

10. Associated Press, "Lawmakers Push."

11. Alan Judd, "Bill Could Affect School Playoffs," *Atlanta Journal-Constitution*, February 2, 2000, 5B.

12. Judd, "Bill Could Affect School Playoffs."

13. Judd, "Bill Could Affect School Playoffs."

14. Judd, "Bill Could Affect School Playoffs."

15. Judd, "Bill Could Affect School Playoffs."

16. Kathey Pruitt and Peter Mantius, "Female Athletes Back Bill for Equal Funding," *Atlanta Journal-Constitution*, February 5, 2000, 5F; Patti Puckett, "Helping Women Athletes Thrive," *Atlanta Journal-Constitution*, February 10, 2000, 2JA.

17. Kathey Pruitt, "Gender Equity Vote Unanimous," *Atlanta Journal-Constitution*, March 18, 2000, 5D.

18. Associated Press, "Barnes Signs Law to Ensure Equal Sports Opportunities for Girls," April 29, 2000.

19. David Pendered, "Stuckey Resolute about Altering Current State Flag," *Atlanta Journal-Constitution*, April 13, 2000, 7JD.

20. Mark Bixler, "Bill Would Define Hispanics as Minorities under State Law," *Atlanta Journal-Constitution*, February 12, 2001, 3B.

21. Chad Roedemeier, "Democrats Propose Giving Patients Access to Doctors' Criminal, Medical History," *Atlanta Journal-Constitution*, January 12, 2001.

22. Ben Smith, "Multimember Districts Confusing, Challenging," *Atlanta Journal-Constitution* (DeKalb edition), May 23, 2002, 1JA.

23. Dick Pettys, "Barnes Squeezing in Fund-Raisers This Week before the Window Closes," *Atlanta Journal-Constitution*, January 7, 2002.

24. Salazar, "Legislative Ambition a Genetic Trait," 1E.

# Dirigo  8

It's hard to lead a cavalry charge if you think you look funny on a horse.

—Adlai Stevenson

MOST LEGISLATORS at the end of a career might shirk their duties and leave the hard decisions or unenviable tasks to the next guy. Mike Saxl was not such a legislator. Days before the fall 2002 elections, he was still working on fund-raising, campaigning for Democratic candidates, doing get-out-the-vote projects, and coming to his office in Augusta almost every day to deal with an ongoing state revenue crisis. Even as his term ended and he moved into lame duck status, as speaker of the House, he presided over a special session of the Maine legislature. The session was to be the scene of his last effort as a legislator to implement an ambitious plan to overhaul the state tax code. A few weeks after the November election, Mike was out of office due to term limits, serving less than eight years in office. He had just turned thirty-five.

## A Circumscribed Legislative Career

Mike Saxl's political career was framed by term limits. Elected in a special election in the winter of 1994–1995, he entered the state House in Augusta as one of the youngest members of the legislature, but with the knowledge that his legislative career would be brief. Maine voters ratified a term limits provision for their legislature, constraining legislators to eight consecutive years of service. Saxl arrived just as the term limits law displaced the longtime Democratic speaker of the House, John Martin, and most of the senior political leadership. The vacuum of experience and the clearing of a backlog of ambitious legislators created an opportunity for upward mobility that Saxl earnestly asserts he did not seek but nonetheless pursued because of the urging of others. Eight years after arriving as one of a group of twenty-something Democrats who banded together under the banner of the "Kids' Caucus," Saxl was a strong speaker of a strong legislature, one of the most powerful politicians in Maine, and, as of December 2002, out of a job.

When we visited in the summer of 2002, Mike had just turned thirty-five. The former middle school teacher was always a leader. In high school, he was hockey team captain, and he kept playing through college (Bowdoin) and as an amateur. Before working for the Democratic Congressional Campaign Committee, he served as an aide to state senate majority leader Nancy Clark in 1990. If he ever had stress, it was well managed and quite hidden. Sitting in his office, talking with him as he makes his way through the midst of a major political campaign and a fiscal crisis, it was fun to note that he still found time to run home and walk the dog, spend time with his new wife, and make time for curious political researchers. In my notes from one of our first meetings, I wrote, "Saxl is an unassuming man, who seems simultaneously very young and very old." Athletic, he also had an appearance that defied age. When he smiled, he was a young man who radiated energy and warmth. In more serious moments, one is uncertain whether the bearded, thinned-hair man in the pinstripe suit was twenty-five or fifty.

Saxl was born to politics. His father and mother were longtime political activists in Maine; at the time of his initial election to the state House in 1995, his mother, Representative Jane Saxl, was an incumbent state legislator who had previously served on the Bangor Council and would later run for the state senate. Saxl's father, the late Joseph Saxl, was the widely respected superintendent of the Bangor Mental Health Institute and, according to the *Bangor Daily News,* "driven by a desire to improve the standard of patient care at the facility."[1] *Horizon Magazine* in 1999 noted that "Mike grew up listening to his parents hash out politics . . . he grew up understanding how important it is to introduce legislation that makes communities work better, to craft the language of bills carefully, and to make the necessary deals to get things passed."[2] Local media and political activists described the family as "respected social activists and community leaders who were committed to improving the lives of all Maine residents." As such, the son was clearly the product of a powerful, positive socialization to public service.

## Political Context: Maine

Maine has a long-established two-party system. While politics "down east" are partisan, both parties have a powerful liberal political tradition, a strong sense of self-government arising from the tradition of the Maine town hall meeting, and a powerful small-town influence over nearly everything in state government. The state has strong Protestant Yankee influences and a substantial Catholic population, and in many respects Canada seemed as relevant to Maine's everyday existence and politics as the lower forty-seven states to the west.

The state legislature has a tradition of access for young politicians. The longtime speaker of the Maine House, John Martin, was in his early twenties when he came to the chamber, and he became one of the youngest speakers in history. Young candidates and young legislators are common in the assembly, and college students and law school students are not uncommon to the corridors of power in the old Charles Bulfinch–designed capitol building in tiny Augusta.

Legislative elections are held in single-member districts of about eight thousand residents; there are 151 total members in the assembly. There is no one geographic concentration of political power in the state, though metropolitan Portland, the Kennebec Valley, and the coast below Bangor and Bar Harbor contain most of the state's population. Election costs are fairly low, and incumbents and challengers run campaigns for just a few thousand dollars. Term limits are highly constraining (four terms), but members can leave one chamber and pursue a seat in the other legislative chamber. One consequence of term limits was the movement of some House members to the senate, and vice versa. Maine legislators are not well paid, but the demands placed on legislators are substantial; serving in the assembly is not a full-time job, but committee meetings and constituency work create year-round demands on time. Much like legislators in Nebraska, those with money or time are best able to serve, though the institution is more attractive to the young than the Unicameral is.

## Beginnings

During one of our first meetings, Mike looked across the table at me with smiling eyes and said, "The first thing I tell people when we talk about this is that I did not set out to do any of this." This statement communicated much about Saxl's own understanding of politics, that "politics is about opportunity, luck, and risk." In late 1994, as a law student in Portland who had just finished a stint with the Democratic Congressional Campaign Committee, Saxl had no particular ambitions to be in the legislature. When a vacancy occurred in his Portland neighborhood, he was approached by his mother, Jane Saxl, and the new speaker to help find a candidate to defend the seat and help preserve the Democrats' fragile majority.

The 1994 legislative elections were hard on Maine Democrats. Term limits double-decimated the Democratic caucus in the Maine House. Republicans sought to tie Democrats to the opposition of term limits, and they characterized John Martin's long-term leadership as a form of cronyism. The Republicans surged in the elections, gaining sixteen seats and leaving the Democrats with the slimmest of majorities in the lower chamber. The governor's office was won by Angus King, an independent, and the senate was in Republican hands. Subsequent to the general election, a death and a vacancy threw the slender Democratic majority into doubt. The loss of two special elections would shift control of the legislature to the GOP. Portland District 31 was closely watched by Maine political observers, and Democratic speaker Dan Gwadosky observed with some trepidation.

The *Bangor Daily News* characterized District 31 as a district that "has traditionally returned liberal Democrats to Augusta."[3] Saxl observed that the real opposition in the district was not the Republicans but rather the Green Party. His predecessor, James Oliver, resigned the seat effective January 1995 to join the Peace Corps. Saxl was approached by his mother and by Dan Gwadosky to help find a candidate to represent the very liberal, urbane Portland districts. Saxl took up the task of contacting potential candidates in the community. As he tells it, "I must have called a dozen people. I talked to the mayor [of Portland], to local community activists, to all sorts of good Democrats. And no one was thinking about running or willing to run. They all said, 'You need to run for this, Mike.' Next thing I know, I'm running, and suddenly everyone else in the constituency is also in the race."

Saxl did not place himself first on the list of possible candidates. As a veteran staffer and organizer, his first impetus was to find a candidate rather than to be the candidate. His actions are like that of many other candidates we have visited with. He first sounded out the potential opposition and found that many potential challengers in the district were uninterested in making the run. Having ascertained that the opportunity was simply too good to pass up, Saxl entered the contest in December. He would have ten weeks to make his case to his neighbors.

The new candidate was not deterred by the political setback suffered by the Democrats in the previous month. Instead, as he put it to Maine political reporter Jay Higgins, "I tried to identify good things in our community, and to turn things around."[4] In other words, instead of hiding like so many Democrats were tempted to do in December 1994, Saxl ran a visible campaign that focused on the positive dimensions of being a Democrat.

After surviving a multicandidate nomination process, Saxl went into a three-way general election race. Maine Democratic leaders watched the election returns less with excitement than with trepidation. Speaker Gwadosky faced the loss of control of the lower chamber after twenty years of Democratic domination after just weeks in office. The loss of one seat would throw the lower chamber into a tie and create a nightmarish conflict over organization that could only be broken with the filing of another vacancy. The principal GOP contender for the Portland seat was a fighter pilot, Duncan Roberts. Another candidate was Green Party activist John D. Herrick, who campaigned hard and was a threat in this affluent, liberal, urbane constituency.

Saxl delivered. Some Democrats were deeply concerned that Herrick would pull sufficient ballots in the very liberal constituency to allow Republican Hopkins to slip through with the type of plurality victories that Maine had entertained for governor in 1994 and president in 1992. At least one Democrat indicated no concerns; floor leader Paul Jacques declared, "I always said if you had good candidates and you run good issue-based campaigns and you talk about what the people want to talk about, you'll do all right." In the end, Saxl pulled 61 percent—about 636 ballots out of 1,100 cast.

Reflecting on his initial campaign, Saxl observed that it was very nearly "overkill, because of my time with the DCCC [Democratic Congressional Campaign Committee]. We had some of the best political talent in the Democratic Party up here working this campaign." From nationally experienced copywriters and professional fund-raising to sophisticated phone banking, Saxl and his crew of twenty-something buddies brought the model of the successful congressional campaign down to the grassroots level. And, in the process, he crafted a model for campaign success in Maine that would be replicated in other races and that is the model for management of a strategy to solidify Democratic control of the Maine House.

## Legislator

Saxl's almost unbridled excitement at being elected to the legislature was evident to Maine political observers. Also in evidence was a powerful desire to bring a new approach to legislative politics and to push what would prove to be a continuing issue, tax reform. Jay Higgins, writing a week after Saxl's victory, observed:

> Between mouthfuls of turkey vegetable stew and accepting the best wishes of restaurant patrons, Saxl could barely conceal his excitement as he looked forward to being sworn into office. . . . [Saxl observed that] "my most pressing concerns have to do with funding for education in Maine and making it equitable for taxpayers while making sure that we have sufficient resources to educate our children and adults in the best way possible."[5]

In his first term in the Maine legislature, Mike Saxl was among the most prolific legislators in the chamber. The freshman, second-most junior member in the chamber passed eight pieces of legislation. Among his major successes was a significant antistalking law, which Saxl had publicly stated was his main legislative priority in his first term.

The volume of legislation passed by Saxl was, as he notes often in describing his career, the product of good fortune. As a member elected in a special election after the session started, Saxl was allowed to introduce new legislation after the call for bills had closed. With such an opportunity, he was able to bring forward bills that favored his policy agenda and that also had other sponsors who could not introduce bills because of the close of the legislative call.

One bill in particular, the antistalking legislation, stands out in the review of Saxl's record. The stalking bill passed out of the Maine House just three weeks after Saxl arrived in the House, with bipartisan support, 107–32, after just a half-hour of debate. To the extent that there was disagreement over this new, tougher law, it focused on the inclusion of computer systems to track stalkers in the state, rather than any particular need to deal with stalking crimes. The chair of the committee that reported the legislation referred to it as the "most significant" legislation to come out of the Criminal Justice Committee, if not the most significant legislation in the session. Mike Saxl had passed significant legislation and initiated strong relationships with other legislators by showing an ability to cooperate to advance notable legislation.

In his first reelection bid in 1996, Saxl drew a single opponent on filing day: Portland Republican Frank G. Akers. Portland voters sent all of the city's legislators back for another term in 1996. Saxl devastated Akers 80 percent to 20 percent. The two men were wildly differentiated on nearly every issue facing the legislature, which no doubt helped Saxl marginalize his opponent in this very liberal district. The contest was a classic confrontation experienced by young candidates. Akers, a businessman two generations removed in age, was a property manager and developer. Running out of the business community, he likely mistook support in the circle of Republican businessmen for a general level of support that could carry the district against the younger incumbent. Saxl ended up with one of the widest victory margins of any opposed incumbent.

Saxl's victory was likely, given the liberal nature of his district and the strong national Democratic Party effort in 1996. Still, Saxl ran in an environment that invited national party action. The national Republican Party targeted Maine state legislative contests, in an effort to follow up on the near-victory that eluded them in 1994. National Democratic sources directed large amounts money into Maine legislative contests. Former DNCC staffer Saxl received $5,000 in direct cash from the Democrats, which was more than sufficient to cover his original, estimated campaign budget. The local media became critical of the infusion of big money into the state legislative contests. The *Portland Press/Herald* observed, just days before the 1996 general election, that "the top spenders in this year's races for the state legislature received most of their money from big contributors, and much of it's from businesses and political committees—not from the little guy."

Common Cause was concerned about how the influx of money would affect the role of special interests in the legislature. Saxl became intertwined in this debate, as he was both a recipient and distributor of financial largesse, while also attempting to certify himself as a "clean" candidate under Maine's new, progressive campaign finance law. In 1996, freshman Saxl was one of the biggest money collectors in the chamber, pulling in almost $23,000, most of it from large-dollar donors, defined in Maine as any contribution over $100. Saxl was popular with party committees; ultimately, $5,000 in contributions came into his campaign just from the Democratic Congressional Campaign Committee.

## Leader

The Pine Tree State adopted term limits in 1992, and the law hit the legislature especially hard in 1994. The longtime speaker of the House, three-decade Democratic leader John Martin, was swept out along with over a third of the legislature. Martin loomed large over the legislature. Very young when he was first elected and became speaker, Martin was a relentless leader of the legislature who would drive the very limits of human endurance. Unmarried and having no family, legislative life was Martin's spouse and love, if not an all-encompassing existence. He was known for keeping the legislature in session until the wee hours of the morning, pushing debate and driving forward legislative initiatives.

With the new, severe term limits, members started to cycle quickly through the legislature. Whereas Martin had been speaker for two decades, no speaker since him has held the gavel for more than two years. The leadership became dynamic and changing. A series of legislators moved into the speakership, often identifying and advancing the prospects of junior legislators.

Mike Saxl was drafted early for the leadership ladder, becoming majority floor whip at the beginning of his second term. He credits the leaders before him with recognizing his potential and promoting his opportunities. Mike became majority floor leader in his third term, and after managing a decisive gain by House Democrats in the 2000 election, he became speaker in his last term. The legislature settled into a stable queue of leadership, with a body of potential presiding officers being identified in the first term, and one of these being elevated to floor leader at the end of the second term before succeeding to the speaker's chair. Members who desire to lead in Maine must make their intentions known early and quickly demonstrate their legislative and political skill. There is simply no time for political mistakes when the political life cycle is so short. Whether one possesses institutional ambitions or has them cultivated, the recognition and pursuit of those ambitions will occur at the very beginning of the legislative career.[6]

With Mike Saxl, one observes the seamless movement from presiding officer to policy innovator to campaigner. Underlying all this is Saxl's view that "everything is a campaign." His efforts on behalf of Democratic candidates for legislative office are not so far removed from his efforts to campaign for his own district. It is about contacting, calling, asking, and cajoling individuals and groups toward the preferred electoral outcome. As a speaker, he works his candidates like a candidate working voters, calling, prompting, and urging them to get out and work. Free moments are taken up calling candidates, massaging them, and encouraging candidates to work the phones and the doors that are so important to winning legislative elections.

Saxl and the Maine Democrats are among the current generation of campaign innovators who make the most of limited resources. Much of what Saxl promotes in raising funds and disbursing them is a rapidly emerging form of campaigning that combines intensive, grassroots effort with consumer technology to target messages effectively through direct mail. This approach has quickly taken on the nickname "tech-n-touch" in politics.

How does tech-n-touch work? A big part of the Maine Democratic GOTV operations illustrates. The program used volunteers in southern and central Maine to go door to door, talking to potential swing voters about issues. They identify no candidate or party in this effort. Each field operative has a personal digital assistant (PDA; e.g., a PalmPilot), which they use to build a database, by household, of issue concerns. Every few hours the PDA databases are uploaded to a general database. When the central database has thirty responses on an issue within a ZIP code, a custom mailing is generated on that issue and sent to those households. Voters are personally solicited for their opinions and then have that "touch" contact followed up with a highly personalized, issue-specific mailing.

One can still see Mike Saxl, the grassroots campaigner, within Mike Saxl, the state party leader. When working a political event, it is evident that Saxl is a man of little pretense, almost retiring when confronted with adulation and praise. Nonetheless, he has a presence, and he is adept at working a room or a crowd. Mike attracts and holds the attention of others because he is acting as an advocate who steps to the fore. During a visit with a meeting of the Maine Association of Interdependent Neighborhoods (MAIN), a liberal, Democratic activist group that is mainly focused on health and social welfare issues, Saxl was clearly complimented and humbled by the laudatory language heaped on him for his good works. For him, this was a chance to rally the faithful, to impress on them the importance of their work, and to mobilize an important part of the Democratic base around Augusta. During a fundraiser the previous evening, Mike was similarly the center of attention, but in this instance he was acting as entertainment, serving as a rallying point for people to open their checkbooks for the final electoral push. The venues and goals were very different, but the general campaign technique was the same: Establish a presence, communicate a message, and develop goodwill with the audience. Saxl as politician displays Bear Bryant's hallmark of leadership: Victory belongs to the team, failure to the coach.

## ''Ruling the Media''

The campaign orientation of Mike Saxl is evident in all of his undertakings. One morning, while I was waiting with the chief of staff in the speaker's office, Saxl came through the door with a burst of energy (as he always does) and tossed me a short monograph by Nick Nichols and Andy Shea, titled "Ruling the Media." "Take a look at this," he said. "We need everyone to read this before they start dealing with the press." Nichols and Shea lay out a set of rules for dealing with the press, in order to avoid negative spin and to have control of a story where you are a potential subject. It is a volume written mainly for corporate spokespersons, but, as such, it has broader application for anyone dealing with the press. The topics in the text reflect Saxl's "Everything's a campaign" mind-set. These "Rules of Engagement" are primarily designed to ensure a degree of control over the interview by the subject and to avoid any embarrassment by limiting the scope of inquiry and the persons, materials, or places accessed in the interview. These rules are unexpectedly similar to the rules of discovery in judicial proceedings

It is not at all surprising that Saxl would want any help possible in handling Maine's independent, critical media. While Saxl is at ease in dealing with the media, he has not always enjoyed a holiday with the state press. Historically, the state media, especially the newspapers, report the beginnings of legislative sessions as having great hope, great potential. Almost invariably, however, this same press subsequently laments the failures of the capital gang and especially the apparent inability of the legislature to finish what it starts.

As the budget battle began, Saxl and the Democratic legislative leadership prepared press strategy for the coming special session. This particular session was held to prepare the current majority leader—and speaker-designate—Pat Colwell for an afternoon television forum on the fiscal crisis. The preparation, which occurred in the speaker's office, consisted of a half-dozen legislators and staff sitting with Colwell, helping him prepare questions, comment, and rebuttal. The first half of the meeting was dedicated to developing the core Democratic budget message; the second part of the meeting, which continued as the speaker ran home to walk the dog, was a simulated Q&A in which everyone peppered the majority leader with questions and worked over possible answers.

## Institution Building

The most interesting dimension of Mike Saxl's public service was his dedication to institution building, especially as an antidote to the detrimental effects of term limits. A concern about term limits held by both academic observers and practical politicians is the emergence of an empowered but unresponsive bureaucratic class in public agencies, and an empowered and selectively responsive class of interest groups who will shape public policy. To that end, Mike Saxl and other House members have worked since the imposition of term limits to actively mentor new legislators and quickly develop issue awareness and expertise to keep the legislature in a position of strength in crafting state policy. This goal is pursued through a variety of formal and informal mechanisms. There has emerged a formal orientation of new legislators that immerses them in the role within days of their election.

With only weeks left to serve, Saxl takes a strong role in the legislative council meetings to set up the bicameral orientation of new members. At least a fifth of each chamber will be newly elected due to mandated and voluntary retirements, or about forty persons. The goal of the revised orientation is to make the process more personal and intimate; one thing to be done, through the caucuses, is to assign mentors to members to work with them to learn the process and foster ties in the institution. When asked whether the mentoring program should be "bipartisan," the answer was "No; it might prove too awkward." The problem was best left to the caucuses.

The orientation, which is designed in a public meeting by a bipartisan, bicameral panel, includes not only the orientation items all members of all legislatures are exposed to, such as how to introduce a bill, how to vote, how to find your seat, and how to access e-mail and file reimbursement. It also includes a variety of very practical, sophisticated training exercises that are more reminiscent of an M.B.A. program or a corporate retreat. Members engage in mock legislative sessions to learn the formal rules operation, but they will also engage in role playing and problem-solving sessions related to existing policy challenges. Sessions are set up to train people in consensus building. Working groups will allow veteran members who coordinate those groups to observe the leadership and problem-solving skills of new members.

These exercises are important, because they will allow the leadership to spot potential leaders early in their brief careers. Mike Saxl confirms the importance of this to his general model of politics—the "art of the possible. You have to have people who are smart enough to understand the problems but who can also look down the road and see the big picture. They have to be willing to work and compromise to get part of what we want now, and maybe wait to get the rest later on. They have to be patient and able to work with people to find good solutions. . . . What do I look for in people? Passion and intellectual ability, and the ability to develop pragmatic skills; . . . they have to be able to look beyond today."

Other sessions will deal with other practical challenges for politicians, such as media training, and meetings with executive agency personnel to learn how to deal with these important actors. Saxl and the other members of the curriculum committee have laid aside any partisan issues in developing this orientation. "This is not a partisan cabal," to quote from one member. Instead, the body is focused on the mission of orienting new members, instead of forcing a partisan or ideological perspective.

The orientation meeting included a variety of ideas that would make good sense in a strict corporate environment—issue orientations, or the appointing of formal mentors for new members—but in the end Saxl and his Leg Council colleagues agree that the more politicized nature of some of these undertakings might be better left to the party caucuses. The group agrees to invite strong, knowledgeable speakers to address working groups on the "major challenges" facing the state—in other words, Saxl gets most of what he wants by getting to frame the major issues for the next legislature, while also, in his own words, "nurturing their abilities." Nothing is said about communicating norms. Much like norms themselves, the communication of those norms appears to be left to informal processes, despite the importance of those norms to the institution.

What is not necessarily evident to most people is the extent of the institutional political apparatuses Speaker Saxl is constructing, even in the waning days of his incumbency. He is dedicated to growing talent to continue the broader agenda he has for Maine ("nurture talent and give them the tools to get the job done"). Because of term limits, this also involves transmission of values and institutional power. The apparatus for accomplishing this goal exists on at least four dimensions:

1. A candidate recruitment organization, to identify and activate potential Democrats to run for the legislature
2. A campaign finance organization, to help both candidates and the Democratic Caucus in general secure funding and finance credible campaigns
3. A mechanism in the legislature for training and indoctrinating new legislators
4. A recruitment program to identify potential, rising leaders in the Democratic caucus and to train them in leadership skills and prepare them as experts on important policy issues

These last two mechanism are integrated into the legislator orientation program. To what extent Republicans exploit these opportunities is not within the scope of my observations. But, as Saxl describes these activities, they are all direct consequences of the term limits law in Maine.

## A Decade of Budget Woes

When Mike Saxl first came to the legislature in 1995, he cited as his most pressing concerns the funding for education and the problems of taxpayer equity. These concerns are rooted in a much broader problem: the creation and maintenance of a stream of revenue for Maine government.

How does the state of Maine manage its budget? For all of Mike's tenure, an independent governor has been in Blaine House, and the senate has passed back and forth from Republican to Democratic to split control. A consequence is that the legislature often ends the regular session without a firm agreement on the budget. Conflicts erupt over the disposition of surpluses, the design of and beneficiaries from possible tax cuts, and ways to deal with budget shortfalls. Financial instability and fiscal equity have been on Saxl's agenda since the day he arrived in the legislature. It is the last issue he is dealing with in his truncated career. It is a problem that will likely not be resolved in his legislative career.

Why does the budget matter? All legislative priorities, and all new initiatives, flow from the budget. If there are insufficient funds to cover all priorities, states must deal with the scarcity of resources by setting priorities. The more acute the scarcity, the tougher decisions become. One policy priority is set against another, and partisan or factional tensions are intensified. While there were years of prosperity in Maine, unstable revenues plagued the state. The fiscal crisis of 2002 reflects this ongoing instability, which has resulted in a budget shortfall of over $200 million. The challenge for the legislature and the governor is to craft a budget resolution and to find a balance between generating new revenues and making cuts in existing programs. For a national Democrat like Saxl, the prospect of service cuts is not attractive, if only because Maine has such tremendous demands placed on it by the population for government services.

Since becoming speaker, Saxl has been conducting an investigation into the problems associated with Maine's ongoing revenue challenges. In October 2001, Speaker Saxl announced the formation of an advisory committee, the nonpartisan Speaker's Advisory Commission on Tax Reform, to explore options for revamping the tax code in Maine. More than a political entity, it includes participants from the business sectors, economic and trade interests, and the academic community. The mission of the advisory committee was to enter into meaningful debate on tax reform to end Maine's perpetual fiscal stress. Public statements by Saxl and private conversations indicate that the existing tax code in Maine was not working in the best interests of the government or the residents of the state. By design, it does not facilitate the effective governance of the state.

Public meetings for the speaker's committee are in the Legislative Council chambers. The three-hour meeting served two purposes: first, to allow the committee to enter into a substantive discussion regarding the direction and scope of tax reform in Maine; and, second, to allow for the presentation of a series of subcommittee recommendations regarding streamlining education policy that are substantively linked to the design of the tax code. The meetings highlighted many of the talents that Mike Saxl has cultivated over the past seven years, and they reflected the goals and values repeatedly articulated in our previous conversations. They also revealed, subtly, his anxiety over pushing forward a tax code revision.

The presentations weighed toward the issues of school funding and delivery of services and highlighted the need for funding equity across school systems. Maine has dramatic disparities in the ability of school systems to pay for local services relative to the fiscal capacity of those systems to pay for such services. A 1789 state law requires each town of fifty or more people to provide at least six months of schooling. For isolated island communities, towns have opted to pay tuition for children to attend private academies, rather than endure even greater costs of providing local schooling.

Education funding is not the only problem. Government and the service sector, along with retailing and wholesaling, make up the bulk of the state economy. Does the tax code promote evolution and diversification of the economy? Does it effectively draw revenues from areas of economic growth and dependency? Do these shortcomings contribute to fiscal stress Down East? The answer, in the eyes and words of the Tax Committee, are no, no, and yes. Maine is in fiscal and economic crisis in part because it cannot stabilize revenues, and instability is in part a function of an imbalanced and outdated tax code that has failed to keep up with the evolution of the state economy. Because the tax code does not encourage investment or the development of small business, and because it is steeply progressive in taxing income, the state also suffers a brain drain of smart and young natives. Mike Saxl envisioned a state economy that will reverse the brain drain of Maine (the state is one of the poorest in the nation, with low levels of college degree attainment and the third-oldest population in America). "We have way too many people leaving, way too few entrepreneurs," he said. "We have to grow microenterprise in the state. . . . We're caught in the 1940s with our tax code. It is geared to a manufacturing and mill industry, and not toward a diversified economy." Saxl is warming to any idea that will encourage budget stabilization. "We have to provide relief and reform that works."

Could he get enough political support out of the Advisory Committee to compel the passage of meaningful reform before his term is up? In one of our last meetings, as we returned from a midday GOTV event in Augusta, Saxl was up front about the need to act, immediately, on tax reform in Maine. There was a "strategic opportunity here. Sometimes, you have the right people in the right place at the right time to take decisive action. At the moment we have the expertise to develop fundamental change in the tax code, the political will to do it, and a set of circumstances with the fiscal crisis that make it possible. The support will disappear unless we act very soon."

My own notes reflect a caution: "Is Mike Saxl pushing too hard, too soon? He has no mandate for fundamental tax change, and he may force a stalemate or backlash that is not necessarily in his party's best interest. . . . OTOH [On the other hand,] he is advancing a policy that should attract conservatives, because it moves revenue generation from property and income, and toward consumption."

To say that Mike Saxl sees everything as a campaign is not to indicate that he has no long-term vision or goals. In fact, the opposite is the case. Saxl came to the legislature with four very clear, broad goals for his home state. That vision included the creation of a more stable, steady revenue stream and a more diversified state economy to fund that revenue stream. He has not accomplished that goal, but he articulated it and pursued it doggedly to the end of his term.

## Conclusion

All of the issues confronting Mike Saxl—legislative elections, the budget, tax code reform—are linked. The immediate fiscal crisis of the state remains in the hands of his legislature and the current governor to resolve. As such, one party or the other may seek to make political capital out of the resolution of the crisis. Saxl and other Democrats, along with the chief of staff for the governor, were quite concerned about having complete buy-in from all political parties on any call for a special session and also about having a bipartisan support for any legislation to address the budget shortfall. "I am not going to let them turn this into a campaign issue. They have to come along." Policy is the campaign; the campaign is policy.

Saxl readily admits that he views everything through the context of a campaign. "I treat everything as a campaign . . . there is a nexus between policy and politics." They flow from each other in his eyes. The campaign perspective likely derives itself from Saxl's career with the DCCC and from the impression one gets that Mike just likes campaigns best. His efforts to reform the state financial system engage the best of his political abilities—namely, working toward a tangible goal in a frenzied environment of uncertainty and pressing need. The crisis mentality of a campaign fits the circumstances of Saxl's last effort at policymaking, long-term economic change couched in the short-term environment of crisis.

However, both those who work around him and anyone who takes the time to observe this leader up close note the same thing, captured succinctly by Rich Pelletier, veteran staffer for the House Democratic Caucus: "The speaker understands better than anyone I have seen that politics and policy are seamless." Saxl himself readily volunteers that where he exists, as a legislator and especially as speaker, is at the "nexus between policy and campaigns." This is telling, because all of these cases reveal that this is true. Politics, and the products of politics, are dynamic. Politics is the ongoing effort to control the physical environment in reflection of the broad-based preferences of the governed. Elections translate those preferences into government. In turn, government crafts policy, which affects the environment that elected the government. Saxl as speaker sat at the nexus, the place where the politics and inputs of the environment made their way into David Easton's (1957) black box.

# Notes

1. A. Jay Higgins, "Young Saxl to Carry on Political Legacy," *Bangor Daily News*, March 6, 1995.
2. Sarah Eilers, "The Maine Phenomenon," *Horizon Magazine*, n.d., 1999; available online: www.horizonmag.com/2/maine.htm.
3. Higgins, "Young Saxl."
4. Higgins, "Young Saxl."
5. Higgins, "Young Saxl."
6. A similar experience of dislocation and a scrambling of the leadership ladder was felt in California, where longtime assembly speaker Willie Brown was ousted by term limits in the early 1990s (see Beiler 1999).

# The Man in the Middle

> In politics, nothing happens by accident. If it happens, you can bet it was planned that way.
>
> —Franklin Delano Roosevelt

THE HEART OF THE Oklahoma Democratic Party is LeFlore County. Nestled in the east Oklahoma hills, this county helped propel the careers of Carl Albert and Robert S. Kerr. The Democratic Party is still king in this part of the state, where the New Deal never ended. In the summer of 1998, political observers whispered that another great political career was starting in the person of twenty-one-year-old Kenneth Corn. Corn sought the open House District 3, previously held by retiring Appropriations Committee chair Jim Hamilton. In 1998, Corn was an intern on the staff of the House Appropriations Committee. Interns can engage in real policymaking if they are bright and show initiative. Kenneth Corn had both of these attributes, and it was initiative and insight that propelled him to political prominence.

Kenneth Corn was always inspired by politics. When he was nine, he gave his first political speech, at the LeFlore Democratic Party fish fry on behalf of David Boren. As a young man growing up in Howe, he listened to the political stories of former representative Charlie Wilson. As a family friend of the Corn's related, "Charlie would sit with Ken and tell him all of the stories about politics and the legislature. And Ken would just sit there and soak it all up, and Charlie loved to sit there and tell him all the stories when Ken would walk over. Politics became the center of his life. When he got to high school, Ken ran the Young Democrats, and he just couldn't wait to vote."

Political involvement ran in the family, not so much as candidates or as political leaders but as organization people, canvassers, and campaign workers. LeFlore County exhibited an attribute of political behavior that is fast disappearing from the American political landscape: the extended family as a political unit. In parts of rural Oklahoma, patriarchs or matriarchs still headed extended families. Before elections, the family head would call everyone together, typically for a Sunday supper after church, and then explain to everyone in the family who the family was backing, and why. Since he was a teenager, Kenneth had assumed that role in his family, if only because he followed politics more closely. Many political candidates in LeFlore knew that getting the Corn's vote meant talking to Kenneth. The array of friends that gathered around Kenneth's candidacy was vast, varying in age from the very young to the elderly. Most of his support came from working-class rural families and retirees who had watched him grow up.

It was fortunate that Kenneth has so many friends and family members to rely on; without them, he might not have gotten his campaign off the ground. He made the decision to run in June, just two weeks before the filing date. He was in China on a university trip and was unaware of Hamilton's retirement until just before he returned. On the Delta Airlines flight to the states, he discussed his potential campaign with two close friends on the trip. Kenneth admitted he was "anxious" for the rest of his visit to China and that he wanted to get back home and run. Within a week, he had decided to run and announced his candidacy from the front steps of the LeFlore County courthouse on June 18.[1] On August 27, he led a five-candidate field for the Democratic nomination. On September 25, he won 64 percent of the vote in a runoff primary. And, on November 3, he carried 68 percent of the vote to be elected to the state legislature.

At age twenty-one, Kenneth Corn went from being an unpaid legislative intern to representing a safe Democratic district. This chapter is an account of his emergence and socialization as a legislator and the development and pursuit of his progressive ambitions.

## "A Stunning Victory"

Multicandidate contests typically boil down to two types. The first type is the free-for-all, where all of the candidates have relatively equal weight and similar chances of winning, and the outcome is quite uncertain until the votes are counted. This type of campaign is especially prevalent when sectionalism and "friends-and-neighbors" voting predominates (Key 1949). The second type of multicandidate election is what former Georgia gubernatorial candidate Bubba MacDonald characterized to me as the "twin pissing matches": the "big pissing match, between the real front-runners, and the little pissing match where all the piss-ant candidates squabble with each other. The key is to have your man in the big pissing match instead of down with the piss ants." What was not clear until primary day was who were front-runners and who were piss ants.

Five other candidates were seeking the District 3 seat, including a Republican who was given little chance in a district with a 90 percent Democratic registration advantage. The talk of local political observers was that there were two other contending candidates besides Kenneth Corn: Paul Plummer, a member of a prominent local family who had taken a leave from his state job to run, and Wayne Hoffman, a former University of Oklahoma football player in the 1970s and nursing home operator who had also lobbied the legislature on behalf of the nursing care industry. Other candidates were initially dismissive of Corn, but they developed a grudging respect for his candidacy. As I navigated a political crowd at Wister Lake, a recreational area in west LeFlore County, asking about the prospects for the Third District, Corn's name was the first one to come up. Noted one observer, "Wayne Hoffman says everywhere he goes, 'There's that Corn kid'; he's for real," and several prominent Democrats confided a month before the election that Corn "should make a runoff." Whether he would win a runoff was not certain, but what was left unsaid spoke volumes: "The kid was for real," if he kept it all together.

Later I asked Kenneth about negative campaigning and the age issue. His youth came up early, and he has suffered the barbs thrown at him. But he was steadfast against going negative.

"Oh, we could go negative if we wanted, . . . but the fact is that I'm too young to get away with it, and it conflicts with my values. I'm not taking special interest or PAC money, and I won't . . . go negative. When a young man goes negative, he looks immature, and he loses credibility with the voters. . . . They've been trying to say that I'm too young, that I don't know budgets. But, when they hear me talk, the age thing goes away; and I worked for Representative Hamilton on the Appropriations Committee last year, so I know that budget better than anyone here. . . . If I go to the capitol, those folks up there don't have to train me or break me in; I already understand the system, I know people, and they know I can work with them. And that will be good for the county."

The attacks did not stop with age. A whispering campaign, the origin of which is unknown, was started alleging that Kenneth was gay. I recall him discussing this rumor when it first started, back around July 4. "First they say I'm too young; then they say I don't know the budget, but I helped write it; and now they're saying I'm gay! I don't know what they'll do next. . . . Well, I've got this rumor beat, though. Shawntel Smith [a friend who was Ms. America] is coming down to visit and do a fund-raiser. We go back a ways, and she is going to make sure that everyone knows that *she came down just to help me out.*"

Although the rumors and criticisms continued into the primary and runoff election, Kenneth was able to lay them aside. During a late July campaign swing, he talked about what was going to happen in the coming weeks.

"Well, they already have tried to hit me with my age, my lack of experience, and now this gay thing. None of it has stuck. Everywhere I go, after I talk, people start to forget my age. There are too many real problems confronting the people of this district that need to be talked about. Every time we have a candidate forum, I bring up something new, and then the next time we meet, all the other candidates are talking about what I talked about the last time out. But I am sure they will keep up this negative stuff. I just don't think it will work with the people of this district."

The negative campaigning did continue. At a candidate forum held by the cattleman's association on the Thursday before the primary, Kenneth found himself under fire from friends of his principal opponent. One audience member stood up and said, point-blank, "I think you're too young—you don't know anything. I worked hard all my life, and you never even had a job. I don't see how you can represent me." The questioner, who I later learned was something of a gadfly, was not prepared for the response he received.

"I decided to lay that issue to rest right there," Kenneth said. "I looked up at him and I said, '[Sir], let me tell you about my life and how I grew up.' And I told him about my parents working hard but always just getting by, and having to work to have things like clothes for school, and how life didn't hand me anything. That fellah, he inherited everything he has; he can't tell me I haven't worked hard. When I finished with him, he sat down, and that was the last we heard about age in a forum."[2]

Kenneth had suspected a hostile reception at the cattleman's meeting. "They're businessmen, and a lot of them support Wayne [Hoffman]." The tack he took to avert a potentially ugly reception indicates the depth of his political acumen and a real understanding of his constituency. "The cattlemen said everyone could bring one guest," he observed, "so I brought my [maternal] grandfather. He's a mechanic who has repaired tractors and farm machinery around here for over fifty years. At some point in time he has worked on machinery for every man in that room, and they know and respect him. So I took him with me, and introduced him, and reminded everyone there how much he had done for them over the years and how much their business had meant to him. . . . They couldn't take me down in front of him."

The campaigning would get even uglier in the runoff, as his opponent tried to paint Kenneth as a "do-nothing, done-nothing opportunist." These efforts did not succeed in derailing Kenneth from his campaign plan.

Corn was in a political fight where he was clearly a contender. He came into direct contact with his opponents and his critics. He sought to establish his political credentials and define the campaign on the issues with which he was comfortable. Part of that effort entailed dealing with negative attacks on his character, personality, and age. It also meant establishing his personal and political maturity in the face of such attacks.

## Organization and Constituency

The first day I traveled with Kenneth, we were accompanied by a high school classmate of Kenneth's and a former neighbor who was a "third grandmother" and also the campaign treasurer. Sou, the third grandmother, was once secretary to another state legislator in the area and demonstrated an inti-mate knowledge of the vote in parts of the county. Everywhere, Kenneth was known and well received. He had tremendous support in this campaign effort. He was clearly a popular young man, though not in the sense of Rich-ard Fenno's Congressman B, the athletic hero. Instead, he was the boy next door, the nice kid who did well in school and who everyone knew to be upright and honest. He was also the kind of kid who fought for kids who couldn't fight for themselves.

In Corn's case, these perceptions were built on his academic accomplish-ment. As a young man in Poteau, he had come from a working-class family with neither credentials nor money. Kenneth worked hard in school, earning himself distinction as a student and as a leader. As a high school senior, he was elected international president of the Future Business Leaders of America. A scholarship winner, he attended the University of Oklahoma and was elected president of the University Housing Association.

The core of support that he relied on was drawn from two universes: the local universe of his family and friends from childhood, and the larger uni-verse of friends made in civic activities and at the University of Oklahoma. Kenneth's campaign officers—the treasurer, manager, committee chair—were drawn largely from a collection of older family friends who looked to him as another grandson. His volunteers were a collection of high school friends, cousins, aunts, uncles, and neighbors from Howe and Heavenor. And, on the weekends, college friends and friends in state politics would drive down to help the campaign.

The campaign was Kenneth. When I asked him about organization—scheduling, fund-raising, scripting—he indicated that he did most of it him-self. Days on the campaign trail included not only door-to-door campaigning and events but also calls on local newspapers and radio stations to place advertising. He clearly had trouble letting go of control of the campaign, even as the demands on his time increased. Still, he appeared to have a very clear perception of where his political strengths and weaknesses were entering the campaign. His greatest strengths were his intimate knowledge of the con-stituency, his speaking ability and command of the issues, and his energy on the campaign trail. His weaknesses were age and the perception that his prin-cipal political opponent was so well funded that he could not be defeated. This last perception caused Kenneth to attract little support from the estab-lished business community. Most of the Chamber of Commerce types were lined up behind Wayne Hoffman, and they had given heavily. So how did a twenty-one-year-old from a working-class family pay for a political campaign against one of the most successful businessmen in his community?

"This campaign was about the common folk," was the explanation offered by a close family friend. "That boy has everything because of himself. No one gave it to him. You look in his reports, and there aren't any big contributions, no $1,000 checks. People are giving him $20 here, $40 there. He is the people's candidate." The same person intimated what was apparent in early August: Kenneth was running on a shoestring. "About two weeks before the primary, he was almost out of money. We didn't know if he would make it, . . . I went around and passed the hat and found about $2,000, and that kept the bills paid until the primary." I asked the older gentleman why he had invested in Kenneth's campaign. The answer, accompanied by a steady, smiling gaze: "Oh, I believe in him. He is an outstanding young man, and I believe in him. He'll do good for people." The same theme recurred again and again throughout the primary. Kenneth's campaign took on a bandwagon quality of supporters headed into primary day; however, a lot of the people hanging on the wagon threw some money into the political kitty. They invested in the youngest, least experienced candidate in the field, based on their belief in him.[3]

To understand how Kenneth Corn related to his electoral constituency, it is helpful to look at the experiences of another Poteau politician, Larry Dickerson. If anyone knew about youth, adversity, and success, it was Dickerson. A twelve-year legislator, Dickerson was initially elected to the state senate in 1986. He survived a difficult reelection bid in 1990 and then had no opposition in 1994 before being reelected in 1998. When we met during the primary, Dickerson was the principal moderator for a Democratic Party function in LeFlore County. After he had finished his duties of introducing the contestants and had made his own speech, we took a walk along the lake, discussing the candidates for District 3 and the challenges of the young candidate.

"It's hard for a young candidate to get taken seriously," Dickerson told me. "I was a young candidate the first time I ran, back in 1986. . . . I made a point of waiting until after my thirtieth birthday to file my paperwork, because I didn't want to [appear on the official filings and in the paper as] 'Larry Dickerson, D, Poteau, 29'; I needed to be 'Larry Dickerson, D, Poteau, 30.' That 3 at the front makes all the difference for some people. . . . We have also sent three other men in their late twenties to the state House in the last few decades . . . down here we elect people and we tend to keep them there."

The importance of starting a young legislator and keeping him (or her) in office was emphasized by Dickerson in a subsequent forum. While giving a talk to a group of about ninety college students, Dickerson was asked specifically about Kenneth Corn and his candidacy. The senator observed that rural districts have a vested interest in electing and reelecting young legislators.

"Term limits are not really good for rural counties," he said. "They count on electing a person to the legislature, and then keeping that person there for a while. The cities have a lot of legislators to look out for their interests. . . . In a rural community, you can elect a relatively young, smart legislator and then keep him in office. He has the energy for the job and also the seniority and smarts to take care of the district. I'll tell you one thing, though. You will get the chance to vote for Ken Corn in a statewide election in eight or ten years."

Kenneth was marked as a man on the progressive career track before he ever took office.

## Erecting Entry Barriers

Whether stumping the small houses and trailers of Spiro or working a crowd in Poteau, Corn gave the impression of a mature, energetic campaigner. As we drove around the south end of the district, he looked over and said, "I just *have* to keep going. I wake up dead tired, but I know I have to get out here and work the doors; after I send the volunteers home, I go back out and knock on more doors." We campaigned subdivisions, subsidized housing, and retirement communities. Kenneth was especially at ease with the "old folks," who took to him like a lost grandson. At one campaign stop on a hot July morning, we sat for twenty minutes discussing watermelon and the problems of growing tomatoes in the summer heat with an ancient woman, her neighbor, and the neighbor's oxygen tank. By the time we left he had their votes. His campaign treasurer said that "the little gray-haired ladies will win this election for him," and, to watch him with the old folks, you understand: He really listened and cared about them. It was easy to forget his age when he talked about the problems of the elderly.

His deliberate gait, with long strides, carried him quickly from door to door; he was literally running, even late in the day. When he got to a door, he knocked, smiled, and asked, "Can I campaign you?" If someone wasn't home, a personal note was left for the voter. This approach to campaigning mattered in Little Dixie; as we walked a neighborhood in 108-degree heat, he observed that "people down here want to see politicians sweat. They want you to work for their vote. If you come see them, talk with them, and give them some time, they'll probably vote for you. Now some of them have their minds made up, and you can't get them. But if you work, they'll respond."

Personal politics were still common in rural Oklahoma. As I observed in the suburbs of Oklahoma City and Cobb County, suburban neighborhoods are not as easy to penetrate using door-to-door as in the past, though doors remain part of state legislative campaigns. People don't always want to be bothered at home, and the hyperactive life of the suburban family—most of the votes are still in family households in the suburbs—means that working doors means lots of missed contacts. Candidates rely more on targeted mailings and phone banking to supplement their door knocking and personal canvassing. Down in LeFlore County, a chat at the cattle grate or a handwritten note in the doorjamb are remembered and appreciated, and dropping in on business districts is still part of the campaign, as is a courthouse round or an hour in front of the Wal-Mart. Corn's campaign style was one with which he was personally comfortable and that also was expected in his community. How long would it stay that way? According to Kenneth, "Forever. Until this town gets big enough to support a TV station; then the politics will change. Our races are too small to advertise over in Fort Smith [Arkansas], and the local papers don't make much of a difference. Direct mail is not as effective as walking, because people really want to see you. Politics here won't ever change until the place changes a lot."

But the politics of the county are changing. One of Kenneth's opponents employed a professional, full-time campaign manager, and another candidate, an incumbent state legislator in another district, contracted Washington-based pollster Alan Secrest to do his preliminary polling. Corn purchased television on cable and on the Fort Smith, Arkansas, television stations. But the real campaign was fought on the ground.

Candidates can set entry barriers for other opponents, even in an open seat, by setting the campaign pace (Ehrenhalt 1991). In this case, we observe the youngest candidate upsetting the plans of the best-funded, heavyweight candidate by taking his campaign to the streets. Kenneth Corn was the first candidate going door-to-door in the Third District, and he spent more time on retail politics than any other candidate. In terms of style he set the tempo of the race with an aggressive campaign to work doors and campaign people. Kenneth observed that "I forced them all outside . . . I can outwalk any of them." Like Matt Dollar, time and energy were his equity.

He also erected entry barriers on a substantive level as well. In Kenneth's campaign appearances, he demonstrated an exceptional degree of issue knowledge, and he used that knowledge to set the tenor of the candidate forums and debates. One observer intimated at a candidate forum that "Kenneth sets the tone. Watch. They'll be talking about what he brought up yesterday, and he'll bring something new in tonight. *They—can't—keep—up.*" By taking control of the issue debate and demonstrating a high level of knowledge and sophistication, Kenneth established himself as the standard other candidates had to meet.

Ten minutes later, one of the crowd asked a question about the new truth-in-sentencing law, a hot political issue in Oklahoma in 1998. Before this event, Kenneth had indicated to me how he would respond to such a question, should his main opponent go first; the scenario played out as expected. Wayne Hoffman replied to a question about truth-in-sentencing by saying that the bill was "too long to read, . . . several hundred pages," but that he was sure it was a good law and he would look into it. Kenneth reached into his briefcase during his response time and produced a copy of the thirty-two-page bill. "This is the truth-in-sentencing bill," Corn said, "and I *have* read the bill [emphasizing its brevity], and it's a bad bill." Kenneth waylaid the age issue by demonstrating superior technical political knowledge.

## Three Elections, Three Wins

The biggest surprise of the August primary was not that Kenneth Corn led the primary field, but by how much. In a field of five candidates, Kenneth pulled 46 percent of the vote and led his nearest challenger by 11 percentage points. The night of the primary, I called Larry Dickerson, and he related to me the scope of Kenneth Corn's win.

"Your boy did good tonight. Kenneth is in a runoff, and it looks like he's going to win big. He's leading Hoffman by about nine hundred votes, and the only boxes out are in areas where Ken will split with him. . . . What happened is that all of the old folks got out and voted for him; they really turned out. . . . Kenneth really connected with people. You know, I got started young myself. I was thirty when I was elected to the state senate. And I used to be the best speaker around these parts. But after last Thursday, I don't know. . . . Dee [Larry's wife] came up to me after the speaking down at the courthouse, and she said, 'Honey, you used to be the best public speaker around here; now you're second best.' And now I stay as far away from Kenneth as possible in the order of speakers. When he spoke to the crowd in front of the courthouse, with [a crew from PBS's] *NewsHour with Jim Lehrer* and the Fort Smith media around, he just took over the crowd. And that changed a lot of folks minds about his age."

The magnitude of Corn's primary victory was a tribute to his stump style and his hustle. He campaigned every neighborhood in the district, wearing out several pairs of shoes in the process. He remarked to me after an all-day campaign session in Arkomo, in the far reaches of the district, "I looked at Arkomo, and I saw that there were maybe two hundred homes up there, and I thought, 'Oh, I can knock this out in no time. Then I got walking around, and I realized that this town went all over the place! I walked twenty-three miles to knock on two hundred doors!" The efforts are evident in the distribution of his vote in the twenty-four voting precincts in his district. Kenneth carried eighteen precincts, including fifteen with a majority of the vote. The support for his candidacy was greatest near his home in Howe as well as in Heavener and Poteau. His runoff opponent, Wayne Hoffman, carried six boxes, all in the northern part of the district.

The emotional energy behind Kenneth's campaign had helped turn out his primary, friends-and-neighbors constituency; however, the presence of a county commission race and a hot district attorney race also drew out many voters, especially in Kenneth's bailiwick of Howe. As Dickerson related it, "Kenneth turned [the friends and neighbors] vote out once, but it was easier because these people had a lot of reasons to go vote. Now he has to identify his vote and keep it mobilized." I then prompted him, asking what turnout would be for the runoff. "I figure that the turnout will fall 40 percent, and it's across the board. If Kenneth can keep his vote and split the vote of Plummer and the others . . . he'll take this thing." He also indicated that *"someone should really tell Kenneth these things."*

The differences between the front-running candidates crystallized in the days leading to the runoff. While waiting to meet Kenneth at a local restaurant, I found myself chatting up the cashier, who was related to an eliminated candidate. Her observations about the race indicated not only that Kenneth would win but that, in a runoff, he would have a real advantage over his opponent.

"Well, we see Kenneth in here all the time," the cashier told me. "He is a nice boy, young but smart. Wayne Hoffman, well, he has all that money, and everyone knows who he is, but he really is running into some problems. You see those men over there [she gestured toward a table with four middle-aged men in short sleeves and ties]—they all did business with Wayne and thought they had a deal, and he didn't come through. They won't back him. A lot of people here think that he doesn't take care of business in the community, that he looks out for himself, and he doesn't care who he runs over . . . and now he is coming around asking for support?"

Wayne Hoffman was, among his business ventures, a nursing home operator. During 1998, a scandal had broken across Oklahoma regarding the oversight and regulation of nursing homes. Allegations of financial misconduct and patient abuse appeared in the media, and the topic was on the lips of many potential voters. One volunteer observed to me, "Where we will get votes is from those old folks, and their families. Wayne Hoffman, well, look at this [she points to Hoffman's brochure]; it says here he is nursing home operator who has lobbied for nursing home operator's legislation. What that means is that he has worked to get rid of assisted care and home care companies. . . . The nursing homes are a scandal. . . . There isn't a working family in this district that doesn't have some relative up in one of those homes, and they don't like how they're treated."

This dichotomy set up a confrontation in the runoff that had a predictable outcome. One in three residents of District 3 receives Social Security (eleven thousand individuals). These are mostly elderly residents, and collectively they are half of registered voters. Their level of turnout is higher than that of young people. They are almost all Democrats. Kenneth organized their support and gave them a reason to vote.

The runoff campaign was rough. Kenneth's opponent, Wayne Hoffman, drew parallels between their respective ages and, on a radio forum, made the argument that "in the armed services, they don't send a private to tell the troops what to do; they send a sergeant. And I know how to lead." This statement, typical of many made in his effort to undo the Corn candidacy, left Kenneth with an opening to respond. "I'm not a sergeant, but the job of the legislator is not to tell people what to do; it's to listen to the people, who tell the member what to do." This articulation of a delegate perspective on representation continued to serve Kenneth well when he was contrasted against his opponent. Young Corn looked thoughtful and serious; his opponent, by contrast, appeared to be heavy-handed and, in the words of a state political reporter, "sometimes downright mean." This was the apparent judgment of the voters, who nominated Corn 2:1.

If Kenneth held Democratic voters at a rate typical of Democratic candidates in LeFlore County, he would win about two-thirds of the vote. Because of the certainty of his general election victory, state Democrats sent Kenneth campaigning on behalf of other candidates. He worked hard in the general election, to be sure, but the outcome was not in doubt. Money flowed in from individual contributors throughout the state. On November 3, Kenneth Corn garnered 68 percent of the vote.

The night of the runoff primary, I talked to a longtime political observer down in Poteau. He summed up the results of the evening. "This election was Wayne Hoffman's to lose. He had the money, the connections, and the profile. But when he went out he turned people off; they didn't want to vote for him. Wayne has himself to blame as much as anyone for getting Kenneth elected."

About a week after winning the Democratic nomination, Kenneth traveled to Oklahoma City to meet with the speaker of the House and the Democratic Party leadership. We had the chance to engage in a postmortem on the primary and runoff campaign. His observations on the election and the experience of being the candidate are relevant to any person considering a political candidacy.

"I don't think anyone can imagine what it is like to be the candidate," Corn said. "I mean, I volunteered for candidates and walked the neighborhoods and all that. But nothing is like being the candidate. You're the man in the middle, everything comes back to you, all the decisions have to be made by you. . . . When I worked for other people, I could go home from the campaign and leave it behind, but now I can't help but think about it, when I get up in the morning, when I get home at night. I'm always tired but I can't rest because my mind is going around so fast."

Despite the limits of prior political activism in preparing him for the role of candidate, Kenneth Corn benefited from the lessons of prior campaigns. This is common among state legislative candidates, especially the young ones. A sizeable majority of young candidates indicated that their general, prior political experiences contributed to preparing for the campaign. Far and away the most common experience among all candidates, indicated by over 80 percent of young respondents, was campaign work (65 percent of responses between thirty-five and fifty-five, and 54 percent of responses over fifty-five, also indicated the role of prior campaign work in helping them prepare their own campaign). No other experiences were widely cited by candidates as contributing to the preparation for the campaign.

Our initial conversations after Kenneth's swearing-in indicated that he was picking up the habits of the incumbent legislator. He was trying to be visible at public events and mending fences with the business community that had largely supported his runoff opponent. He would make one concession to the demands of modern campaigning and his incumbency by hiring a campaign manager. In the campaign described here, Kenneth handled most of his own scheduling, strategy, and the management of volunteers. Our post-election conversations indicated that he felt overextended and exhausted from handling all aspects of the campaign.

## Legislator

Kenneth Corn entered the Oklahoma House of Representatives as the youngest representative elected in over twenty years. The trappings of the freshman legislator stand in stark contrast to the perks of Congress. Corn, a member of the majority and vice chairman of the Revenue and Taxation Committee, shared an office and a secretary with another freshman legislator. Corn's seat was at the rear of the House chamber, amid a variety of other junior members and members who liked to be at the back of the room; the main entry to the chamber passes beside Kenneth's desk.

Kenneth developed a reputation very early as a hardworking legislator. "I always try to get to the capitol by seven, so that I am already in the building and pass the governor as he arrives." When the legislature was out of session, Corn still spent at least three half-days each week at the Capitol, and full weeks when committees were meeting. He developed a reputation for reading and understanding complex legislation and for asking questions. On the floor this translated into influence among junior Democrats sitting in back. Members of the majority party usually followed party lines; however, Oklahoma politics has another dimension, a rural-urban split, that still divides the Democratic Party (Patterson 1962). When these divisions emerged, Kenneth is often a cue for back-bench rural Democrats.

Corn's emergence has not been without controversy. In the special session that preceded the general session in 1999, Kenneth voted against a compromise tax bill designed to deal with a revenue short-fall. "It was a bad bill, and I voted against it . . . some people think I'll pay for that later, but I told leadership that I couldn't support the bill; it wasn't good for the district, it wasn't good for poor folks." Then, he again voted against leadership, opposing legislation to give authority to raise college tuition to the state board of regents, stating, "I feel like that's our [the legislature's] role. We're closer to the people. We're responsible . . . it is a responsibility of the legislature."[4]

The district defined Kenneth Corn in his first legislative session. As one senior GOP staffer related it, "Ken has two perspectives on any spending bill: 'If it's anywhere else, it's pork; if it's for Poteau, it's progress." As the representative of a poor and aging constituency, Corn's constituency service efforts were directed at bringing state funds and development into his county. Many of his legislative efforts in 1999 entailed assisting with the development of tourism and outside investment in southeastern Oklahoma, including the development of roads.

Aside from these initiatives, most of Corn's efforts in the legislature were directed at developing a serious reputation in the chamber, cultivating a network of political support among Democratic Party elites, and finding issues to expand his political profile. He turned aside a feeler to take the chairmanship of the Agriculture Committee. The committee is important to his district, but it deals with controversial issues that Kenneth sees as a "threat" to his political safety. Instead, Kenneth turned his efforts to a comprehensive drug enforcement policy for the state, seeing in that legislation an opportunity to address a serious social problem. In late October 1999, we went to dinner at an Oklahoma City political hangout known for highly solicitous service. Kenneth talked about the session, reelection, ambition, and many other things. But we spent a lot of time going over his new policy initiative. He laid it out in clear, crisp fashion. He was advancing an initiative to deal with the "alarming" increase in methamphetamine traffic in his rural districts. As he described it to me, "We're going to call it 'Deep Six.' . . . The idea is to turn the focus from going after the end used [of the drug] and instead turn attention to the people who choose to profit from selling this poison to kids. . . . you know, we rank in the top five in the nation in meth traffic, and that is just not right. It's dimming the future for all of us. It's just not right."

The idea subsequently outlined in a legislative proposal Kenneth advanced in November had six key points, including mandated 85 percent sentence time served before eligibility for parole for those convicted of the sale of controlled substances, no suspended or deferred sentences for selling to minors, increased drivers' license suspensions, no appeal bonds for those convicted of manufacture or sale of controlled substances, tougher property forfeiture provisions, and an appropriation of $10 million in new funds to hire more law enforcement officers and increase prevention programs.[5]

Kenneth admitted that the bill "wouldn't be easy to get through." He was concerned not just with policy but also with the press. He was seeking publicity and was chagrined when, four days after announcing his plan to the press amid tepid coverage, the governor's office announced a similar initiative that received broad coverage. Perhaps the lesson, as one Republican legislative staffer noted, was that an important initiative should not be announced the Friday before the Texas–Oklahoma football game. While Fridays are typically slow news days, they are not the best days to showcase new initiatives.

Another staffer, in the governor's office, observed, "Well, Kenneth's a first-term, down-state Democrat, and Frank is governor. The press reacted in proportion."

Corn was not deterred, however, and he did not back down from confronting Frank Keating on other issues. In the 2000 legislative session, the young representative challenged the growing size of the governor's cabinet (elected state agency executives are not part of the personal cabinet, but governors are allowed to appoint advisory "secretaries"). In January, Corn introduced HB 2352, a measure to make government more efficient by reducing the size of the personal cabinet.[6] The legislation did not pass in 2000, but the legislature authorized a study by Corn's Rules Subcommittee. Kenneth placed this action in perspective, denying partisan motivations. "I have nothing against this governor . . . but that cabinet needs to be well organized, cost-effective, and have its powers clearly defined."[7]

The concept of proportion appeared in other political encounters. Republican members pressed Kenneth early in his term whenever he would rise in debate. This was in part reaction to the exceptional coverage of the new member. Corn's arrival at the legislature was a front-page human interest story for both of the state's major papers (the *Tulsa World* and the Oklahoma City *Daily Oklahoman*), complete with photographs and extensive interviews. Kenneth was highly visible as the vice chair of the major tax-writing committee in the chamber, and he has used the power to hold legislation in order to exact support from other members. The leadership has tolerated moments of "insolence"—such as the bolt on the emergency tax provision to benefit Oklahoma's ailing oil industry—that might not go unpunished for other members. His presence in the chamber was conspicuous and the behavior of the Democratic leadership indicated that he was being groomed for larger things. This attention from leadership and the press had created some expectations in terms of deference and attention in the freshman that might not be borne out during his longer legislative tenure. Kenneth Corn in 1999 was a prodigy and a novelty; at some point, as one powerful statewide elected Democrat observed to me, "he'll need to slow down and just be Kenneth, or he'll never survive."

Conversations with veteran legislators in 1999 often turn to speculation about higher office, about Corn's timetable for political advancement. He is assumed to have progressive ambition by his new peers. Whatever the consequences were of this assumption for his performance in his present position remained to be seen, but the political future of Kenneth Corn are potentially unlimited. Having attained political success at the earliest age possible, he was the object of political curiosity and much speculation. At a fund-raising event during the general election campaign, Corn and Dickerson were photographed with the popular former Oklahoma governor George Nigh. Just before the photographer took the picture, Nigh switched places with Kenneth, placing the young politician in the middle of the group. As the photographer shot his picture, Nigh told Kenneth, "Son, remember, the man in the middle is always *the man*." A torch was passed.

## Representative

Despite his presence in weighty political matters and the undue attention accorded to his age, Corn still goes about the tasks of representing as well as legislating. He handwrites correspondence. Every Thursday during session he returned to the district to work district events. He indicated that "someone will be gunning for me in 2000," most probably from within the Democratic primary; he was already preparing to deal with a tough renomination fight. If he wins again, he will likely be safe for a long time. "Down here they like to keep someone in for a while; once you win it and make it your own, they won't try and take you out."

Part of the strategy to insulate against a potential challenge was to vote with the wishes of his predominantly conservative, rural, populist district. A strong streak of Christian fundamentalism runs through Oklahoma, nowhere more so than in LeFlore County. In March 1999, Kenneth crossed lines to vote against most Democrats and most of the leadership on legislation that would have added sexual orientation to the list of state hate crimes. He was one of several rural Democrats who defected and joined the minority Republicans to defeat the bill. In explaining his vote, Kenneth stated that "my folks back home" might not know that explicit language classifying homosexuals had been removed.[8] Other efforts were directed at the economic challenges confronting his rural district, such as the organization of a forum in Poteau during the summer of 1999 to bring attention to the financial hardships confronted by small farmers. And there was still more, always more to be done. Whether it was getting together with other local legislators to announce a grant to build a new fire station in Spiro or negotiating tax breaks to try to keep Johnson Controls from moving its manufacturing facility out of state (a failed effort), Representative Corn was visibly active.

## Ambition and Career Decisions

Kenneth Corn allowed his personal career to be shaped by the opportunity to run for state House District 3, and every campaign that will follow will be affected by his decisions as a legislator. His other, nonpolitical career choices would be influenced by the campaign cycle and the demands of governing. During one of our debriefing conversations after the September 1998 runoff, I asked Kenneth about his long-term political and personal goals, such as going to law school.

"I don't think I will go to law school now, Dr. Gaddie. The whole idea behind going to law school was to mark time until Representative Hamilton decided to step aside. Now, a lot of people think that I jumped in too soon, that I am really too young for this. [Pause] I know that. They tried to keep me out of this race, promising that, in eight or ten years they would run me for the congressional seat . . . this seat, the state House, is where I can serve my community and my state."

Subsequent conversations indicated that law school might again be a possibility, because it complemented his political career, but it appears that law school "is more the speculation of the people around [Kenneth Corn]," rather than an undertaking he is seriously considering. His thoughts reflect Joseph Schlesinger's speculation about young politicians. Schlesinger found that the successful politicians who started very young were more likely to choose law as a career because it complemented the skills of politics, without presenting a potential conflict with the constraints that public office places on the private career (see also Eulau and Sprague 1964). Kenneth said he would likely abandon elective politics if he could no longer serve as a full-time legislator. To serve full-time as a politician—and now an elected official—meant looking up the political ladder, to the next, larger campaign. He was "thinking up."

Corn's path of progression was not decided in 1998. In political circles, one would hear two offices typically mentioned: governor and Congress. The governor's mansion was a more remote possibility, in part because of the numerous interested players in state politics, making for a large challenger pool, and in part because it was so remote in time. In 1998, Kenneth had a dozen years to wait before an election where he was constitutionally eligible to run. Congress seemed to be a more immediate option. But, if you listen carefully, governor was where his heart was.

In my notes from 1999, I had penned, "Will this particular career turn into a permanent political career? Certainly the opportunity is there. Such a career will have to be progressive due to Oklahoma's twelve-year term limit on legislators; at age thirty-three, if still in office, Corn will either have to find another office or get out of elective politics. Other career options might beckon." Later, I had noted an observation of one of Kenneth's college friends from just after the primary election: "Kenneth isn't going to change for politics; it will have to change for him. If he doesn't seem happy doing elective office, he'll leave." Kenneth confirmed this sentiment in a conversation during the general election season.

"If I quit enjoying this, if I find that I cannot be effective as an elected official, I will find another way to serve. There are a lot of good not-for-profit organizations that need good fund-raisers as directors and operating officers. I can see myself doing that if I get tired of politics, if I think staying in politics challenges my values, who I am."

The degree of dedication to a future candidacy derives from the circum-

stances surrounding each candidate. Writing in 1999, Kenneth Corn necessarily had a political career and a political future because of his success.

## Reluctant Advancement

Conversations with Kenneth Corn throughout 2001 indicated that his ambitions ran toward the governor's mansion or possibly to the U.S. House. But
those ambitions were not imminent. Kenneth always saw himself serving out
his terms in the state House of Representatives, and there was ample reason
to stay. Although just twenty-five, he had substantial legislative successes. He
had been willing to go head-to-head with the chief executive, but he also
showed that he could work with all parties in pursuit of economic goals for
the state. With the arrival of term limits in 2004, the backlog of senior Democrats would be swept aside, and Corn would be poised to jump on the leadership ladder, with a significant committee chairmanship, maybe a floor
leadership position, and eventually the speaker's chair.

Kenneth described himself as a man of the House, and, like Thad Balkman, he viewed his institution as more egalitarian than the state senate. He
had close ties to senators, most notably Larry Dickerson, and he worked
closely with senate colleagues on legislation and other matters of interest.
Slowly, inevitably, starting in early 2000, events beyond his control would
propel him into a run for the state senate.

In 2000, Larry Dickerson, state senator and longtime friend and mentor
to Kenneth Corn, learned that his cancer, long in remission, was returning.
Dickerson would undergo extensive treatments at the M. D. Anderson Cancer Treatment Center. The treatments would tap his physical strength; Larry
lost a great deal of weight and found his ability to conduct the business of
government severely limited. Kenneth, as his counterpart, attended to the
needs of his own House district and Larry's senate district. In the process, he
introduced himself to a larger constituency and started interacting with local
elected officials and political activists in Sallisaw and a variety of other communities in Sequoyah County that made up the balance of senate District 4
outside the boundaries of Kenneth's House constituency.

By spring 2002, Larry Dickerson seemed to be on the road to recovery.
He was beating cancer again, making an amazing recovery to resume his legislative duties. Initially using a wheelchair and then a walker, Dickerson
returned to the senate, where he was working with Kenneth to pass an expansive health benefit package for teachers. Then, during the first week of March,
during an afternoon floor session, Dickerson had just completed participating
in debate when he complained that he was light-headed and needed to leave.
It had been a busy day; the ailing senator passed eight different pieces of legislation that day before leaving the chamber. He collapsed soon afterward and
never regained consciousness.

Kenneth spoke to me from the hospital where he was sitting with Dee Ann Dickerson and others of Larry's circle of friends. The news was not good. Larry had suffered a dramatic collapse, and there were no prospects of recovery. He was on life support so that his family would have time to visit with him and make their final good-byes to a father, husband, and loved one. Media speculation about who would be the successor started before the day was out. There was little doubt that Kenneth would be tapped to run as Larry's successor. Dickerson's widow made her belief known that it was Larry's wish that Kenneth should take over. Dickerson's political adviser shielded Kenneth and the Dickerson family from inquiries about the succession. Despite the lack of statements to the press, Kenneth Corn was immediately identified by various news outlets as the heir apparent.

Larry Dickerson had been grooming Kenneth as a possible successor. After the November 2002 election, Kenneth and I talked about his succeeding Larry. "As soon as it was apparent that he was getting sick again, Larry started taking me around and getting me acquainted with the district and his operation. He really did grease the skids for me to take over for him, should the time come." Dickerson had recognized his successor and was passing the torch.

## Transitions

Larry Dickerson's passing dramatically disrupted every aspect of Kenneth's life. For as long as he had been involved in politics, Dickerson had been there, to work with, call on for help, talk to, argue with, and fight alongside. Now, for the first time that Kenneth could remember, he was going about the business of politics without his oldest political friend and most important mentor.

"We really should talk about this at some length, Dr. Gaddie. . . . When Larry died, I had a really hard time for a very long time. It was very hard to accept that he was gone, and sometimes I would just forget. I would be sitting on the floor, listening to debate, trying to work through a problem with legislation, and I would think, 'I need to talk to Larry about this.' I would be halfway to the senate chamber before I would remember that he was gone. . . . It was very hard to function, because for as long as I had been here I had relied on him to talk to and work with. We had legislation pending, and were working together on the teacher's insurance bill. And now he was gone."

Kenneth was navigating the sea of politics completely on his own. Long-time legislative leaders from his part of the state were departing—Dickerson had died, majority leader Mike Mass was leaving the legislature to run for Congress—and Kenneth now found himself increasingly taking the lead on a variety of issues without the counsel of veteran legislators. The transition was complete. He was no longer a protégé.

There was still business to be done, and politics, while emotional, does not stop for the sentiments of a young legislator. The previous fall, Kenneth had pushed to have the legislature call itself into special session, to consider legislation to expand health benefits for state public teachers and other elementary and secondary education employees. The problem, under the program in force, was that teachers paid such large shares of their health care premiums that it significantly reduced take-home pay. Out-of-pocket costs for a family of four could run as high as $7,500. When combined with generally low teacher pay in Oklahoma, the heavy insurance premium contributed to high rates of teacher attrition. He had succeeded in getting two-thirds of state House members to sign on for a special session call, but fell short in the senate. The effort had impressed institutional leaders. In late November, the speaker of the House and senate pro tempore agreed to appoint a special committee to explore the issue and recommend reforms. The special panel confronted tremendous barriers to crafting an expansion of state teacher health benefits. The state confronted a budget crisis, and a revenue shortfall threatened and would necessitate budget cuts.

The legislative proposal that resulted from Corn's special study (HB 1968) would increase the state's contribution to cover health benefits to 100 percent of the individual premium for teachers and support personnel. The bill was one of the first measures considered in the 2002 session, and it passed out of the House in late February with overwhelming, bipartisan support. The depth of support for the measure in the House was underscored by the decision to not make the legislation contingent on finding a funding source and by the restoration of the legislation's title, which ensured it would go directly to the governor after passing the senate. In the senate, the fight would be led by the senate author, Larry Dickerson. It seemed especially appropriate that the ailing but persuasive Dickerson lead the fight in the senate. In public appearances, he regularly spoke of the need to improve and expand health care benefits for Oklahomans. His own bout with cancer as a college student had been won only because his father, a firefighter, had quality health insurance that allowed Larry to get treatment.

The legislation did not advance before Larry died in early March, and it languished in the senate. It was a high–price tag item, and the state was already confronting budgetary challenges and a governor who was not disposed to increase taxes. Then, in late April, as the legislature advanced toward the end of session, new senate sponsor Johnnie Crutchfield (Dem.-Ardmore) advanced the legislation coincident to a day of intensive lobbying by numerous state education interest groups and public school systems. The bill, retitled the "Larry Dickerson Educational Flexible Benefits Allowance Act," passed out of the senate on April 18 by a 42–0 vote and was returned to the House for approval of changes in the legislation, where it passed in final form on May 15 by a 93–4 vote. Governor Keating signed the legislation on May 21.

The teacher health benefits bill was landmark legislation for several reasons. It was the largest increase in teacher benefits in recent memory. The bill passed both chambers by large margins in a very lean budget year. The state entered the legislative session confronting a $350 million shortfall, and this legislation could increase costs by $35 million in year one and $85 million in year two. Even as state agencies were hit with emergency budget cuts of up to 17 percent and the legislature combined budget cuts for the coming fiscal year with a raid on the rainy day fund, legislators found the political will to increase teacher benefits.

It was the single greatest achievement of Kenneth Corn's political career. His persistence and politicking had led the legislature to consider the benefits crisis of teachers, and the initiative prevailed despite a desperate budgetary environment. "I think it is the most important piece of legislation this session," he told me. "We addressed a major crisis in Oklahoma. We are losing our best and brightest teachers to other states because we're not competitive." Kenneth was insistent on sharing the credit with his departed mentor. "Larry was my partner in trying to pass this plan. It's appropriate that we name a piece of legislation after him. He really knows what it meant to have health insurance and to be able to see a doctor."

## Election

Kenneth Corn announced for the state senate the week after Dickerson's funeral. The result was a profound dampening effect on the potential competition for the district. In a two-county senate district that overlapped four state legislative districts, the homes of six county commissioners, dozens of other city and county officials, and countless lawyers, exactly one other candidate, a gadfly Republican, filed against the twenty-five-year-old state House member. There would be no primaries for senate District 4; both candidates looked to November. Unlike his run for the House four years prior, Kenneth Corn was the favorite and the presumed winner.

The last day of the 2002 campaign I went back on the campaign trail with Kenneth. We would be working the northern end of senate District 4, up in Sequoyah County. The confidence that Kenneth exhibited was quiet, but he was certain of victory the following day. However, to look at his efforts the weekend before the election, you would think he was involved in one of the closest contests of his life.

The first part of the day was taken up with meetings, mainly with local officials in small towns along I-40 in Sequoyah County. We then worked several local community centers, as Kenneth spent time visiting with individual retirees and also spoke about his efforts on behalf of elder care and programs to ensure activities and nutrition programs for the elderly. While Kenneth continued to exhibit charm and persuasiveness with his elderly audiences, one local observed, "That boy sure can sling the shit." After finishing the round of retiree lunches, we took lunch at a Mexican restaurant across the state line in Fort Smith, Arkansas, with a new state representative from a district in Sallisaw and some other local politicians. The talk was about politics and mainly about the single hottest issue of the 2002 campaign in rural Oklahoma: cockfighting.[9] The balance of the day was taken up with all the typical activities of local campaigning. Whatever Kenneth Corn had become in terms of a policymaker or a dealmaker, he was unchanged as a campaigner. We put out about one hundred yard signs and then worked doors in a rural, black community. He was running radio and some TV, but it was really another ground campaign.

In seeking Larry Dickerson's seat, Kenneth inherited many of Larry's relationships and many of the activists and supporters who helped maintain Dickerson's reelection constituency. Oklahoma state senators have no small amount of patronage at their disposal, and the desire of the beneficiaries of Dickerson's favor were now investing in his successor. Larry's tag agent, the local contractor who provides car tags in the district, worked the rural neighborhoods until well after dark and then accompanied us to a meeting of the Sequoyah County Democratic Women's Organization at the local Western Sizzler.

In all, it was a fairly uneventful election for Corn. His polls showed him running in the high 70s or low 80s. His opponent was invisible. Most of Kenneth's efforts went into cultivating and consolidating support in areas outside his old House district and in campaigning for other candidates for state and local office. Half of the senate district was his old House constituency; in light of his accomplishments in the legislature and his activities on behalf of the ailing Senator Dickerson during the previous two years, Kenneth's election took on all the qualities of an incumbent reelection. He carried the district in a landslide.

# Conclusion

The beginning of Kenneth Corn's career is very informative as to the process of legitimation and transition that is experienced by the new politician. The young candidate had little in the way of political résumé or life experience to draw on, yet his tireless efforts and involvement as a young person in party politics, and his knowledge of practical politics as a young adult, facilitated his election. While the similarly situated Matt Dollar ran an energetic campaign in an environment where issues didn't matter, Corn ran in an environment where issues, policy, and expertise were everything. His innate qualities as a candidate shone through his limited résumé. His subsequent legislative career indicates the speed with which youth and inexperience are quickly forgotten in the new political career. Representative Corn had to adjust to being one member among many, and his successful socialization quickly laid to rest any concerns about age and prior experiences.

A talented, successful young politician might look to a long career in the legislature. But, as described earlier, we observed that for Kenneth Corn, term limits loomed large because they would necessarily circumscribe his career at an early age. It is therefore reasonable to expect Corn and other state legislators to react to term limits in part by considering other political opportunities. In addition to the historically noted factors that affect the decision to move up or move on—opportunity, ambition, and odds of success—a new factor has entered the equation.

Legislators who are advantaged by an institution with an organizational structure that values seniority, or legislators who either have static ambitions or intrainstitutional ambitions inside the legislative body, find their political careers disrupted, if not ultimately terminated. For Kenneth Corn, he had institutional ambitions. He had indicated during his first campaign that the notion of being speaker was attractive and that he might have an opportunity to lead the chamber because of term limits. But Corn recognized that if he did not start on the path to the chair early, he might not get there before his own time was up. The Oklahoma legislature allowed him early access to positions of responsibility, including a chairmanship, and he was able to pass significant legislation. He might have been speaker eventually, under the right circumstances.

Corn's political ambitions turned to matters of policy and the pursuit of progressive ambitions. Term limits are ostensibly designed to curb the detrimental effects of political ambition, such as long-term incumbency and the perceived nonresponsiveness of legislative bodies that is presumed to accompany high incumbent security. But, as a brake on incumbency, limits also compel turnover in legislatures that outstrip the hard effect of limits on the most senior members.[10] For Kenneth Corn, the state senate offered many benefits to the progressive politician. Representing a larger constituency creates a larger political base, and, in the senate, his individual vote is worth more. The four-year term allows him a lull in reelection fights, and the long term also means that he could take a "free shot" at another office without placing his seat at risk. Kenneth observed in a self-deprecating moment that "the main difference between the House and the senate is that the rooms are bigger and the furniture is nicer in the senate."

For young people just starting a political career, like Kenneth Corn or Thad Balkman, term limits hold intriguing, sometimes conflicting implications. A legislative body that has term limits holds out the prospect for more frequent incumbent turnover and increased open seats, thereby creating more avenues for the pursuit of political ambition. The opportunity to initiate a legislative career is heightened because there will be more open seats, more often. And, once in the chamber, members will be less likely to find themselves situated behind a backlog of senior members who block the way to coveted committee assignments. Ascension of the leadership ladder will be similarly quick, as we saw with Mike Saxl, because there will be constant turn-over of presiding officers, committee chairs, and floor leaders. But there are also dilemmas. Members who hold institutional ambitions may get stuck behind a short queue of fast-charging members, or they may end up spending an abbreviated legislative career in the minority party and therefore on the wrong side of the opportunity structure in a more partisan legislative body. Legislators who find that they like the job of state legislator and who are good at the job, based on some subjective, qualitative criterion, will have their political ambitions effectively quashed by the mandated truncation of service. For Senator Corn, the move from state House to state senate appears to be just one stop on the way up. As a Republican legislator observed to me, "Kenneth? Oh, he's headed places."

## Notes

1. *Tulsa World*, "Howe Man to Vie for Seat in House," June 25, 1998.

2. The age issue came up again, in the runoff. In debate, Corn, all of twenty-one, argued that he had "more experience in government and the political system" than the forty-six-year-old Hoffman. Hoffman countered that his experience as a father, businessman, and University of Oklahoma football player on the 1974 national championship team would compensate. A local politician button-holed me and observed, "Doc, the more mature candidate will win the runoff"; he then winked and added, "You know I mean Kenneth."

3. Money came easier in the runoff. The night of the primary, I asked Kenneth how much money he needed for the three-week runoff, and he estimated $3,000 in new expenditures. In the end, he spent an additional $3,044. The general election campaign was well financed, as Corn raised almost $25,000 from a variety of sources, all in amounts less than $1,000. His overall funds raised were just under $33,000, which placed him just above the median for a winning House candidate in 1998.

4. Tim Talley, "Committee Approves Tuition Bill," Associated Press, February 2, 1999.

5. Ron Jenkins, "Freshman Lawmaker Pushes Anti-Drug Plan," Associated Press, November 9, 1999.

6. Tim Talley, "Committee Approves Bill to Revamp Governor's Cabinet," Associated Press, February 24, 2000.

7. Ron Jenkins, "Howe Democrat to Lead Study," Associated Press, September 21, 2000.

8. Tim Talley, "House Defeats Hate Crimes Bill," Associated Press, March 10, 1999.

9. A state initiative to ban the breeding and fighting of game fowl was on the November ballot. The game fowl industry had fought to keep the measure off the ballot, and now groups in eastern and southern Oklahoma were working frantically to defeat the measure. Cockfighters and other groups in rural Oklahoma were working hard to guarantee a heavy turnout for the antivote, using door-to-door get-out-the-vote efforts and phone banking to mobilize voters. In areas like LeFlore and Sequoyah Counties, these efforts often blended with local Democratic Party GOTV efforts.

10. Moncrief et al. (1992) and Opheim (1994) observe that, among incumbent state House members, the choice of reelection over retirement or progressive ambition occurs 75 percent and 80 percent of the time, respectively. The low rate of progressivity results because the pursuit of progressive ambition carries a low probability of success, while incumbent reelection carries a high probability of success (Brace 1984; Rohde 1979; Francis and Kenny 1997).

# The Man with the Plan 10

The quiet calculations made by unseen candidates in February or March
. . . or even earlier, have as much to with the eventual outcome in
November as do the noisy fall campaigns.

—Linda Fowler and James McClure

EVEN AS MEMBERS PURSUE their legislative goals, those with progressive ambition will find that it influences their political behavior.
Defining representation as a "set of relationships between a House
member and the member's constituency," Richard Fenno (2000) indicates
that any activity engaged in by the representative that relates to his or her
constituency involves the activity of representation. Each representative
chooses a strategy of representation, albeit one constrained by a variety of
factors, including the predispositions and goals of the member. To the three
goals advanced by David Mayhew (1974), Fenno (1996) notes a fourth: winning higher office, which we can also think of as the pursuit of progressive
ambition. The goals members pursue are influenced by their ambitions and
by the contexts in which they pursue those ambitions. Goals themselves may
be shaped by an initial decision to go into politics or by early career experiences. Therefore, legislator behavior among the young and progressively
ambitious will be influenced by the pursuit of progressive goals. For the
young legislator, this means playing two games: a short game, of crafting
institutional reputation, legislative accomplishments, and constituency ties to
sustain the member in her current representative role; and the long game, of
using reputation, accomplishments, and incumbency to prepare for the pursuit of her political ambitions.

Entering the third year of his first term, Jon Bruning was thinking about
reelection, about policy, and about his career. Bruning's district is in Sarpy
County, a suburban area outside Omaha. Nestled in the midst of several old
farming communities, the district straddles a major interstate. It is off of these
exchanges where Republican opportunities have blossomed. Although the
district is clearly Republican, it has elected Democrats in the past, including
the incumbent whom Bruning defeated in 1996. It is a district with potential
for substantial political competition. The incumbent is aware of this, calling
it "a very proactive district."

The son of two university professors, Bruning was a student leader and

Phi Beta Kappa key holder at the University of Nebraska. As a law student, he was editor of the law review and one of the top students in his class. Within a year of leaving law school, he was earning a solid six-figure salary with an educational technology company. At age twenty-seven, he gave it all up to run for a legislative office that pays $12,000 year. Within one minute of meeting Jon on the floor of the Unicam, he summed up what I had guessed the moment I saw him coming: "I like the campaigning the best. I am good at it, maybe too good."

Jon is a believer in the permanent campaign. He is obviously well read and well versed on campaign technique, the use of consultants and expertise, and voter contacting. In our conversations recalling his initial campaign, Bruning placed a premium on two things: information and energy. In his first campaign, he relied heavily on the expertise of the national Republican Party, as reflected in its publications for candidates, and on the expertise of consultants, especially in the areas of mailing and publication design, and in survey research. Jon Bruning does many things very well, but he also seems to be aware of the things that other people might be able to do better for him.

He used information in an effective and efficient manner, because information was important to his representative style—the retail-oriented, permanent campaign. His office was a flurry of activity, with consistently moving correspondence and e-mail traffic piled on top of legislation, on top of phone messages. Bruning himself was also always in motion, moving paper, returning calls, and propelling ideas forward while balancing his legislative career with his legal practice and his family life. Jon's administrative assistant summed it up: "He's a gunner. . . . What I like about working in this office is that there is always something going on." Other staffers at the capitol remarked on the sheer level of activity that emanates from his office. The franking privilege of senators allows each to send out one thousand pieces of mail per month. Jon used his entire frank every month on constituent surveys and responses to the individuals who return the surveys. Those surveys allowed him to tap undercurrents that are running through the district and to better explain his actions to his constituents. He was not going to lose "on some roll call that made the wrong person mad for the wrong reason." Jon was converting his district into a safe district, to use as a springboard to run for higher state office. Malcolm Jewell (1982) and Cherie Maestas (2000a) have observed this same behavior—a greater commitment of resources and time to communication with the constituency—among younger and more ambitious state legislators.

What is interesting about the style is that it is personal yet also distant. Jon's engaging personality and relatively small, rural-to-suburban district would seem to encourage personalized politics, but Bruning's style promotes a personalized form of indirect contacting via correspondence and interaction through his surveys. This style reflects the changing nature of Sarpy County and of politics. The American suburban life has built itself up around activities, rather than community and organization. From work to car pool to after-school activities to bed, the suburban American family flies through the day. The time for cozy chats, front-door visits, and small-town politics is not there. Virtual communication, either mail or e-mail, facilitates the interaction of suburbanites. Jon connects with his constituency in the way suburbanites are connected to each other—letters, e-mail, passive interactions that can be absorbed and thought about in the nanomoments of leisure presented by modern life.

## Legislator

During my first day in Lincoln in the winter of 1999, Adrian Smith and I were sitting together in the capitol cafeteria, having hamburgers and discussing Adrian's experiences in city government. Bruning walked into the cafeteria, a Cheshire cat grin on his face, and looked at us both. Leaning over the table, he recounted his just-ended encounter with the Unicam's executive committee. "I really stuck my foot in it. . . . I was a smart-ass, and I will pay for what I said." Bruning grinned.

Nearly every day I was in Lincoln, he expressed his disgust that he did not have e-mail access on his notebook computer at his legislative chamber desk. Web access was cut off on the floor by the executive committee of the chamber, which administers the operational issues of the Unicam. "They're worried that someone might actually get something done down on the floor. . . . [Another senator] said, 'Well, Jon, one of you young guys might be looking at pornography or something on the floor, and we can't have that.' The average age on that committee is sixty-six. . . . I looked at them and asked them if any of them used a computer or if they were too busy trying to crank up the old Model T. . . . I want my e-mail this afternoon!" Bruning grinned and headed off for another meeting.

Such challenges to authority and norms were not unusual in the nascent period of Bruning's legislative career. Elected to a four-year term in 1996, Jon initially served as chair of the Enrollment and Review Committee, a position that he handed off to Adrian Smith. Though he saw value in the experience, he also found it constraining. "That was really frustrating . . . it is important to be in there and to learn the process, and you have to be on the ball. . . . I just have a hard time sitting on the floor waiting for things to happen." Bruning was sometimes controversial, not so much because he failed to defer to norms but because he was active in the process immediately, proposing legislation and talking to the press about the needs for political reform. Bruning generated substantial press coverage, and sometimes it earned him unwanted attention from colleagues.

After that very harried first session, Jon Bruning moved to consolidate his political position. No longer the chairman of enrollment and review, he moved off the front row, to the rear of the chamber, where he could "see all the action. I want to know what is going on." He was named vice chair of the principal environmental committee in the legislature, where he demonstrated expertise and commanded respect. During one visit to Lincoln, the committee chairman was called away, leaving Bruning in the chair. In executive session (far less formal that the more public general sessions), Bruning exuded a quiet authority that made him not only a capable chair but an expert in the balancing of discussion and debate. It is this ability, to interact as a quiet expert in small groups, that was probably his greatest asset. He is a natural executive.

Bruning accessed multiple constituencies within the legislature, and his youth is apparently part of this ability. The female senators, who made up a larger portion of the Unicam than in most state legislatures, were willing to work with him, as were the urban legislators who shared some common interests with him and viewed Jon as more open-minded than some elder, rural Republican senators. Even the noted "conscience" of the chamber, Senator Ernie Chambers, would work with Jon on occasion, especially when Jon's expertise came into play. But, more often, Chambers and Bruning were at odds.

An example of the ability of a senator to have influence beyond the scope of his or her seniority came during the debate on LB 514, legislation designed to ensure the continuation of the "Life-Line" program, which subsidizes rural phone service and emergency phone service. The proposed legislation would have added an additional fee to local phone service, to pay for the cost of the program. The dean of the legislature, Ernie Chambers, objected to the legislation and sought to amend the bill to make the cost come from the general fund, rather than from a special, additional fee on phone use. When Chambers halted the progress of this legislation, Jon became very active on the floor. In four days on the floor of the Unicam, in what Adrian and Jon called "a typical week," Bruning rarely participated in debate, instead concentrating on paperwork or listening from his chair. When Jon is deep in thought, he rocks his chair vigorously, at an almost frantic pace. Then he stopped, bolted up, and entered into a fifteen-minute flurry of activity, moving from member to member. He then came over to me, on the side of the chamber; I inquired, "What happened?" Jon explained that this bill was important, not so much for the source of revenue as for the service provided. It was being bogged down and could completely stop the flow of legislative business. He first approached a group of the bill sponsors, inquiring as to their goals in passing the bill. He then disappeared into the lobby, where he convened telecommunications lobbyists to identify a compromise they would accept in the legislation. He then consulted with Chambers to ascertain what he would accept as a compromise. In the end, he "brokered the deal" and freed up the flow of legislation.

Queried later about the event, Jon indicated that "telecommunications is one of the few areas where I might be considered to be something of an expert" in the chamber. Jon was the general counsel for Cox Communications in Omaha. When telecommunications bills came up, he knew that he would have a voice in legislation because of his expertise and his rapport with the industry representatives. Other senators recognized that expertise in this particular area, making Bruning an inadvertent policy entrepreneur.

## Unbridled Ambition

As I went through my notes, I found, scribbled on the back of an envelope, "Bruning is GOP, but also a careerist?" Political science literature finds political careerism more often among Democrats (Ehrenhalt 1991). Government does not have the same emotional or tangible benefits for conservatives (the financial rewards are too small, and those who disdain government do not make a career of it). The best prospect for conservative careerism comes from Republicans who are Christian activists; these activists envision a positive, activist role for government in their social agenda, so government becomes a tangible ends to their political goals and therefore also a tangible career. Jon Bruning is a Christian and a conservative, but his politics originally emanated from the pragmatic, economic side of the conservative movement. As he tells it, "When I was in college, I was out there, a Democrat and a liberal, . . . and my parents are Democrats." For Jon, a former Democrat, his realigning moment came "when I got out of college and started paying my own way. . . . My parents would give me [a check] at the beginning of every semester, and anything that I got in addition—scholarship, award—was like a bonus. . . . When you have a situation like that, it is easy to be liberal; . . . taking financial responsibility for myself made me a Republican. There wasn't a pot of unlimited money to go to from Mom and Dad. I think a lot of students become more conservative once they have to manage their own finances."

Despite his political change of heart from his parents, they and their friends helped him with the early fund-raising that established him as a serious political player.

In a conversation at his Sarpy County home, the topic turned to getting started. Jon's thoughts were quite explicit and were shaped by his felling of an incumbent Democrat. He touched on three particular aspects of the beginner's career: the need for financial support, the importance of information, and the necessity of hard work.

"The biggest problem with a lot of people who want to get into politics is that they won't listen . . . and not just young people, but especially young people. I had a guy in my office, not a month ago, who said he wanted to run for the Unicam. I told him the names of eighty people he could go to, and if he just said that he was a Republican and that he wanted their financial support, they would have given him money. . . . This guy just wanted to sit there and talk about ideology and his political philosophy; the people who can help you in politics don't want to hear that. They want you to sit down, listen to their concerns, and then they'll give you money. Sometimes you don't even have to ask."

Bruning's observations are especially relevant to the experience of Adrian Smith. During the course of my visit, I became aware of their close relationship; in my next visit, I was told of just how far back it went.

"In college," Bruning told me, "Adrian Smith wrote a letter to the campus paper blasting a liberal column I authored, and Adrian Smith is smart . . . a true believer in Reagan and conservative Republicanism. And, before he ran, years later, he comes to see me, and about thirty other people, because someone suggested it, and he asked the right questions. He listened to people who had been in politics longer, or before, and who were willing to help him. And he won, because he knew what to ask, when to ask, and how to listen."

While the styles may be different and the origins of their political beliefs are dissimilar, Smith and Bruning share at least one common denominator: They are smart enough to go and find out how to do things right and to listen to good advice.

Bruning was in the midst of his first term of office, yet this bright, charismatic man was already demonstrating progressive ambition, which he freely discussed. In our first, brief contact on the floor of the Unicam, he noted that he planned to run for attorney general, after winning reelection, in 2002. The 2000 reelection would serve as a springboard for fund-raising for the statewide campaign. Jon indicated that his eyes were on the governor's mansion; while he would not rule out a run for Congress back in early 1999, it was apparent that he does not place the same premium on congressional service as many of the progressive politicians observed in Kazee's (1994) study.

## Family

To discuss Jon Bruning's political career is to discuss his family. Family was a top priority to Jon. As a two-career family in 1999 with a small child, Jon and Deonne's personal time was limited and precious, and they tried to avoid impositions on their time outside workdays. They made professional and lifestyle decisions so Jon could stay in politics, and Jon made political-style decisions to maintain the family's personal life. Whether those choices can be continued as they pursue Jon's progressive ambition remains to be seen.

In 1999, Deonne was general counsel for AT&T. Her office was across the street from the capitol, so she and Jon commuted to work together. It was a hectic life; they had full-time child care arrangements with an old friend in Omaha, and every day started with taking their daughter into Omaha, then driving to Lincoln to work, and returning home for a family evening and an early bedtime. At lunch one day in her Lincoln office, Deonne observed that the life of a senator includes numerous intrusions: "People don't think anything of calling you at six in the morning or eleven at night, of bothering you at church or in the grocery. Everything you do is a public event. Jon handles it real well, but he really doesn't want to be bothered on the weekends or when he is doing family things." The intrusions were not sufficiently imposing for Deonne to think that Jon should get out of elective office. She was very supportive of his efforts to move up to statewide office and believed that, in the long term there were substantial family benefits should Jon become attorney general. "My family lives to the west [of Lincoln], and Jon's family is here in Lincoln. . . . With Jon as [attorney general] we could move to Lincoln and also move the children's care arrangements down here. The commute would disappear, and we would probably have more personal time." Further conversation revealed that other intrusions would disappear, because Jon would move out of a constituency service–oriented office. He would work in a policy area that would bring interests to him. Political time would become policymaking time or family time.

Unlike members who take in the social activities of Lincoln during the legislative session, Bruning limited his activities to lunches and the occasional reception. I found this surprising, given the extensive social life that often surrounds legislative sessions and the amount of extracurricular politics that is conducted after five. For many legislators, especially the politically ambitious who may have designs on other office, the after-hours work would be mandatory: There are connections to be made and cultivated, opportunities to establish a presence, and, indeed, even the simple benefits of enjoying a social occasion. If Jon Bruning goes to an after-hours event, it is in part because of these motivations, but the motivation underscores his progressive ambition and Jon's almost-religious belief in the permanent campaign: "You do not have to go to their events to get their money." But, despite the concessions of political life to personal life in Jon's career, his spouse observed that, in the pursuit of political goals, Jon is "relentless. He is the type of person who, if he decides to do a thing, he will do it. When he would get up during the campaign and say 'I am going to knock on one thousand doors today,' you can bet that he won't be home until he does. . . . If Jon came in the door and said, 'I am going to be president,' I am certain he would go out and do it."

## Initial Observations on Ambition

Of the politicians we have met so far, Jon Bruning had the most clearly spelled-out and obvious progressive ambition. He has a plan. In this case, the structure of the progressive ambition that the politician mapped out was determined by family constraints. The decision for Jon to run for the legislature was part of a long-term plan; the sacrifice of his prepolitical career was probably not worth the benefits of a state senator's salary and position. The political positions that can be derived from legislative service, such as attorney general, would be beyond the grasp of a thirty-two-year-old private practice attorney with no political portfolio. Not so for the thirty-two-year-old, two-term state senator, who has instant political credibility. But, to look at Jon Bruning's start in elective politics, he was the embodiment of where our politics have taken us. What Fowler and McClure (1989) observe about congressional politics is applicable here as well:

> Specialization has reached the realm of political ambition . . . in the modern era, each level of public office has its own network of influential leaders, its own body of knowledge and expertise, and its own rewards, making it difficult to run for Congress if a politician has not already got on the fast track and been warming up for the big race for a long time. (228)

A statewide campaign would require more resources and time than a state legislative campaign, and much of Bruning's efforts in creating a safe constituency and cultivating his capital connections were directed toward making the jump to higher office. All of his actions were geared toward the end goal of his ambitions, lest he not succeed in the very demanding and specialized world of modern electoral politics.

## AG Stands for Attorney General

Three years after our 1999 visits in Lincoln and Omaha, Jon Bruning and I hooked up again during October 2002. He was in the stretch run of a months-long statewide campaign for office that he had been planning since before his previous reelection to the Unicameral. As we drove away from suburban Omaha in the early-morning light, toward the Loess Hills to the northwest, Jon was already in full campaign mode. His Ford Expedition cut along the farm-to-market roads of Nebraska cattle country as he took phone calls over the headset of his mobile phone. I perused the itinerary and sipped coffee, while, between frequent calls to donors and party people and calls from the media and staff, we talked about the campaign, his family, and his future.

After about twenty minutes of catch-up, I asked, "How's it going?" The answer was immediate: "Keith, it is going fantastic. The money is coming in, and we have good, solid support. . . . Our polls show us up by fifteen points, which is probably about right. Now I just have to keep working to the last day. We're going to win." The optimism, drive, and determination that had impressed me about Jon Bruning during our initial meetings were still evident.

In our visits in 1999, the importance of his family in his life was obvious. The product of a strong, intellectual family, Jon placed his spouse and his children (a son was born in the spring of 1999) ahead of other demands. Three years later, he was still not one to partake of the legislative social scene in Lincoln, though he indicated that "occasionally" he and Deonne had started to make some events. Aspects of the Brunings' life had changed since we last visited. Deonne had cut back on her career commitments to spend more time at home with the children; she was essentially a full-time mom now, which Jon indicated was one of their long-term goals as a family. Jon's law practice had grown substantially over the past three years, leading to the degree of financial independence that made their preferred family arrangement possible. As Jon related to me, "For us, the best thing for the family is to have a mom at home . . . and for me to have a schedule that has the entire family together at the end of every day."

Even in the midst of what the papers called a "highly contentious" statewide campaigns, Jon's public life ended at the driveway. "One reason I'm always on the phone out here [in the car on the road] is that I can't take the work inside with me. I have to have all of my messages cleared and my calls made before I go in the house." Jon Bruning still endeavored to make it home every evening, if not by dinner, then certainly by a reasonable hour.

The key, Jon said, to managing a full-time political career and a professional career while also having a complete family life was discipline and commitment. As we drove down the road, three hundred miles of highway behind us, discussing the imbalance that permeated so many professional lives, the struggle between work and family, Jon's observation was telling and spoke to the underlying discipline he has developed. "Look, you are in control of this. Take control of it. Don't take press calls after six o'clock. Do you really need to be quoted again? You make the decision to commit yourself to dividing your work time from your personal time, and make sure that the family time is sacred."

## First Out of the Gate

The second week of June 2001, Jon Bruning announced his campaign for attorney general. Bruning had not been quiet about his ambitions, and had related to me (and doubtlessly to others) his intention to run two years prior. Scott Bauer, in covering Bruning's campaign committee, said, "Bruning, a 32-year-old lawyer, has long been considered a likely candidate for attorney general,"[1] and Robynn Tysver, of the *Omaha World-Herald*, observed in an article on legislators seeking other positions that Jon Bruning "is hoping his long-term vision pays off. Bruning, who has never hidden his political ambitions, wants to become attorney general. He's been running for the job, more or less, for two years."[2] The previous year Jon had applied for the vacant position of secretary of state and had made a list of eight finalists; his progressive ambitions were expressed and public.[3]

It was not clear that Bruning would get a free ride. David Kramer, chair of the Nebraska Republican Party, remarked at the time that he "anticipates a couple of others may join the race in the coming months." One potential contender, Deputy Attorney General Steve Grasz, stated he was "weighing options." Ernie Chambers, the independent liberal from Omaha, "chided Bruning, saying he is more focused on running for attorney general than fulfilling his legislative duties."[4]

Bruning's initial filing effectively cleared the field of candidates. Under Nebraska state law, candidates must file paperwork when their campaign committee for an office raises more than $5,000. On June 11, when Bruning opened his AG campaign account, he transferred $72,000 from his state senate account to his AG committee.[5] Four weeks later, sixteen months before the election, Steve Grasz took his name out of contention for attorney general and announced he would back Bruning for the AG post. His reasons for not running were cast in the personal context: "I've been mulling it over for eight months. I have four children, ages two, four, seven, and nine, and I just concluded that I didn't want to be away from them for the next twelve months."[6]

Jon continued to run his permanent campaign, raising money and lining up support. Throughout the summer, the Republican field cleared for Bruning, who announced his belief that the campaign would cost "about $300,000,"[7] a daunting figure for most politicians in a small state. By October, Jon was out front on fund-raising. In the classic form of the veteran politician he was

> raising cash for his attorney general campaign like someone worried about a challenger, but there is none in sight. Bruning formally launched his bid in stops across the state. . . . It has been known for more than a year that Bruning would run, and he has been raising money for months. . . . With money in the bank and no declared opponent, the Republican apparently can breathe a little easier. Not likely, said the 32-year-old lawyer. "I guess I still have a fear that some rich person will enter the campaign, buy lots of advertising and get out ahead."[8]

The Democrats still had no candidate, though the state party chairman, Steve Achelpohl, said, "We're talking to people, and certainly people are considering it . . . obviously we would like to have people come forward, and the sooner the better." By Labor Day, when the field of candidates for major office in Nebraska is usually known, "the Democratic Party [was] still trolling for candidates to run for Attorney General."[9]

The press focused on Jon's "law-and-order" credentials, especially his legislative initiatives in regard to the death penalty, and referred to him as "a staunch supporter of the death penalty, [who] has led the fight to change Nebraska's method of execution." He was the favored candidate of law enforcement. The major law enforcement orders endorsed his candidacy, making him "law enforcement's choice." He attempted to present a more well-rounded candidacy than just law and order, however. Over pretzels and Cokes at a small roadside grocery, we talked about other aspects of his campaign besides the death penalty issue. "I see myself as a consumer advocate. As attorney general, I want to use the office to defend consumer rights, especially in areas like telecom. It is a place where I have experience and a track record of performance."[10]

Nonetheless, this campaign would ultimately, mainly, be about law-and-order issues. And, as a law-and-order candidate with a record of fighting for tougher treatment of criminals, as an attorney general candidate in a nation facing challenges in fighting terrorism and preserving civil liberties, Bruning was a logical source to talk to about how to defend against future skyjackings.

When asked about using profiling of passengers as a method of security, Jon's remarks that he would "support racial profiling" set off a flurry of criticism from the left. In the wake of the September 11 attacks on the United States and still without a candidate for attorney general, the Democratic chair stepped into the campaign as a surrogate to criticize Bruning for his comments: "[I]t is appalling that any lawyer would make such statements," [Nebraska Democratic chairman Steve] Achelpohl said. "It's so far out of bounds."[11] Bruning clarified his remarks, saying he would not condone racial profiling of blacks or Hispanics but that "an Arab on an airplane by himself is different. . . . I said we don't want to go back to a time like during the Second World War where we had internment camps for Japanese Americans. . . . We just need to use our common sense to protect our national security." Achelpohl attempted to sustain the story, arguing that "[Bruning is] playing to people's basest instincts and fears for political gain, and that's extremely irresponsible." The story faded, but it was not the last firestorm that Bruning would endure on the campaign trail.

## Jon Bruning and Death Penalty Reform

In the wake of the challenge to Alabama's use of the electric chair as a sole method of execution, in December 2000 the Unicameral was considering revising the Nebraska death penalty to address potential constitutional defects in the law. An Associated Press survey of state lawmakers revealed that three-quarters of forty-nine senators said they either were "supporting or were leaning towards"[12] supporting replacing the electric chair as the sole form of execution in Nebraska. Jon Bruning had already been politically active on this issue and was out front as advocating change, stating, "We should have done this years ago."[13]

At the beginning of the regular legislative session in January, Jon decided again to introduce his lethal injection legislation, LB 62. His arguments echoed earlier concerns about the dubious constitutionality of the Nebraska death penalty. "We've waited far too long to do this. At some point the electric chair is going to be unconstitutional in all fifty states. That time is near." Later, speaking to the press, he argued, "It is only a matter of time before the United States Supreme Court or the Nebraska Supreme Court declares electrocution unconstitutional," adding that by 2000, Nebraska was one of four states that offered electrocution as the sole means of execution. Much like his 1999 proposal, the 2001 bill was modeled on a recent Florida reform, which offered the condemned a choice of method. "I do not see any reason for us to pick the most brutal method we can think of to carry out punishment . . . if the punishment is death, that's not something I'm proud of, but let's carry it out in the most humane way possible."[14] Jon introduced the bill early in the session in order to ensure some attention on the issue agenda. The coming legislative session would have a very full schedule, with a looming budget debate and also the task of legislative redistricting. Bruning observed that "If . . . I have a good idea I have to get it in right away so it has a chance to be heard and debated prior to those huge issues coming up."[15]

Bruning quickly found himself across the battle lines from Ernie Chambers, an ardent death penalty opponent. "This is one of those issues," Chambers declared, "as long as I am in the legislature, that I must address full-bore."[16] Chambers had successfully passed legislation to abolish the death penalty in Nebraska in 1979, only to see the measure vetoed. Another of Bruning's concerns was that state or federal courts would strike down the state law. All of the legislature was aware that, the previous May, a state court judge had upheld Nebraska's death penalty law but had also ruled that the "procedure used during electrocutions amounts to cruel and unusual punishment."[17] At the beginning of the regular legislative session in January, Jon Bruning again introduced his bill: "It is only a matter of time before the United States Supreme Court or the Nebraska Supreme Court declares electrocution unconstitutional." By 2000, Nebraska was one of four states that offered electrocution as the sole means of execution.[18]

By March, when legislators have to set their priority bill, Bruning placed his priority marker on the lethal injection bill, though talk around the capitol building was that the bill might not even emerge from committee. The Bruning bill and a competing measure drafted by Judiciary Committee chair Kermit Brashear were bottled up in Judiciary, and committee member Ernie Chambers vowed to kill both measures. Bruning, realistic about the bill's prospects, fully expected the bill to be the target of a filibuster action by opponents if it came to the floor. The opponents of his legislation, most notably Chambers, were vocal in opposition to the bill and condemned Jon for using the issue to further his own ambitions. Robynn Tysver observed that Senator Chambers "on Tuesday scoffed at the idea that the Bruning bill would make it onto the floor. He accused Bruning of playing politics with the death penalty. 'It's one of the pebbles in his campaign for attorney general.'"[19]

Part of the challenge to passing the bill resided in the cumbersome nature of the Unicameral's procedures, which can empower one senator who knows procedure to stop most any initiative. The other problem was one of the context of the political times. The 2001 legislature was beset with a variety of contentious issues, including arguably the most divisive issue in legislative politics, redistricting. With the sixty-day clock ticking on the legislative calendar, lawmakers such as Chairman Brashear and Speaker Kristenson were reluctant to open another contentious legislative debate, and there was intense, vocal minority opposition from the procedurally adept Chambers. "Omaha Senator Ernie Chambers, known for his ability to stall or kill bills, is opposed to all three proposals and has vowed to block them."[20] Chambers was fully on the offensive, attempting to stall the move toward a reformed death penalty and to discredit the "humanity" of lethal injection. In hearings before the Judiciary Committee, he argued that injections can be botched. "I think 'Humane Execution' is an oxymoron."[21] Medical witnesses argued against the use of an execution technique under the guise of a medical procedure on ethical grounds.

By the end of March, it was all over but the shouting. Jon Bruning had campaigned hard to pass a reform to the death penalty. He sought to marshal positive press attention and to enlist support from his colleagues, and he used every procedural trick available to him to compel debate on his legislation. However, the political forces, competing issues, and determination of the opposition frustrated his effort. But Bruning did not want to wait and was worried that the Supreme Court would rule the electric chair a "cruel and unusual" punishment. Jon opined in frustration, "We're rolling the dice by waiting."[22] He would doubtlessly have wanted to have passed this major legislative reform in time for his coming campaign for attorney general. A major legislative accomplishment of this sort is valuable to members seeking reelection and to those with progressive ambition. Regardless of whatever personal motivations Bruning alleges to possess for advancing the proposal, the issue debate would ultimately move in his direction.

# January 2002

Jon Bruning was out of the gate fast, again proposing the lethal injection reform of the death penalty. Now a declared candidate for attorney general, he acted quickly and set the tenor for the coming legislative session by placing this controversial topic at the center of the first day's work.

> Less than ten minutes into the first day of the 2002 legislative session, Jon Bruning introduced a bill Wednesday to change the state's method of execution from the electric chair to lethal injection. And it wasn't long after that that Omaha Senator Ernie Chambers, a longtime opponent of capital punishment, was vowing to fight the measure. "I will not vote for any death penalty bill, no matter how they sugarcoat it, other than one to abolish it," Chambers said. Bruning knows Chambers' words are not hollow. . . . Bruning, who is running for the Republican nomination for attorney general, [is] concerned that recent challenges to the use of the electric chair might lead the U.S. Supreme Court to decide it is cruel and unusual punishment.[23]

Having traveled this road on two other occasions, Bruning was cautious regarding the prospects for his legislation. He noted the formidable presence of Ernie Chambers, observing, "It can be very difficult to amend a bill in the Judiciary Committee with Senator Chambers standing watch."[24]

There was more than sufficient support technically to pass the death penalty reform, and Governor Johanns would certainly pass the reform legislation. Bruning again prioritized the bill, to heighten its prospects of getting to the floor. And again the bill confronted competition from Kermit Brashear, who again introduced his own bill. Unlike Bruning's bill, which dealt only with the issue of lethal injection, Senator Brashear's bill was an omnibus measure, addressing sentencing issues in addition to method.[25]

The lethal injection proposal languished in committee. By mid-March, Jon was again fighting to get his lethal injection bill out of committee and down to the floor. Despite a relatively high number of priority on the docket and Jon's efforts, the committee wouldn't move. Chairman Brashear said there was "no rush" to advance the bill, because time would be better spent on budget issues. Bruning indicated to the press that he might force the issue, and he did file a motion to pull the bill from committee. "This subject is never going to be easy to deal with but that doesn't mean we should avoid it. If not this year, when?" said Bruning.[26] By April, as the 2002 session winded down, both bills remained tied up in committee, and with eight days left in the session, there was insufficient time to consider the legislation and also complete the budget. The legal community waited for the Supreme

Court to rule on the constitutionality of several aspects of state death penalties, including the determination of extenuating circumstances by judges instead of juries. The uncertainty surrounding other aspects of the death penalty emboldened those who supported abolition.[27]

Two months later, in June, the United States Supreme Court ruled that the guarantee of a jury trial extends to the penalty phase of assigning the death sentence, thus effectively nullifying Nebraska's use of judicial troikas to determine the extenuating circumstances that merit capital punishment. (Ironically, the state had redesigned its law in the 1970s because of the perception that juries might be biased in their imposition of the death penalty.) This ruling vindicated opponents of Brashear's legislation, which would have only revamped Nebraska's use of three judge panels. The various death penalty decisions from the summer of 2002 were mute on the use of the electric chair. As the summer came to the plains, Nebraskans had a flawed, nonfunctioning death penalty law.

The issue divided the legislature and was unpleasant to consider and debate. But, it would soon explode onto the front pages and provide a powerful issue for Jon Bruning.

## September 2002: Murder in the Heartland

Norfolk, Nebraska, is a tiny plains town near the South Dakota border. Best known as the hometown of the legendary comedian Johnny Carson, Norfolk evolved into a diverse community with urban problems. A growing Hispanic community has been accompanied by a dramatic increase in crime. On Thursday, September 23, four men entered the branch of the U.S. Bank in Norfolk and committed the bloodiest bank robbery in recent U.S. history. Four bank employees—Lola Elwood, Jo Mausbach, Lisa Bryant, and Samuel Sun—and one customer—Evonne Tuttle—were killed in the robbery shortly before 9:00 A.M. By noon, three of the alleged gunmen—José Sandoval, Jorge Galindo, and Erick Fernando Vela, all locals—were in custody, and a fourth suspect, Gabriel Rodriguez, was being sought. Under Nebraska law, a murder in the commission of a felony carries either life in prison or a trip to the electric chair.

The crime made national headlines and set off a debate in Nebraska over the crippled state death penalty statute. Within a week, local senator Gene Tyson called for the legislature to revisit Bruning's legislation. Tyson spent much of his weekend polling his forty-eight legislative colleagues to see whether there was support for a special session. "And right now, I have more yes votes than turn-downs," he said. Tyson was adamant about reforming the death penalty and soon enlisted Jon in his cause. "If we get the laws changed, then these trials could go ahead with no ambiguity," argued Tyson.[28]

## October 2002: Norfolk, Nebraska

Jon and I were on the campaign trail. The first stop, at nine o'clock, was in Madison County, Nebraska, in Norfolk. We would be making several stops up this way, and our first visit was with the county attorney, Joe Smith, at his office in the county courthouse and jail. In tiny Madison County, which has a population of about twenty-five thousand, nine homicides had been committed since the summer. Eight of the killings were part of two crimes. The first was the fouled bank robbery; the others were gang-style slayings that took place in the countryside outside town. As Smith related, "These other slayings were real gangland killings. [The ring leader] comes out of L.A., and him and these other guys are real believers in this Latin Kings stuff. They're all wrapped up in it . . . our big concern is that someone is going to try and bust these guys out."

The prosecutor had several worries, not the least of which was the potential constitutional defects in the state's death penalty law. The Nebraska death penalty had two possible legal defects. The first was the sentencing provision. Smith was justifiably concerned about fixing this flaw. "I have a trial starting October 21 where the death penalty is clearly called for." Both the prosecutor and Bruning noted to the press after their private meeting that the prosecution was impaired because of these legal defects. If Nebraska did not fix the defects in the law before the trial finished and moved to the sentencing phase, it would take a tool away from the prosecutor and affect his prosecutorial strategy.

Other deliberations that day gave insight to the respect Jon commanded. He was a force, a serious man who was respected by serious people. Despite his youth, Bruning enjoyed the respect and deference of senior legislative colleagues and members of the law enforcement community. In this meeting, Bruning articulated a course of action and communicated his expectation that the legislature and governor would act quickly to correct defects in the sentencing portion of state law, if only because it was, as he noted at a press conference in Norfolk, "an appropriate role for the governor and the legislature." Those in the meeting also discussed legislative strategy for a possible special session, which Jon confided he expected to be called for November 7, immediately after the election.

The second defect in the capital punishment law, the method of application, is the one that Jon Bruning found troubling, as mentioned earlier. As we drove from the courthouse to a meeting of the county Republican Party, he reiterated his argument that other states provide for alternative means of execution besides the electric chair. "That makes our death penalty law unusual. If someone comes along and successfully makes the argument that the electric chair is a needlessly cruel form of execution, and we have no alternative to fall back on, we may have no death penalty in Nebraska."

Any effort to correct the death penalty not only would ultimately have to address the concerns from the Court's decision regarding the method of sentencing but, as a preemptive matter, would have to allow alternative means of execution.

Later, as we headed up a country road to visit a donor, Jon received a phone call from one of his staff members in Lincoln. After a brief chat, he hung up and smiled at me as we pulled up the driveway. "The governor just called and said that he will call a special session to deal with the death penalty right after the election, November 7." As we turned into the carport, the smile faded a bit. "That won't make Deonne happy. We were going to take a vacation right after the election, sort of a reward for surviving the campaign. Now I'll have to put that off."

The killings in Madison County served as an impetus to address the defects in the death penalty law, brought media attention, and caused conversation among lawmakers. During this campaign tour, Republicans who met the press with Jon emphasized that he was a longtime advocate of reforming the state death penalty law and that he was therefore a good man to help fix the defects in the process. Were Jon to win the election, he would not take office until January, so he could be involved in any legislative session called before. I asked him whether he intended to take a role in the session. His answer at the time was "Yes, definitely. I am going to introduce a bill, just like I have in the last three sessions, to deal with the lethal injection issue. And I'll be down there on the floor fighting for a new, constitutional death penalty law for Nebraska. As attorney general, I have to implement that law." He also wanted a hand in shaping the policy he would have to enforce and defend. But, he added, the need for death penalty reform was not driven by the events in Madison County. "A case like this shines light on a more general problem."

This would not be the first special session; the governor called the Unicam into session during the summer to deal with the fiscal crisis. Now the state would absorb the cost of a second special session to address the defects in the death penalty statute, which had been known to the legislature both before the first special session call and also during the regular session in the spring. Why didn't they address the problem sooner?

"I suppose we might have dealt with the issue earlier," Jon told me, "but it would have created a political mess. Ernie Chambers would have tied up the legislature, held up everyone's legislation during the regular session and the special, to try and kill the death penalty. . . . If we deal with it in special session, and it is the only issue on the call, then Ernie doesn't have leverage over other members of the legislature. He can't tie up their district projects or their favored legislation hostage to procedure. We can clip Ernie's wings by focusing on a single issue. The special session offers us eight days to focus on the problem; we would only get bits of days in the regular session."

The strategic planning relative to Chambers reflected the respect political players in Nebraska have for the self-appointed "defender of the downtrodden." Joe Smith, in both public and private, when asked whether Chambers would fight an effort to revise the death penalty, observed, "I respect his honest opinion, and I value our relationship. We have respect, with dissent."

The killings in Norfolk focused attention on the problems with the death penalty law and created an opportunity for policy reform. Bruning's comments echoed those of Mike Saxl of Maine, whom I had visited the previous week. As we drove down the highway, a clearly saddened Bruning observed that "sometimes unique opportunities exist to make changes in public policy. . . . We couldn't take this up during the last special because it would have conflicted with the budget. . . . Now we have an opportunity to react and change the law to reflect what the people want and what society expects [from government]." When asked about waiting for regular session, Jon echoed the words of Joe Smith to the press: "There are pressing cases that merit clarity in the law. We cannot wait any longer . . . these killings in this community are one perfect example of why the legislature should act now."

## October 2002: Observations

As we rolled along the impeccable two-lane highways of rural Nebraska, the sun started to shrink behind us, and we picked up traffic from Lincoln and Omaha. I made a note that we had not really seen a lot of people that day, maybe seventy if you include the thirty folks at the Madison County GOP lunch and the employees whom we campaigned at the courthouse.

The attendance at the Madison County GOP luncheon reflects the challenges to civic life in Nebraska and America writ large—namely, the graying of American politics. As noted in the chapter on Adrian Smith, politics in Nebraska is not a game typically played by the young. Most officeholders are older, often in their fifties and sixties, and the politics of Nebraska allows for relatively easy entry to higher office without extensive office-holding experience. Of the thirty attendees, most were over forty. There were few young people in attendance, and Bruning and I were among the youngest in the room. It was, however, an enthusiastic group. His fifteen-minute talk addressed the subject on the minds of everyone, the death penalty and the pending special session. He held the audience in rapt attention. Jon appeared serious, far more serious in making this public presentation than in any other venue I had observed. He commanded the room, holding the attention of his audience. Most of his remarks I had heard throughout the day, but now I saw the entire pitch being made at once. He conveyed his sympathies for the tragedies visited on this community and called for the legislature to reform the death penalty law.

The rhetoric changed, subtly, from his private presentations, and the met-

aphors became more pointed. He asked for the Unicameral to give prosecu-
tors "the arrow in the quiver" they need to prosecute these crimes to the full
extent of the law. The rhetorical device about "clipping the wings" of the
opposition returned, but Jon was respectful of Chambers's power, calling him
an "able foe . . . who knows how to play hardball." When asked about the
prospects for passage, he said he was "absolutely confident. We have thirty-
nine or forty votes [out of forty-nine] to fix the sentencing problems with the
death penalty. We need thirty-three to pass an emergency measure."

Throughout this visit, I observed a more ideologically defined Jon Bruning. He was a more determined, hardened conservative and described himself in conservative terms. While the conservatism of his politics is not
necessarily new, the sharpness of the ideological contrast is. It was a conservatism circumscribed by thoughtfulness and an appreciation of the challenges
confronted by increasingly diverse communities in his state and around the
nation. As he closed his remarks, he reflected on the growing debate in rural
Nebraska about the relationship between the growing Hispanic population
and the challenges to law enforcement. Bruning segued into an informed
exposition on Hispanic culture, tying that culture to the goals of many in the
GOP. "This is not a Hispanic problem that we face. I have traveled around
the world and have spent time in South America and in Hispanic culture. The
basis of that culture is family and God. These are also the bases for the GOP.
. . . We are all immigrants, and your ancestors were not kings. They all came
here for an opportunity, and we have to welcome immigrants into our larger
communities." Bruning was out front with the press on this issue, positioned
with the leading edge of the national GOP in promoting efforts toward Hispanic communities.

We distributed almost every lawn sign in the back of the truck to excited
activists, and Jon held another impromptu press session in the parking lot.
When I queried him about the paucity of contacts, he responded, "This is a
different type of campaigning than running for the legislature. When I ran
for the Unicam, I would knock on six hundred doors a day and make big-
crown events. . . . Now, in this race, if I can come into town and meet with
three really good, well-respected residents and also get by the newspaper,
that's really better. When I ran for the Unicam, it was about the quantity of
contacts. . . . This is about the quality of contacts. These were the people
who lead business, shape opinion, and give money to candidates. They were
people who went out and generated votes from other people."

This evolution is evidenced in Jon's studied efforts to further develop and
sharpen his stump style. Already an accomplished speaker and debater, he
continues to hone his presentation skills through practice and the study of
other speakers. Jon is the one admitted student of political presentation I
have met on the campaign trail. "I love C-Span. . . . I like to watch the
debates, to watch candidates as they present themselves. I study their man-

nerisms, their presentation, their hand gestures, everything." In my notes from a press conference Jon conducted, I found the following: "He has a good presentation style. It is evident that he has a sense of his physical self, of how his mannerisms, gestures, and expressions appear to others. When conducting television interviews, he strikes the almost-classic TV anchor pose, head set slightly to one side, leaning slightly forward and with his hands clasped before him." This subtle technique is also used by actors in film when they are attempting to steal the focus of the camera in a scene. For Jon Bruning, whom the camera favors, the result was the projection of a thoughtful presence that was also part of his private demeanor. What was not communicated was the steely discipline that underlies his existence. He was in the transition from grassroots door-knocking legislator to major media candidate.

## "A Contentious Campaign"

Early in the campaign, days after filing, Bruning criticized his opponent for part ownership of a bar that was cited for violation of the state alcohol beverage control laws. His comments struck at the credibility of his opponent and called into question Mike Meister's suitability to serve as attorney general. Bruning stated that "the attorney general is the highest law enforcement position in the state, and we expect that person to follow the letter of the law, not break it." He asked that his opponent sell his stake in the bar, as a matter of ethical prudence. Meister called the violation a "technical mistake."[29]

Then, Jon stepped four-square into the Catholic priest abuse scandal, chastising the local archbishop for his handling of pedophile priests. He used his position on the floor of the Unicameral to call for the removal of the local archbishop. "If a priest in the church, under the archbishop's direct employ, was looking at child pornography, and instead of disciplining him or getting him treatment, he was reassigned to another parish, then [the archbishop] is not worthy of his position."[30] His effort to clarify the remarks did not diffuse the issue. "My comments speak for themselves. My concern is that in this case, the archbishop made a grave mistake. . . . For me, this isn't about the Catholic Church. I have a deep respect for the Catholic Church. My concern is for the safety of kids." Catholic Republican legislator Mike Foley threatened to withdraw his support of Bruning, stating from the floor, "I think you failed us today, Jon." Further criticism was forthcoming from the major paper in the state, the *Omaha World-Herald*, which observed, "Bruning wants to persuade voters that he has the temperament to be Nebraska's next attorney general. After Thursday, that temperament is up for discussion."[31] The following Monday, after a weekend of "reflection and consultation" with Catholic friends, Jon retracted his remarks and apologized.[32]

Bruning's opponent was unforgiving. Mike Meister, age forty-one, said the incident "demonstrated Bruning's inexperience and lack of judgment."

. . . When you're looking at an office or public service, you have to have the kind of maturity to distance yourself from your emotion and be a professional. . . . Bruning softened his position because of politics. He realized that he shot himself in the political foot, and now he's got to back-pedal to protect himself."[33]

The exchanges of March continued through the summer. In mid-July, Mike Meister produced documentary evidence of legal run-ins that Jon had had with Lincoln police while in college and law school. On July 15, at a press conference where he distributed copies of documents, Meister "called on his opponent . . . to explain three run-ins with the law that occurred during Bruning's undergraduate and law school days at the University of Nebraska."[34] The records provided at a press conference indicated an arrest in Lincoln on misdemeanor larceny charges in 1991, when Jon was an undergraduate, and for disturbing the peace in 1992. He also had a 1989 ticket for negligent driving and failing to appear in court. All of these charges were either dismissed or never filed. The Omaha paper quoted Jon as saying the incidents were "youthful mistakes," and he "plead[ed] guilty to being an idiot on Husker game days. A lot of us did things in college we are not especially proud of." The larceny arrest resulted from a postgame dispute with a bouncer at a Lincoln bar.[35]

Meister questioned whether Bruning made these disputes known to the law school and the state bar association, and Bruning replied in the affirmative. Bruning countered Meister's innuendoes by again calling attention to his previous criticism of Meister's liquor license woes. Meister then tried to flip Bruning's March comments: "Bruning's dubious record makes him politically unelectable and morally unacceptable as a candidate for attorney general. . . . I don't have a public record. Jon Bruning has a public record."[36] He went on to say that "his past actions disqualify him from holding the office of attorney general."[37] Jon, far ahead in the money game, challenged the motivation behind Meister's tactic. "This guy is desperate because his campaign is dead in the water. . . . When I was young and irresponsible, I was young and irresponsible. When I was young, I thought beer was food. I'm not proud of this stuff, but the fact remains it was college foolishness. Nebraskans are not interested in somebody's foolishness during college."[38] The allegations were sufficiently prominent in the media to warrant comment by incumbent governor Mike Johanns, who was seeking reelection on the Republican ticket. In response to Meister's questioning the governor's continued support for Bruning, he observed, "The tickets were dropped, making them a non-issue. If anything, it causes me to question Mr. Meister's grasp of the law if he doesn't recognize the difference between a dismissed ticket and a conviction."[39]

The editors of the Omaha newspaper said what many were no doubt thinking as they watched the campaign: "Neither candidate for attorney general is covering himself with glory during the campaign's slow season. . . . If either or both want to be taken seriously by the bulk of voters, we believe they'll stand a better chance when they start talking about topics with some heft to them."[40] Jon Bruning responded to the challenge by returning to the core themes of his campaign: water rights, law enforcement, consumer protection, and the death penalty.[41]

The battle to succeed the longtime attorney general Stenberg devolved into accusations of competence, ideology, and ambition. Meister characterized Jon Bruning as "all politician, with little legal experience."[42] Robynn Tysver reported that "[Jon]Bruning has never hidden his ambition. He said it is doubtful that attorney general is the last office he will seek. [Bruning said,] 'I'd be lying to you if I said I never dreamed of being governor, but the only way that is going to happen is if I do a fantastic job as attorney general.' "[43] In response to Meister's criticism of Bruning's record as a litigator, and particularly noting that Jon had never prosecuted a criminal case, Bruning countered that he had appeared before the Nebraska Supreme Court and also appears on behalf of clients at frequent state Public Service Commission hearings. He also pointed to his "thriving" corporate law practice—he represents over a half-dozen telephone companies—and his six years as a legislator in the Unicameral.

Jon did not want to endure those criticisms but had definitely become circumspect about the tenor of the campaign. "You can say it, but he can't pay for it. . . . The papers will only run a negative story so many times before it is no longer news. . . . Going negative doesn't work, because you can't sustain it through time." Now that the press's patience and attentiveness to the personal negative campaign had been exhausted, Jon Bruning felt he was left with a clear shot to make his pitch in the media with advertising, and to set the issue debate.

## Money, Facts, Ernie Chambers

Jon's race for attorney general was the most expensive in the history of the state. "When Don Stenberg [the current attorney general] ran for office last time, he spent about a quarter-million dollars. We raised over $450,000." As Associated Press reporter Kevin O'Hanlon observed a year before the election:

> State Senator Jon Bruning wants to be Nebraska's attorney general—and he's willing to spend big bucks to win the office. . . . Bruning, who already raised $175,000, said he's willing to spend at least $800,000 on his campaign despite having no opposition so far for the GOP nomination or from the Democrats. . . . "That doesn't mean I'm going to let grass grow under my feet. Money is

never going to win you a race, but you can lose one for a lack of it." If Bruning spends that much, it would be the most ever laid out [in a race for attorney general of Nebraska].[44]

By contrast, in his first campaign for attorney general in 1990, retiring incumbent Don Stenberg spent $299,000, $255,000 in his 1994 reelection, and $215,000 in his 1998 reelection.

The money has been well spent. According to the figures Jon recalled to me as we drove down the highways, about $15,000 went for polling, which was "cheap because we're using the same pollster as the governor," so he gets to dip into the same sample on the same instrument and gets more extensive information. A lot of money—over $150,000—went into television.[45] Like most candidates with money, Bruning bought lots of television. The campaign produced two different advertisements. The first advertisement was a "law-and-order" spot that focused on efforts to get rid of methamphetamine labs in Nebraska. The ad has a dark feel and draws attention to one of the most serious addictive drug problems plaguing a variety of suburban and rural communities. When Jon talked about the methamphetamine problem in Nebraska, it mirrored his advertisement. But, as both a candidate and a senator, he had rode along with law enforcement in some of the roughest neighborhoods in Nebraska, so he spoke from firsthand experience. As we headed from Madison County to visit a contributor, I asked him to elaborate.

"Keith, it is a real problem for us, growing out of control. In 1998, we busted twenty meth labs in the state of Nebraska; in 2002, that number jumped to two hundred meth labs busted. Almost 40 percent of the violent crimes in Nebraska are related to methamphetamine. The problem is that any idiot can make it. . . . We have to increase education and awareness regarding the problem, and teach retailers, cops, teachers, parents, and neighbors to know what they're looking for. . . . We had a bust recently because a Wal-Mart clerk got suspicious when a teenager bought $300 worth of a twenty-four-hour cold medicine."

Both the ad and his description of the causal relationship between uncontrolled drug dealing and crime were consistent with Jon's law-and-order theme and reflects his political record of going after violent crime.

The other advertisement was positive, in the classic "qualifications and accomplishments" video style (Kaid, Nimmo, and Sanders 1986). Titled "He Did It!" after the ad's tagline, the emphasis of the thirty-second spot is on Bruning's areas of legislative accomplishment and policy emphasis in the Unicameral and in the campaign, with an emphasis on law enforcement and consumers' rights. His television campaign started on October 15 and would run through election day. And there was mail, always mail, targeted to likely voters.

As with most of the aspects of Jon's political career since he had arrived in the Unicameral, the television advertising came under fire from Senator Ernie Chambers. Speaking to the press the week before the election, Chambers referred to the "He Did It!" ad as "deceptive" and characterized it as an effort to

> cover up a poor legislative record. State Senator Ernie Chambers of Omaha accused Bruning of taking credit for someone else's hard work. Bruning responded that Chambers was throwing a "temper tantrum" in the final days of the campaign, because he realized that Bruning is going to win the election for attorney general. He said Chambers' ire revolves around their differences on the death penalty. . . . The television advertisement shows Bruning working as a lawmaker, and a voice intones "[Bruning] said he would strengthen the death penalty. He did it."[46]

Bruning said the ad referred to a 1998 measure he cosponsored to make the murder of a police officer a capital offense (he indicated the same thing to me weeks before the ad appeared). While the main author and moving force on the floor was Gerald Matzke, Bruning had set the bill as his priority.[47]

The purpose of the media campaign was to build name recognition and put Jon's image and message before the electorate. Despite being one of the most covered members of the Unicameral, Bruning started the campaign with "next to no name recognition. We might have been at 5 percent, maximum, and even now"—that is, three weeks before the election—his name recognition was not nearly universal, though it was far higher than that of his Democratic opponent. Jon continued on name recognition, observing that "the problem with a lot of politicians, a lot of potential candidates, is that they think they are better known than really they are. No one knows you, and it is a very hard thing to learn. You have to go out and get known, again and again." To do otherwise was to allow ego to intrude on getting things done.

## Observations on Ambition

Earlier, I wrote that Jon Bruning "clearly has progressive ambitions." Four years after that observation, he acted on those ambitions, and I do not doubt that he will act on them again. In one of our conversations, I asked him again, "If offered a seat in the U.S. House at no cost, would you take it?" and the answer was no. We then talked about the U.S. Senate, and the answer was more qualified. "I might be able to do the Senate, later, after the kids are older. In the Senate you don't have to be campaigning constantly—you have six years." Jon Bruning was not the arrogant sort of man who would say he wanted to be president. That aside, he is on a trajectory to be able to make such a run some day, should he become the chief executive of Nebraska. To aspire so high at a young age invites that observation, whether it is desired or not.

When he came into the Unicameral, he gave up a full-time job that had him earning in the six figures. Now, after building a successful law practice, he will lay it aside to take a substantial pay cut to become attorney general of Nebraska. "Some folks, they look up and say, 'Man, $70,000—that's a lot of money; he must be doing it for the money.' But I can make much more than that practicing law, and I will sacrifice earnings to take this job." Bruning has confronted the challenge of choosing between avarice and ambition, and ambition has won.

The people watching Bruning were clearly intrigued by his electoral prospects. As we left a GOP meeting, Bruning held an impromptu interview session with a small group of TV and print reporters in the parking lot. He fielded questions about politics, policy, and especially the death penalty law. The last question a reporter asked as we headed for his truck was "Do you think you'll run for governor in four years?"

## Conclusion

The following was published in the *Omaha World-Herald* during the week before the 2002 general election:

> Nebraska is best served when the lawyer in this position is characterized by caution and, in general, non-activism. That makes Jon Bruning . . . our choice . . . Bruning's avowed top priority, is to assure Nebraskans, as far as possible, of being safe in their streets. He supports the death penalty and believes in dealing firmly with violent criminals. He would come to the job well-versed in the ways of the capitol. . . . *His opponent has criticized him as too much politician and too little lawyer. We reject both notions. First, we don't view ambition as a flaw. If Bruning someday wants to be governor, more power to him. He's 33; there's plenty of time. And, he'll have to turn in an outstanding performance as attorney general in order to be taken seriously thereafter* [emphasis added.] . . . Jon Bruning [has] all of the tools to be an excellent Attorney General.[48]

Jon Bruning transcended the criticisms of his candidacy and the questioning of his experience and character to emerge as a respected, highly regarded politician in Nebraska. His issue for the previous three years resonated with voters and found an added impetus in the tragic shootings in Norfolk. Press coverage from early in the campaign, which emphasized foibles, faults, and failings, was superseded by a ringing endorsement from the state's major paper, which lauded not just his potential but also his intellect and vision, and which endorsed his ambition.

The following Tuesday, Bruning carried ninety-three of ninety-three counties and took 66 percent of the vote en route to a thundering victory. He carried twenty-eight counties with over three-quarters of the vote and took 78 percent in Madison County. He weathered a storm of controversy and criticism, focusing on his behavior as a youth, his beliefs, and his performance in legislative office. He is largely inoculated against such criticism in the future by his success at the ballot box and the assessment of his character by third-party observers. He is considered to be one of the most prolific fund-raisers in Nebraska, and the issues of importance to him are the same issues of concern to his new constituency. Within hours of his election as attorney general, his name was circulating as a potential successor to Governor Mike Johanns.

How Bruning parlays these achievements into future political success remains to be seen, though the reputation, ability, and talent are clearly present. His response to his election belied any ambition, as he observed, "I am really humbled by the support the state has given me. I'm anxious to get to work and do the job."

Bruning's intention to serve out the balance of his legislative term before becoming attorney general changed the day after the election, but before the special session convened to consider reforming the state death penalty. "With the death penalty laws already clouded by recent Supreme Court decisions, I do not want to open up another avenue" for appeal for Nebraska's seven death row inmates. Bruning observed that, "hypothetically, any of those seven people could appeal based on the fact that an attorney general–elect is serving in the legislature in a special session [to strengthen the death penalty law.] . . . It is a chance I am not willing to take with the taxpayers' money."[49]

## Notes

1. Scott Bauer, "State Senator Bruning Will Run for Attorney General," Associated Press, June 12, 2001.

2. Robynn Tysver, "Some Look to Roles outside Legislature," *Omaha World-Herald*, April 21, 2002, 7B.

3. Robynn Tysver, "Jockeying for Moore's Post Begins," *Omaha World-Herald*, November 11, 2000.

4. Tysver, "Some Look."

5. Leslie Reed, "Bruning Makes Move in Bid for State Post," *Omaha World-Herald*, June 12, 2001.

6. *Omaha World-Herald*, "Stenberg Aide Says He'll Back Bruning for Post," July 4, 2001, 16.

7. Like many politicians around the country, Jon Bruning had to figure out

what to do with his Enron money (he received $450 from the Houston-based firm, as did forty other Nebraska politicians in both parties). He gave it to a charity, the Salvation Army Heat Aid Fund.

8. Robynn Tysver, "Bruning Begins His Campaign for the Attorney General's Job," *Omaha World-Herald*, October 10, 2001, 3B.

9. Kevin O'Hanlon, "Democrats Still Vying for Attorney General Candidates," Associated Press, September 1, 2001.

10. Bruning was considered an expert in telecommunications and, like his spouse, represents telephone and cable firms in Nebraska.

11. Kevin O'Hanlon, "Democrats Criticize Bruning over Racial Profiling," Associated Press, October 22, 2001.

12. Kevin O'Hanlon, "Lawmakers to Grapple with Lethal Injection, Death Penalty," Associated Press, December 26, 2000.

13. O'Hanlon, "Lawmakers to Grapple."

14. Kevin O'Hanlon, "Lethal Injection Bill Introduced," Associated Press, January 4, 2001.

15. Robynn Tysver, "Legislature Begins Flow of New Bills," *Omaha World-Herald*, January 4, 2001.

16. Tysver, "Legislature Begins Flow."

17. Tysver, "Legislature Begins Flow."

18. O'Hanlon, "Lethal Injection Bill Introduced."

19. O'Hanlon, "Lethal Injection Bill Introduced."

20. Associated Press, "Lawmakers' Priorities Touch on Death Penalty," March 9, 2001.

21. Associated Press, "Lawmakers' Priorities."

22. Robynn Tysver, "Lethal Injection, Gun Bills May Perish in Committee," *Omaha World-Herald*, March 30, 2001.

23. Kevin O'Hanlon, "Battle Lines Drawn Quickly in Lethal Injection Fight," Associated Press, January 9, 2002.

24. O'Hanlon, "Battle Lines Drawn."

25. Under Nebraska law, judges assigned the death penalty using three-judge panels. The existing Nebraska statute allowed for the assignment of the death penalty if two of three judges concurred that extenuating circumstances were present. Brashear's bill would have required unanimity in the panel. The proposal would abolish the practice of automatically taking first-degree murder cases to the penalty phase at trial to determine if the penalty is warranted. See O'Hanlon, "Battle Lines Drawn."

26. Robynn Tysver, "Priority Bills Face Squeeze," *Omaha World-Herald*, March 18, 2002, 1A.

27. Kevin O'Hanlon, "Senator Says Nebraska Must Change Method of Execution," Associated Press, April 5, 2002.

28. O'Hanlon, "Senator Says."

29. Robynn Tysver, "Bar Ownership an Issue in Attorney General Race," *Omaha World-Herald*, March 6, 2002, 4B.

30. According to a KMTV survey published in the *Omaha World-Herald* ("Most in Poll Differ with Archbishop," March 21, 2002, 1B).

31. *Omaha World-Herald*, "Editorial: Bruning on Thin Ice," March 23, 2002, 10B.

32. Leslie Reed, "Senator Apologizes for Calling Archbishop Unworthy of Post," *Omaha World-Herald*, March 26, 2002.

33. Reed, "Senator Apologizes."

34. Joe Kolman and David C. Kotok, "Attorney General Hopefuls Spar over Run-ins with Law," *Omaha World-Herald*, July 17, 2002, 1B.

35. As it turns out, the larceny arrest was a classic college town dispute. While waiting in the cold outside a bar with several fraternity brothers, Jon observed the bouncer letting several other people from another Greek house jump the queue. Jon chastised the bouncer and then swiped the bouncer's knit cap off his head to get his attention.

36. Kolman and Kotok, "Attorney General Hopefuls."

37. Kevin O'Hanlon, "Meister Questions Bruning's Run-ins with Police during College," *Omaha World-Herald*, July 16, 2002.

38. O'Hanlon, "Meister Questions."

39. O'Hanlon, "Meister Questions"; see also Joe Kolman, "Johanns: Bruning Still the Best Candidate Despite Past Charges," *Omaha World-Herald*, July 17, 2002.

40. *Omaha World-Herald*, "Editorial: Much Ado about . . . ?" July 17 2002, 6B.

41. The arrest issue did not completely die until September, when Ernie Chambers filed a complaint with the Nebraska State Bar Association against Bruning, which was subsequently dismissed.

42. Robynn Tysver, "Two Battle for Office in Stenberg's Shadow," *Omaha World-Herald*, September 30, 2002, 1B.

43. Tysver, "Two Battle for Office."

44. Kevin O'Hanlon, "Bruning Readies to Make Attorney General Bid Official," Associated Press, October 9, 2001.

45. Scott Bauer, "Johanns Heads into Final Week of Election with Plenty of Cash," Associated Press, October 28, 2002.

46. Robynn Tysver, "Senators Spar over Bruning Ad," *Omaha World-Herald*, October 26, 2002, 8B.

47. Chambers remained unconvinced, stating that "to make the claim that he strengthened the death penalty means that he introduced and obtained passage of a bill to accomplish that purpose," while Bruning again countered that "it seems a little strange that the senator who prioritized the bill shouldn't get any credit for its passage. Without that priority status, the bill would have never passed." See Tysver, "Senators Spar over Bruning Ad."

48. *Omaha World-Herald*, "Editorial: Three for Nebraska," October 26, 2002, 6B.

49. Todd van Kampen, "Bruning Will Be Stenberg Successor," *Omaha World-Herald*, November 6, 2002, 2SS.

# Ambition's Edge  11

There are many ways of going forward, but only one way of standing still.
—Franklin Delano Roosevelt

THE BEGINNING OF ANY CAREER is rife with uncertainties, questions, and challenges. The initiation of the political career is no different, as candidates set out to present themselves to a public that has most likely not heard of them, is only somewhat familiar with the office they seek, and is confronted with other political and nonpolitical decisions to make. The initiation of a political career presents myriad uncertainties for the candidate. "Will people support my campaign?" "Can the nomination be won?" "Can the election be won?" "How can I capture the support of the electorate?" All of these uncertainties wrap themselves up in one basic question: "Is my best good enough to persuade other people that I should govern on their behalf?"

All individuals starting out in politics have one common asset: ambition for office. The source of the motivation is at variance, and often not readily observed, but the ambition to move up is there. Those who run have a desire for public position, a drive that propels them beyond citizenship. Among the very young, the reasons for seeking office are as varied as those exhibited by older, more politically prominent politicians: the intense belief in public service, policy goals, personal political advancement; the desire for power; or a need for attention. James Q. Wilson (1962), in his book *The Amateur Democrat*, argues that the political amateur enters politics because some issue or issues motivates him; the political professional enters politics and uses issues as a vehicle for gaining office. From this perspective, all of the young politicians described in this book are closer to professionals than amateurs. They are making career choices because they want to be in government, but not on the basis of any one issue.

What do we learn about the initiation of the political career by the very young, when we evaluate them in their element?

## Running

The elements that are important to describing and explaining the activities of politicians resonate in the beginning of the political career. Young candidates for public office craft organizations to support their efforts and develop networks of contacts to volunteer, contribute, and promote their campaign. The core constituency, as initially described by Richard Fenno, is the inner circle, the advisers, confidants, and personal friends who help sustain the politician. This research did not explicitly set out to explore the core constituency, but in describing these campaigns and the events surrounding the initiation of these careers, it was impossible to ignore the core support available to each candidate. All of the individuals profiled in this volume possessed strong core constituencies, and those constituencies either existed or were quickly constituted in the earliest stages of the political campaign. All of the elements that arise out a core constituency—the emotional support, financial connections, political networks, and potential advisers—were proximate to all of the candidates before they ran for the legislature. What candidacy did was to take discrete and separate elements, and then pull them together into a focused network of support that is the kernel at the heart of the politician's core constituency.

Many of these individuals had relatively strong civic ties and also mentoring relationships with established politicians. The great surprise is that, amid a domestic environment in which civic culture and interaction is presumed to be in decline, these candidates had such strong mentor relationships in their lives. Some, such as Stuckey-Benfield and Saxl, needed to look no further than the dinner table to find a mentor or political hero. Others found mentors elsewhere, from the ranks of existing politicians, neighbors, or in their life experiences as students or political activists.

The candidates often started without substantial connections to centers of power. However, the increasing likelihood of success attracted the attention of the powerful, successful, and connected. Dollar, Handrick, and Hunt developed connections after demonstrating their potential without elite support. Stuckey-Benfield, Corn, Balkman, Bruning, Saxl, and Smith came into the political arena with strong, elite social networks developed through their families or their own efforts. While elite investment in terms of money came later for Corn, the investment in support, advice, and back-channel promotion of his candidacy was more valuable than money. Either successful candidates have direct access to the money required to run a political campaign, or their community and inner circle help make funding available. As one of Corn's retired supporters related to me at an event, "I invested in that boy because I have known him all my life, and I believe in him."

# On the Presentation and Appearances of Campaigns

Campaigns reflect the values and traditions where the campaign takes place. Even then, there are common traits across all of the legislative campaigns examined in this book.

First, legislative campaigns in these states are waged on the ground and are largely low-tech undertakings. Candidates win on the basis of indirect and direct contacting (mailings and working doors) and through the efforts of largely volunteer organizations that are built up from their families and social networks. While money is necessary to win election, money without organization and effort will probably fail. The politicians visited here are largely self-motivated, self-promoting individuals, and they largely designed and managed their own campaigns. Therefore, among young candidates, the organizational success or failure of the campaign rests on the shoulders of the candidate. Technology enters the campaign to facilitate grassroots efforts or because the costs of technology-based communications—especially television—are sufficiently low to merit the investment. The intense, grassroots nature of these campaigns allows young and vigorous candidates to compensate for money and connections with time, effort, and energy.[1]

Survey data bear out these impressions about campaigning on the ground. The primary and general election candidates surveyed by Hogan (1995) agreed that the most effective way of communicating with voters is personal contacting and door-to-door outreach (table 11.1). In primaries, young candidates put less emphasis on the effectiveness of person-to-person contacting, though this strategy ranked just behind door knocking as the most effective form of communicating. Young candidates in primaries also placed greater stock in yard signs as communicating devices, and young candidates were more sold on the effectiveness of direct mail. Where candidates under thirty-five especially differed from other primary candidates was in their greater belief in phone banking as an effective communication tool. General election candidates are largely undistinguished by age group in their evaluation of campaign technique effectiveness. All age groups had over 90 percent agreement on the effectiveness of person-to-person contact and over 80 per-

Table 11.1   The Effectiveness of Different Media and Campaign Techniques in Communicating with Voters in the District (%)

| Candidate Age | Mail | Newspaper | Radio | TV | Yard Signs | Person-to-Person | Doors | Phone Bank |
|---|---|---|---|---|---|---|---|---|
| Primary | | | | | | | | |
| Under 35 (*n* = 46) | 56.5 | 23.9 | 17.4 | 19.6 | 58.7 | 67.4 | 87.0 | 45.7 |
| 35–55 (*n* = 151) | 56.9 | 15.9 | 23.8 | 21.2 | 43.7 | 92.7 | 79.4 | 32.5 |
| Over 55 (*n* = 44) | 47.7 | 18.1 | 13.6 | 9.15 | 4.59 | 3.28 | 1.82 | 9.5 |
| | | | | | | | | |
| General Election | | | | | | | | |
| Under 35 (*n* = 66) | 62.1 | 18.1 | 16.7 | 19.7 | 43.9 | 92.4 | 84.8 | 39.4 |
| 35–55 (*n* = 269) | 66.5 | 19.7 | 25.7 | 24.9 | 43.7 | 92.9 | 83.3 | 34.2 |
| Over 55 (*n* = 106) | 59.4 | 19.8 | 19.8 | 23.6 | 42.5 | 95.2 | 81.1 | 34.0 |

*Source:* Hogan (1995).

cent agreement on the effectiveness of working doors. Solid majorities also espoused the virtues of direct mail. No other technique was evaluated by a majority of respondents in any age group as being an effective means of communicating with voters.

Second, young politicians are largely issue oriented in their campaigns, but, whenever possible, they attempt to run on their limited experience. These impressions are largely borne out by Hogan's survey data (see table 11.2). When surveyed, primary and general election candidates in seven states revealed life cycle differences in their campaign emphasis. In primaries, sizeable majorities of candidates across age groups indicated that they placed "great emphasis" on issues, though, like Joe Handrick, young candidates most often ran issue-oriented campaigns. Issues were most emphasized by candidates under thirty-five (63.8 percent), followed by personal qualities (59.6 percent) and community service (46.8 percent). Candidates between thirty-five and fifty-five had the same order of intensity of emphasis (issue, 68.9 percent; personal qualities, 63.5 percent; community service, 56.1 percent), while candidates over fifty-five most emphasized their personal qualities (74.4 percent), followed by community service (69.8 percent), and placed similar levels of emphasis on partisanship and issues. Among primary candidates, the greatest differences in emphasis were in community service, prior political involvement, and party identification, where the oldest candi-

**Table 11.2   Aspects on Which the Candidate's Campaign Placed "Great Emphasis" (%)**

| Candidate Age | Issues | Personal Qualities | Community Service | Prior Political Involvement | Party Identification | Opponent |
|---|---|---|---|---|---|---|
| Primary |  |  |  |  |  |  |
| Under 35 (n = 47) | 63.8 | 59.6 | 46.8 | 19.1 | 40.4 | 12.7 |
| 35–55 (n = 148) | 68.9 | 63.5 | 56.1 | 34.5 | 45.9 | 17.6 |
| Over 55 (n = 43) | 62.8 | 74.4 | 69.8 | 55.8 | 60.4 | 14.0 |
| General Election |  |  |  |  |  |  |
| Under 35 (n = 66) | 72.7 | 51.5 | 40.9 | 16.7 | 22.7 | 22.7 |
| 35–55 (n = 275) | 69.5 | 53.5 | 43.6 | 34.5 | 25.8 | 27.6 |
| Over 55 (n = 109) | 71.6 | 67.9 | 61.5 | 49.5 | 34.9 | 17.4 |

*Source:* Hogan (1995).
*Note:* Respondent answered that voters "knew something" about them or "knew a great deal" about them before the election because of their issues, their personal qualities, their community service, their prior political involvement, and their party identification.

dates were far more likely to emphasize these aspects of themselves than were young candidates, especially on the dimension of prior experience.

A similar pattern emerges among the general election candidates. All candidates placed the greatest emphasis on issues, followed by personal qualities and community service. But older candidates, and especially candidates over fifty-five, more often placed great emphasis on these dimensions than did the younger candidates. The youngest candidates were half-again less likely to emphasize community service, emphasized prior political experience two-thirds less often, and were about half as likely to place great emphasis on their party identification in the campaign.

The surprise of the interviews and campaign observations was the extent to which young candidates often parlayed limited prior experience into an aura of legitimacy. Corn, Smith, Handrick, Dollar, Saxl, and Stuckey-Benfield all possessed varying degrees of experience in government, as state legislative aides or interns. Saxl also had significant experience in big league politics, with the DCCC. The young lawyers have a bit more legitimacy, due to their legal training; and Balkman, Stuckey-Benfield, Bruning, and, to a lesser extent Saxl (initially a law student) could fall back on the law as further legitimation (see also Meinhold and Hadley 1996). Smith and Handrick both had some experience in small-time local government. Two—Stuckey-Benfield and Saxl—are the progeny of well-known political families. The threshold for legitimation is sufficiently low that a smart candidate can convert limited experience, and the knowledge that comes with it, into political legitimacy. Once the legitimacy threshold is crossed, it does not have to be reestablished, and youth ceases to be a negative issue.

Third, incumbents can be defeated by young candidates and first-timers. In the cases presented here, the young candidates who won ran from the right (Balkman, Bruning, and Smith) and attacked early and often on roll call votes, member activities, and wedge issues to unseat them. Balkman, Bruning, and Smith all unseated incumbents in their initial efforts at the legislature. Hunt and Handrick failed to unseat incumbents in three efforts. Hunt, in particular, probably failed because the "stealth" strategy did not leave sufficient time to disconnect the incumbent from his constituency, though running from the left in his district did not help. Incumbents fell to sustained, unrelenting efforts to systematically undo their incumbency.

Fourth, constituency dictates campaign style. Previous research, especially the work of Fenno, draws this same conclusion about congressional campaigning (see Fenno 1996, 2000), and we see it again in these varied, early political experiences. Across these candidates, the combination of the type of constituency (urban, suburban, rural, or mixed) and the presence or absence of long-standing political traditions affected the initial presentation by the candidates. Kenneth Corn ran a campaign that followed in the political traditions of his constituency. He walked neighborhoods, campaigned at political events, and stood in contrast to other candidates in political forums. Many candidates did this. But, in Corn's district, all of the sweat equity campaigning was conducted in an environment where it was important to know people and to spend time with them in a fashion that mattered. This was a person-to-person campaign: People knew the candidate and expected to be known, not unlike the "congressman A" (Jack Flynt) of Fenno's (1978) *Home Style*. Corn's success was a product of the opportunities for direct comparison and public visibility that were available in his district. Numerous political events were scheduled and well attended. The candidates were often seen together, and the candidate forums presented numerous opportunities for Kenneth to demonstrate his innate technical knowledge of politics and issues.

Adrian Smith and Joe Handrick campaigned in similar environments, though their districts were not so firmly grounded in the intimate, personal connections seen in Corn's case. Their campaigning was largely one-to-one, by themselves or their surrogates, and then supplemented by television and mailing. When Jon Bruning shifted from a local to statewide campaign, his campaign style necessarily evolved to meet this changed context.

Shane Hunt, Thad Balkman, Jon Bruning, and Matt Dollar worked in the environment of the American suburb. Mike Saxl and Stephanie Stuckey-Benfield ran in urbane, liberal districts with large gay populations. But all of them followed a proven plan, similar to the plans advocated by the campaign schools. They engaged in high-visibility activities with great frequency, and they cultivated contacts with party officials, local business people, and voters. Their campaigns were vigorous and emphasized one-to-one contacting and crafting increased name recognition. For Balkman and Bruning, this approach in the suburbs worked against veteran incumbents; it was less effective for Hunt, if only because displacing an incumbent requires a reason. Voters have to be given a credible reason to vote against an incumbent, and while Hunt contrasted himself with the incumbent using comparative advertisements, those issues and comparisons were not sufficient to compel the voters to abandon the incumbent and came too late to create an opportunity.

Fifth, early effort matters. The successful young candidates examined here started planning and implementing their campaigns at the earliest possible moment. Campaign efforts for the state legislature started as much as sixteen months before the general election and entailed efforts to clear potential opponents from the primary field, fund-raising and voter contacting, and laying the foundation for the fall candidacy. Good politicians, regardless of age, think several steps ahead, recognizing that the actions of the previous winter and spring affect the choices of following summer and fall. The campaign does not end.

# Legislative Career

Fenno (1996), in his analysis of the 1992 campaign of Wyche Fowler, observed that "to intrude on a campaign . . . is to discover that the campaign is embedded in a career" (167). But, in conversations with these young politicians, we can also assert that to intrude on a career is to discover it is embedded in a perpetual campaign and that the campaign *is* the career. Every officeholder held that the making of policy, the pursuit of ambition, and their constituency activities are all directed toward the electoral context and are readily interpreted in the context of the campaign. Of the politicians discussed here, Mike Saxl probably came closer than anyone to explaining this dynamic: "Policy and the campaign is the same thing. You campaign on policy, you make policy in the context of the campaign. Politics is the nexus of policy and elections. They are seamless." This is so because down in the states, representative life is seamless, flowing from legislating to campaigning to acting as the ombudsman. Staff resources are few, even for leadership, and legislators and their staffs handle all aspects of representation in greater detail. To disentangle the policy dimension from the electoral and campaign dimension is to ignore the reality of political life, where the two are closely integrated and interdependent.

New legislators, whether seeking only a legislative career or pursuing a career that progresses through offices, must demonstrate both temperament and ability in legislative office. How they go about doing this will vary from institution to institution, but there is some expectation of constituency service and representation and also a demonstration of minimal legislative competence that can be used in seeking reelection. Matt Dollar, looking forward to his first legislative session in Georgia, observed that "the two-year term means you have to think forward. . . . To get reelected, I have to keep my name up in a good way . . . and do what a freshman is supposed to do: kickin' it on constituency service . . . working hard." He concluded by noting, "As a freshman, I need to lay low and also find a way to make my mark. I do not want to look like a maverick. . . . You won't see me sponsoring any landmark legislation." Adrian Smith of Nebraska would doubtlessly agree with this perspective but was also under less pressure to conform and perform simultaneously, due to his four-year term. After showing his easy ability to conform with norms and pass legislation, Smith subsequently became active on numerous legislative matters.

Norms and institutional structure can be constraining. Jon Bruning was ready to wade into legislating from his first days in the Unicameral, and he found his institutional role conflicted with his personal and political style. Joe Handrick confronted challenges in pursuing policy he thought was important, because the institutional design of the assembly, and especially the concentration of power by the speaker, mitigated against his ambitions and goals.

The norms of these bodies, and the expectations of new members, do not have a differential effect on members based on their ambitions. The behaviors that are expected of new legislators at this level—write a bill or two, learn how to take part in debate without being too conspicuous, do your homework, and get reelected—are compatible with the pursuit of progressive ambition, because both static ambition and progressive ambition require the establishment of a professional reputation. For new members, the pursuit of progressive ambition is moot until they can prove their ability in their initial office, with sufficient proof of ability being reelection. Whether they seek to maintain their position or expand to larger venues, these legislators will have to cultivate reputations and establish those reputations with voters and political activists. Because these behaviors will be similar, it may be difficult to distinguish the member who is progressively ambitious from the member who has static ambition or intrainstitutional ambitions. The first step, in either case, is to demonstrate competence in the chamber and an ability to play by the rules, if not all the time, at least often.

The ability to pursue significant legislation was not constrained for all of the legislators in this study. There was no long apprenticeship for Stuckey-Benfield, who passed controversial, significant legislation as a freshman, or for Corn, who actively pursued ambitious policy proposals that affected his district and also his broader political constituencies. Bruning spent almost his entire legislative career fighting to remedy flaws in the Nebraska death penalty statute, and his efforts became an important part of his successful campaign for attorney general, though he never passed the reforms he sought. Balkman and Saxl fought pyrrhic battles for tax code reform, but both also demonstrated as freshmen the ability to pass legislation that was meaningful to their constituencies and to the state.

Once members move past the initial pains of socialization and indoctrination, the age issue fades as a constraint on the political career. Almost all of the legislators in this study acquired positions of responsibility and leadership within their first or second term, in part because the exceptional skill, ability, and energy they demonstrated in getting elected was also evident in their legislative behavior. Term limits contributed to this success, by opening doors to leadership positions because of high turnover in office. Saxl in particular enjoyed the benefits of having the row plowed for him, as he moved quickly through a succession of positions to the speaker's chair. Mike acknowledges that he was mentored, brought along by the speakers who preceded him. This influence is evident in his efforts to craft structures that institutionalize mentoring and identify new talent in the assembly.

Mike Saxl is an extreme example of what is true for all of the politicians in this study: Within the general context of advancement in the legislative body, youth quickly fades as a constraint on the exercise of ability and expertise by legislators. Saxl's role as speaker was possible because of term limits. In

Georgia, the institutional norms of longevity and institutional advancement would have precluded such a rapid advance to the top of the leadership. In contrast, Stephanie Stuckey-Benfield will likely serve at least five terms before she can think about competing for a major leadership position or committee chairmanship. She can still pursue policy goals, but any institutional leadership beyond a committee chairmanship is remote and will require longevity and patience. Her influence and leadership role is informal, arising from innate qualities such as expertise and judgment rather than formal position.

Finally, the legislative career lays the groundwork for the pursuit of progressive ambition, regardless of the motivation of the candidates for pursuing the legislative career. The legislative efforts of the legislators examined in this volume run the gamut from addressing constituency concerns to expanding social benefits statewide to pursuing significant reform of the criminal code. No two policy imperatives examined here are exactly the same, but they all served the purpose of addressing an issue of importance to the legislator, while also advancing the reputation of the legislator. State legislators deal with so many different types of legislation and have access to so many aspects of policymaking, it is difficult to disentangle the motivations arising for legislative initiatives from the nature of the policy created by the initiative.

This leads to a final point about ambition and policy. Observers of politics will not always agree with the policy goals of those they observe, and to evaluate policy requires a recognition of the influence of the personal lens on the evaluation. After turning off my own value lens, I have to conclude that ambition is good for public policy, for the reasons consistent with the findings of researchers into congressional ambitions (see Hibbing 1986; Hall and Van Houweling 1995; Herrick and Moore 1993) and state legislative ambitions (Maestas 2000a, 2000b). Politicians with institutional ambitions and those with progressive ambitions pursue policy goals that expand beyond the scope of their constituency. They develop expertise. And, as we have observed of the young legislators in this volume, they are relentless in the pursuit of broad-based policy goals that benefit individuals beyond their parochial constituency. This is true of both those who have shown progressive ambitions and those with institutional ambitions. Ambition is not just what fuels the recruitment of candidates, as Fowler and McClure (1989) observe, but is also the fuel of efforts to craft creative public policy. Age is no barrier to harnessing ambition in this respect, though the internal dynamics of the legislature do matter.

## The Evolution of Ambition

One aspect of the study of political ambition and political careers is to capture the temporal aspect of how ambition evolves, from the beginning forward. However, the political science literature largely engages in an effort at backward mapping—going to the outcome and seeing how someone got there. That approach is useful to understand the path of successful, progressive ambition. The heavy emphasis is on Congress; the narrow scope of examination is confined to a group of politicians at a time in political life that follows the formation and crystallizing of political ambitions. The experiences that shape ambitions and careers are long past, and the folks who had ambitions and lost them fall out of the analysis.

Chapter 1 asserts that politicians must have had progressive ambition at some point in time, in order to have moved from being private citizens to public servants. Few are drafted, and people are rarely elected against their wishes. In chapter 2, data on political activists, candidates, and legislative incumbents reveals a strong life-cycle effect on progressive ambition. To stand for office in the United States is to declare your competence and willingness to serve, and all candidates have goals—ego, power, policy, or future ambitions—that are not satisfied outside office. But, except among the young, progressive ambitions are rare in our political class.

If ambition is initially progressive, then for there to be other forms of ambition—discrete ambition, static ambition, or intrainstitutional ambition—it must follow that ambition evolves through time. If ambition is not initially progressive beyond the initial office, then that ambition must have grown from the political experience, and it must also mitigate against life cycle trends of declining progressive ambitions. There is no doubt that ambitions evolve. The remaining question of why ambitions evolve, and how quickly ambitions evolve, merits discussion, and the cases and analysis in this volume do shed some light on those questions.

Ambitions evolve for several reasons. At the time one seeks office, the long-term ambitions of the politician are not usually fully conceptualized. For many who seek political office early in life, there is a strong socialization to politics in their early years and an early desire to hold public office. Almost every person profiled in this volume can point to an early socialization experience and a youthful fascination with government and campaign politics. Stuckey-Benfield, Corn, and Smith had it early; Dollar got it later than others. Many of these people ran for office at a very early age—of the individuals profiled here, five ran for the state legislature or city council before age twenty-five, and all but one was in legislative office before age thirty. In many cases, these politicians discovered that their goals and desires changed as they aged. Joe Handrick put it best when he said, "What do you do when you realize that you accomplished everything you wanted to by the time you're twenty-eight?" Only two of them articulated any sort of "plan" for pursuing clearly expressed, progressive ambitions. And both of those individuals— Corn and Bruning—acted on the plan within the time frame of this study.

One of the surprises of the interviews and fieldwork was the lack of congressional ambition among these young politicians. This could be a product of case selection, and I do not seek to generalize from the observations of these politicians. But, even among those individuals with progressive political ambitions, there is no desire for a congressional career. A variety of contexts was advanced to explain why they did not want to pursue congressional ambition, but the personal context, specifically family, and the structural context of the two-year term and constant campaigning weighed against a congressional career for all but one of the politicians. Perhaps this resistance will diminish with time or as contexts change. If Fowler and McClure are correct that an intense desire for a congressional career is required to successfully pursue that career, and if there continues to be a decline of progressive ambitions through the life cycle, then those congressional ambitions will need to develop in the near future if they are to be acted on.

Things do change. Joe Handrick and Stephanie Stuckey-Benfield confronted changing personal contexts and the demands that accompany those changes. In Joe's case, he directed his career in a direction that was far more personally satisfying for him, getting out of elective office and moving to the private sector, where he is now building a consulting and lobbying practice. Legislative life no longer offered to Handrick what he wanted in public service, but he has found a way to do those things he enjoys the most about political life, but without the constraint of legislative ethics rules and running for reelection. Others indicated that they do not see elective office as a career commitment but rather as a service to be performed for a time. Only Stephanie indicated a long-term interest in legislative service at the state level, but even she faces powerful challenges from the personal context, and the resolution of those challenges is not imminent.

Events in the legislature cause politicians to alter or reconsider their ambitions. Some are directed into pursuing intrainstitutional, progressive ambitions, such as moving into leadership. Mike Saxl had almost no choice in the matter; he was advanced for new leadership positions whenever openings occurred. Then, also against his wishes, the youthful speaker of the House found himself term limited and out of work come December 2002. Saxl never saw the legislature as a long-term career; indeed, he knew he was term limited before he ever ran for the open seat in Portland in 1994. Saxl states definitively he never planned on pursuing the leadership, yet he rose to the top of his institution. Now he moves on, in search of new venues and new challenges.

For others, the experiences can lead to the realization that they dislike electoral politics and the representative role and that their ambitions were misplaced. Again, Joe Handrick is a good example, as he saw a limit to his ability to act as an effective legislator due to his perceptions of the distribution of power in the Wisconsin assembly. Still others may run up against the political peter principle, realizing that they are incapable of moving beyond their current station. Then, there are others who find that their policy, political, or ego needs are satisfied in their current station. They will pursue their career in place and not try to make the move up. Stephanie Stuckey-Benfield, in her first campaign for the legislature, said she was in for "twenty years." Her ambition has not yet changed. Others have vague notions of their ambitions that crystallize through time. Kenneth Corn and Matt Dollar were the subject of speculation about their progressive ambitions before they ever took the oath of office. For Dollar, progressive ambitions are not present, and he expects them not to develop. For Corn, the progressive ambitions were always there, but they were not clearly articulated. Now they are taking shape, as he builds a body of legislative accomplishment and assesses the political opportunities that lay before him. He wants to be governor but cannot rule out a run for U.S. Congress if the opportunity were to present itself. Only Jon Bruning had a definite plan.

Ambitions evolve, and in most cases, there is a rapid decline of progressive ambition. In the political activist communities surveyed and also among officeholders, progressive ambition rapidly disappears by the midthirties. Many political activists who hold progressive ambitions are never able to act successfully on those ambitions; some may try and fail, and find that the pain of losing is too great to endure again. Others never find the intestinal fortitude to step up and offer themselves. Still others redirect their ambitions or lose interest. In any case, the intensity for distinction and position that is held in youth dissipates rapidly, and only those few who either intensely hold their ambitions or are on their own path toward some political goal hold those ambitions in later years. Political scientists would prefer that political ambition look like Jon Bruning, Kenneth Corn, or Stephanie Stuckey-Benfield, individuals who lay out their intentions for a career and describe their institutional or progressive ambitions in frank terms. These are people who have some concept of where they are going and are committed to the journey. More often, though, ambition looks like Matt Dollar, who is shaping his ambition, or Joe Handrick, who evolved away from politics and has eschewed any progressive ambitions.

So, if we model the evolution of ambition and the political career, what would the model look like? Relying on literature and the analysis presented here, we find a picture emerging that resembles figure 11.1. First, all political ambition is initially progressive, because it entails the activation of ambitions though candidacy and the effort to attain public office. The assumption of public obligations and station beyond those of the private citizen are inherently progressive. Some politicians will have more refined ambitions than others, for either policy goals or personal career goals. The clarity and intensity of those goals affect the evolution of their political ambitions and their evaluation of their current institutional position. Losers reassess their ambitions and either commit to run again, like Handrick, or walk away.

Second, once in office, politicians evaluate the opportunities placed before them and take actions through their office to advance their goals. This

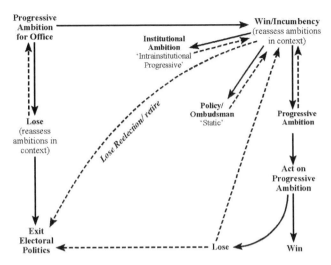

Figure 11.1    Ambition's Evolution

may entail the crafting of public policy through legislation or oversight, the promotion of themselves or a cause through their incumbency, or the positioning of themselves in the institutional hierarchy. Because, unlike in the U.S. Congress, the pursuit of intrainstitutional ambitions in state legislatures does not preclude progressive political ambitions, the behavior of a state legislator pursuing institutional goals is not easily distinguished from the behavior of a legislator pursuing progressive ambition.

Third, through time, with learning and knowledge, members reevaluate their ambitions. In addition, the evolution of other contexts, especially the political and personal contexts, create potential constraints on progressive ambition, or alternatively promote progressive ambition in the politician. This alteration of ambitions through the life cycle is evident in empirical data about officeholders, activists, and the general population. Efforts to craft theories of ambition and careers need to incorporate the notion that ambitions are not always fully conceptualized when a politician seeks office and that personal and political events will shape ambition through the career and the life cycle.

Uncertainty exists in the political future, and it is because of this uncertainty that we can never fully predict the willingness of potential candidates to act on ambitions. The uncertainty—of opportunity, of the political context, of the personal life—often precludes the pursuit of progressive ambition, even by valiant risk takers. Until potential candidates' options narrow to the point where they must run or defer, the uncertainty will exist regarding their ambitions. And, if they do defer, it is possible that avenues of progressive political advancement are forever closed, leaving only those avenues within the institution.

## Note

1. Technology and organizations should take on greater importance in larger constituencies, such as the senates of California and Texas, where legislative districts parallel media markets in their scope and population.

# A Note on the Research Technique

# Appendix

THE STUDY OF POLITICAL AMBITION and political careers has its roots in probing, qualitative studies. Donald Matthews's (1954, 1960) classic studies of political leaders enumerate the attributes of legislators and note the role of sociological factors in determining opportunities to hold major office. It is the interviews and observations in his study that lent depth to our initial understanding of institutional ambition and institutional constraint on legislators. It has been field studies, such as those of Richard Fenno (1978, 1996, 2000), Thomas Kazee and his contributors (1994; see also Kazee and Thornberry 1990), Sandy Maisel (1982), and Linda Fowler and Robert McClure (1989), that have proven most insightful in explaining how congressional candidates act on their ambitions. I adopted a field research technique combined with informal interviews, secondary source research, and supplemental survey data. Fenno (1996), in his Julian Rothbaum Lectures at the University of Oklahoma, published as *Senators on the Campaign Trail*, presents an eloquent rationale for the political scientist to get out of the office and onto the campaign trail:

> Glimpses from the campaign trail . . . remind us that it is, after all, flesh and blood individuals, real people we are talking about when we generalize about our politicians . . . there is something to be gained by occasionally unpacking our analytical categories and our measures to take a first-hand look at the real live human beings subsumed within . . . observation of politicians on the campaign trail is helpful because it takes us to the place where our representative form of government begins and ends—to the home constituency. Representative government has local roots and a bottom-up logic. And that is precisely the perspective of the observational research that is conducted on the campaign trail. (6)

So political science benefits from studying *politics in practice*, rather than confining itself to the study of the residual of politics: political outcomes.

Problems arise from the use of the participant observation, especially when one enters a campaign for a small constituency. The most obvious problem that the researcher encounters is that he is part of the environment, part of the political experience. The voter, standing in her door, cannot help but notice who else is in the background. In the small-town and rural campaigns, rumors of "outsiders" can make their way through the political grapevine with great speed. As Fenno (1978) observes in *Home Style*, "one key to effective participant observation is to blend into each situation as unobtrusively as possible" (267). So you dress appropriately, assume the staff position, and stay out of the way.

Going on the campaign trail with candidates did intrude on the "natural order" of the campaign. It may have altered the environment (though I doubt it; these aren't rhesus monkeys). However, going to the politics allowed me to observe events and behavior directly, and then to hear people offer their interpretation of events. Just "hanging around" was useful. I did not work from a prepared list of questions. I did not carry a recording device. As was the case for Fenno (1978), Dexter (1970), Heard (1950), and, more recently, Fowler and McClure (1989), I believe that the presence of a recording device in particular fundamentally changes the dynamic and richness of the observation experience. I was never far from my laptop, and I was always ready to start writing at the earliest convenient moment. Much of the material for this book was written in the parking lots of Union 76 truck stops and Love's gas stations, at the counters of Krispy Kreme donut shops, at the tables of coffee shops, in various airport terminals, in hotel rooms, and wherever else time and opportunity came together on the road.

Alluding back to Fenno's experiences, the easiest way to blend in is to become an active participant. By avoiding a structured instrument, I was free to navigate interesting events as they unfolded, rather than forcing my subject back to my list of topics. Political people love to talk, and I found myself waving signs, handing out literature, walking neighborhoods, sitting in on strategy sessions, and commiserating with political activists, all the while making notes in my mind. This put me in the mix, but not in the way. In the end, I obtained a more intimate look at the campaigns of these people, their lives as policy entrepreneurs and decision makers, and the candidates as people, and I got to witness the American political process in its most personal setting.

# REFERENCES

Anderson, William. 1975. *The Wild Man from Sugar Creek*. Baton Rouge: Louisiana State University.

Applebome, Peter. 1996. *Dixie Rising*. New York: Harcourt Brace.

Associated Press. 1999a. "April Fools! Motion to Kill Fireworks Bill Catches Freshman Off Guard." April 1.

———. 1999b. "Nine New Senators Begin Settling into Their New Jobs." January 19.

———. 2000a. "Barnes Signs Law to Ensure Equal Sports Opportunities for Girls." April 29.

———. 2000b. "Lawmakers Push Equal Sports Opportunities for Girls." February 1.

———. 2000c. "Other Gambling News." February 24.

———. 2001a. "Bill Prohibiting Discrimination of Gays Related to Housing Advances." April 3.

———. 2001b. "Gays Getting Housing Discrimination Protection." May 31.

———. 2001c. "Johanns Vetoes Housing Discrimination Protection for Gays." May 31.

———. 2001d. "Lawmakers' Priorities Touch on Death Penalty." March 9.

———. 2002. "Three Candidates under 25 Vie for House Seats in Cobb." July 1.

*Atlanta Journal-Constitution*. 1999. "The Gender Gap; Equity Backers Stirring." December 19, 1E.

Barber, James David. 1965. *The Lawmakers: Recruitment and Adaptation to Legislative Life*. New Haven, Conn.: Yale University Press.

———. 1988. *Presidential Character*. Englewood Cliffs, N.J.: Prentice Hall.

Bauer, Scott. 2001. "State Senator Bruning Will Run for Attorney General." Associated Press, June 12.

———. 2002. "Johanns Heads into Final Week of Election with Plenty of Cash." Associated Press, October 28.

Baxter, Tom. 1998. "Qualifying Gives Newcomers Chance to Make First Mark." *Atlanta Journal-Constitution*, April 28, 3B.

Beiler, David. 1999. "The Unsinkable Willie Brown." In *Campaigns and Elec-*

*tions: Contemporary Case Studies*, ed. Michael A. Bailey, Ronald A. Faucheux, Paul S. Herrnson, and Clyde Wilcox. Washington, D.C.: CQ Press.

Bixler, Mark. 2001. "Bill Would Define Hispanics as Minorities under State Law." *Atlanta Journal-Constitution*, February 12, 3B.

Black, Gordon. 1972. "A Theory of Political Ambition: Career Choices and the Role of Structural Incentives." *American Political Science Review* 66: 144–57.

Blocker, C., J. Evans, J. Freeman, J. Mixon, A. Munn, K. Semrad, K. Skibsted, and G. Snow. 1998. "House District 91 Public Opinion Poll." Unpublished ms., University of Oklahoma, Norman.

Brace, Paul. 1984. "Progressive Ambition in the House: A Probabilistic Approach." *Journal of Politics* 46: 556–69.

Breaux, David, and Malcolm Jewell. 1992. "Winning Big: The Incumbency Advantage in State Legislative Elections." In *Changing Patterns in State Legislative Careers*, ed. Gary F. Moncrief and Joel A. Thompson. Ann Arbor: University of Michigan Press.

Bullock, Charles S., III. 2002. "Georgia." In *The New Politics of the Old South*, ed. Charles S. Bullock III and Mark J. Rozell. Lanham, Md.: Rowman & Littlefield.

Bullock, Charles S., III, and Ronald Keith Gaddie. 1993. "Georgia." In *Redistricting in the 1980s: A 50-State Survey*, ed. Leroy Hardy, Alan Heslop, and George S. Blair. Claremont, Calif.: Rose Institute of State and Local Government.

Bullock, Charles S., III, and Harrell R. Rodgers Jr. 1976. *Coercion to Compliance*. Lexington, Mass.: Lexington.

Bullock, Charles S., III, and Michael J. Scicchitano. 2001. "Symbolic Black Representation: An Empirical Test." *Social Science Quarterly* 82: 453–63.

Cain, Bruce, John Ferejohn, and Morris P. Fiorina. 1987. *The Personal Vote: Constituency Service and Electoral Independence*. Cambridge, Mass.: Harvard University Press.

Campbell, James E. 1997. *The Presidential Pulse of Congressional Elections*. Lexington: University of Kentucky Press.

Canon, David T. 1990. *Actors, Athletes, and Astronauts: Political Amateurs in the United States Congress*. Chapel Hill: University of North Carolina Press.

Caress, Stanley M. 1996. "The Impact of Term Limits on Legislative Behavior: An Examination of a Transitional Legislature." *PS: Political Science and Politics* 29: 671–76.

Carey, John M., Richard G. Niemi, and Lynda W. Powell. 2000. *Term Limits in State Legislatures*. Ann Arbor: University of Michigan Press.

Crane, Wilder, and Meredith W. Watts. 1968. *State Legislative Systems*. Englewood Cliffs, N.J.: Prentice Hall.

Dexter, Lewis Anthony. 1970. *Elite and Specialized Interviewing*. Evanston, Ill.: Northwestern University Press.

Drinnon, Elizabeth McCants. 1997. *Stuckey: The Biography of Williamson Sylvester Stuckey, 1909–1977*. Macon, Ga.: Mercer University Press.

Easton, David. 1957. "An Approach to the Analysis of Political Systems" *World Politics* 9: 383–400.

Ehrenhalt, Alan. 1991. *United States of Ambition: Politicians, Power, and the Pursuit of Office.* New York: Times Books.

Eilers, Sarah. 1999. "The Maine Phenomenon." *Horizon Magazine*; available online: www.horizonmag.com/2/maine.htm (accessed July 23, 2003).

Engstrom, Richard L. 1971. "Political Ambitions and the Prosecutorial Office." *Journal of Politics* 33: 190–94.

Eulau, Heinz, and John D. Sprague. 1964. *Lawyers in Politics: A Study in Professional Convergence.* Indianapolis: Bobbs-Merrill.

Fenno, Richard F., Jr. 1978. *Home Style: House Members in Their Districts.* Boston: Little, Brown.

———. 1990. *When Incumbency Fails: The Senate Career of Mark Andrews.* Washington, D.C.: CQ Press.

———. 1991. *Learning to Legislate: The Senate Education of Arlen Specter.* Washington, D.C.: CQ Press.

———. 1994. *Watching Politicians: Essays on Participant Observation.* Berkeley, Calif.: IGS.

———. 1996. *Senators on the Campaign Trail: The Politics of Representation.* Norman: University of Oklahoma Press.

———. 2000. *Congress at the Grassroots: Representational Change in the South, 1970–1998.* Chapel Hill: University of North Carolina Press.

Fiorina, Morris P. 1977; 1989. *Congress: Keystone of the Washington Establishment.* New Haven, Conn.: Yale University Press.

———. 1994. "Divided Government in the American States: A By-product of Legislative Professionalization?" *American Political Science Review* 88: 304–16.

Fowler, Linda L. 1993. *Candidates, Congress, and the American Democracy.* Ann Arbor: University of Michigan Press.

Fowler, Linda L., and Robert D. McClure. 1989. *Political Ambition: Who Decides to Run for Congress?* New Haven, Conn.: Yale University Press.

Francis, Wayne L., and Lawrence W. Kenny. 1997. "Equilibrium Projections of the Consequences of Term Limits upon the Expected Tenure, Institutional Turnover, and Membership Experience." *Journal of Politics* 59: 140–252.

Gaddie, Ronald Keith, and Gary W. Copeland. 2002. "Oklahoma: The Secular Realignment Continues." In *The New Politics of the Old South*, ed. Charles S. Bullock III and Mark J. Rozell. Lanham, Md.: Rowman & Littlefield.

Gelb, Joyce, and Marian Leaf Palley. 1996. *Women and Public Policies: Reassessing Gender Politics.* Charlottesville: University of Virginia Press.

Hadley, Charles D., and Lewis Bowman. *Southern Grassroots Party Activists Project, 1991–1992: [United States]* [Computer file], 2nd ICPSR version. New Orleans, La.: Charles D. Hadley and Lewis Bowman [producers], 1993. Ann Arbor, MI: Inter-university Consortium for Political and Social Research [distributor], 1997.

Hall, Richard L., and Robert P. Van Houweling. 1995. "Avarice and Ambition in Congress: Representatives' Decisions to Run or Retire from the U.S. House." *American Political Science Review* 89: 121–36.

Hamm, Keith, and David M. Olson. 1992. "Midsession Vacancies: Why Do State Legislators Exit and How Are They Replaced?" In *Changing Patterns in State Legislative Careers*, ed. Gary F. Moncrief and Joel A. Thompson. Ann Arbor: University of Michigan Press.

Heard, Alexander. 1950. "Interviewing Southern Politicians." *American Political Science Review* 44: 886–96.

Herrera, Richard, and Warren E. Miller. 1995. "Convention Delegate Study, 1992 [United States]." InterUniversity Consortium for Political and Social Research Study #6353. Ann Arbor: University of Michigan.

Herrick, Rebekah, and Michael K. Moore. 1993. "Political Ambition's Effect on Legislative Behavior: Schlesinger's Typology Reconsidered and Revised." *Journal of Politics* 55: 775–76.

Hibbing, John R. 1986. "Ambition in the House: Behavioral Consequences of Higher Office Goals among U.S. Representatives." *American Journal of Political Science* 30: 651–65.

Higgins, A. Jay. 1995. "Young Saxl to Carry on Political Legacy." *Bangor Daily News*, March 6.

Hogan, Robert. 1995. "Campaigning for the State Legislature: Determining Variations in Campaign Organization, Strategy, and Techniques." Paper presented at the annual meeting of the Southern Political Science Association, Tampa, November 1–4.

Huckshorn, Robert J., and Robert C. Spencer. 1971. *The Politics of Defeat: Campaigning for Congress*. Amherst: University of Massachusetts Press.

Jacobson, Gary C., and Samuel Kernell. 1981. *Strategy and Choice in Congressional Elections*. New Haven, Conn.: Yale University Press.

Jenkins, Ron. 1999. "Freshman Lawmaker Pushes Anti-Drug Plan." Associated Press, November 9.

———. 2000. "Howe Democrat to Lead Study." Associated Press, September 21.

Jewell, Malcolm C. 1982. *Representation in State Legislatures*. Lexington: University of Kentucky Press.

Jewell, Malcolm C., and Samuel C. Patterson. 1977. *The Legislative Process in the United States*, 3d ed. New York: Random House.

Johnson, Dennis W. 2001. *No Place for Amateurs: How Political Consultants Are Reshaping American Democracy*. London: Routledge.

Judd, Alan. 2000. "Bill Could Affect School Playoffs." *Atlanta Journal-Constitution*, February 2, 5B.

Kaid, Lynda Lee, Dan Nimmo, and Keith R. Sanders. 1986. *New Perspectives on Political Advertising*. Carbondale: Southern Illinois University Press.

Kazee, Thomas, ed. 1994. *Who Runs for Congress? Ambition, Context, and Candidate Emergence*. Washington, D.C.: Congressional Quarterly Press.

Kazee, Thomas, and Mary Thornberry. 1990. "Where's the Party? Congressional Candidate Recruitment and American Party Organizations." *Western Political Quarterly* 43: 61–80.

Key, V. O. 1949. *Southern Politics in State and Nation.* New York: Knopf.

Kingdon, John. 1973; 1981. *Congressmen's Voting Decisions.* New York: Harper & Row.

Kolman, Joe. 2002. "Johanns: Bruning Still the Best Candidate Despite Past Charges." *Omaha World-Herald*, July 17.

Kolman, Joe, and David C. Kotok. 2002. "Attorney General Hopefuls Spar over Run-ins with Law." *Omaha World-Herald*, July 17, 1B.

Lenart, Silvu. 1997. "Naming Names in a Midwestern Town: The Salience of Democratic Presidential Hopefuls in Early 1992." *Political Behavior* 19: 365–82.

Loomis, Burdett A. 1988. *The New American Politician: Ambition, Entrepreneurship, and the Changing Face of Political Life.* New York: Basic Books.

Maestas, Cherie D. 2000a. "Professional Legislatures and Ambitious Politicians: Policy Responsiveness of State Institutions." *Legislative Studies Quarterly* 25: 663–90.

———. 2000b. "Uncertain Calculations." Ph.D. diss., University of Colorado.

Maisel, Louis Sandy. 1982. *From Obscurity to Oblivion: Running in the Congressional Primary.* Knoxville: University of Tennessee Press.

Maisel, L. Sandy, and Walter J. Stone. 1997. "Determinants of Emergence in U.S. House Elections: An Exploratory Study." *Legislative Studies Quarterly* 22: 79–96.

Maisel, L. Sandy, Linda L. Fowler, Ruth S. Jones, and Walter J. Stone. 1998. "Nomination Politics: The Roles of Institutional, Contextual, and Personal Variables." In *The Parties Respond: Changes in American Parties and Campaigns*, 3d ed., ed. L. Sandy Maisel. Boulder, Colo.: Westview.

Mann, Thomas, and Raymond Wolfinger. 1980. "Candidates and Parties in Congressional Elections." *American Political Science Review* 74: 617–32.

Matthews, Donald. 1954. *The Social Backgrounds of Political Decision Makers.* New York: Doubleday.

———. 1960. *U.S. Senators and Their World.* Chapel Hill: University of North Carolina Press.

Mayhew, David. 1974. *Congress: The Electoral Connection.* New Haven, Conn.: Yale University Press.

Meinhold, Stephen S., and Charles D. Hadley. 1996. "Lawyers as Political Party Activists." *Social Science Quarterly* 76: 364–80.

Moncrief, Gary F., Peverill Squire, and Karl Kurtz. 1998. "Gateways to the State House: Recruitment Patterns among State Legislative Candidates." Paper presented at the annual meeting of the American Political Science Association, Boston.

Moncrief, Gary F., and Joel A. Thompson. 1992. *Changing Patterns in State Legislative Careers.* Ann Arbor: University of Michigan Press.

Moncrief, Gary F., Joel A. Thompson, Michael Haddon, and Robert Hoyer. 1992. "For Whom the Bell Tolls: Term Limits and State Legislators." *Legislative Studies Quarterly* 17: 37–47.

Monroe, J. P. 2001. *The Party Matrix*. Albany: State University of New York Press.

Nice, David C., and Patricia Frederickson. 1993. *The Politics of Intergovernmental Relations*. Chicago: Nelson-Hall.

O'Hanlon, Kevin. 2000. "Lawmakers to Grapple with Lethal Injection, Death Penalty." Associated Press, December 26.

———. 2001a. "Bruning Readies to Make Attorney General Bid Official." Associated Press, October 9.

———. 2001b. "Democrats Criticize Bruning over Racial Profiling." Associated Press, October 22.

———. 2001c. "Democrats Still Vying for Attorney General Candidates." Associated Press, September 1.

———. 2001d. "Lethal Injection Bill Introduced." Associated Press, January 4.

———. 2002a. "Battle Lines Drawn Quickly in Lethal Injection Fight." Associated Press, January 9.

———. 2002b. "Meister Questions Bruning's Run-ins with Police during College." *Omaha World-Herald*, July 16.

———. 2002c. "Senator Says Nebraska Must Change Method of Execution." Associated Press, April 5.

*Omaha World-Herald*. 1998. "Early Start Led to Newcomer's Success in West." November 5, 13.

———. 2000a. "Anti-Lottery Bill Seeks to Win Points for Cause." January 6.

———. 2000b. "Bill Targets Actors in Lottery Ads." February 6, 1B.

———. 2000c. "In the Legislature." April 11, 15.

———. 2000d. "State Should Ante Up." February 12, 10.

———. 2000e. "Video-Pickle Bill Stalls." February 25.

———. 2001a. "Gay Housing Veto Stands." June 1, 13.

———. 2001b. "Gay-Rights Amendment Sinks Real Estate Bill." May 24, 23.

———. 2001c. "Gay-Rights Measure Advances." April 5.

———. 2001d. "Legislature Races to Finish Line." May 31, 1.

———. 2001e. "Stenberg Aide Says He'll Back Bruning for Post." July 4, 16.

———. 2002a. "Editorial: Bruning on Thin Ice." March 23.

———. 2002b. "Editorial: Much Ado about . . . ?" July 17, 6B.

———. 2002c. "Editorial: Three for Nebraska." October 26, 6B.

———. 2002d. "Most in Poll Differ with Archbishop." March 21, 1B.

Opheim, Cynthia. 1994. "The Effects of U.S. State Term Limits Revisited." *Legislative Studies Quarterly* 19: 49–59.

"Over Half Million Elected Officials in U.S." 1996. *Campaigns and Elections* (May).

Patterson, Samuel C. 1962. "Dimensions of Voting Behavior in a One-party State Legislature." *Public Opinion Quarterly* 26: 185–200.

Pendered, David. 2000. "Stuckey Resolute about Altering Current State Flag." *Atlanta Journal-Constitution*, April 13, 7JD.

Pettys, Dick. 2002. "Barnes Squeezing in Fund-Raisers This Week before the Window Closes." *Atlanta Journal-Constitution*, January 7.

Pitkin, Hannah. 1967. *The Concept of Representation*. Berkeley: University of California Press.

Powell, Lynda W., Richard G. Niemi, and John M. Carey. 1998. "Recruitment of Quality Candidates: State Legislator's Decisions to Run for Congress." Paper presented at the annual meeting of the American Political Science Association, Boston.

Prewitt, Kenneth. 1970. "Political Ambitions, Volunteerism, and Electoral Accountability." *American Political Science Review* 64: 5–17.

Prewitt, Kenneth, and William Nowlin. 1969. "Political Ambitions and the Behavior of Incumbent Politicians." *Western Political Quarterly* 22: 298–308.

Pruitt, Kathey. 1998. "Freshman Legislators Learn the Ropes." *Atlanta Journal-Constitution*, December 6, 5E.

———. 2000. "Gender Equity Vote Unanimous." *Atlanta Journal-Constitution*, March 18, 5D.

Pruitt, Kathey, and Peter Mantius. 2000. "Female Athletes Back Bill for Equal Funding," *Atlanta Journal-Constitution*, February 5, 5F.

Puckett, Patti. 2000. "Helping Women Athletes Thrive." *Atlanta Journal-Constitution*, February 10, 2JA.

Reed, Leslie. 2001. "Bruning Makes Move in Bid for State Post." *Omaha World-Herald*, June 12.

———. 2002. "Senator Apologizes for Calling Archbishop Unworthy of Post." *Omaha World-Herald*, March 26.

Roddy, B. L., and G. Garramone. 1988. "Appeals and Strategies of Negative Political Advertising." *Journal of Advertising and EM* 32: 415–27.

Roedemeier, Chad. 2001. "Democrats Propose Giving Patients Access to Doctors' Criminal, Medical History." *Atlanta Journal-Constitution*, January 12.

Rohde, David. 1979. "Risk-Bearing and Progressive Ambition: The Case of Members of the United States House of Representatives." *American Journal of Political Science* 23: 1–26.

Rosenthal, Cindy Simon. 1998. *When Women Lead: Integrative Leadership in State Legislatures*. New York: Oxford University Press.

Salazar, James. 2002. "Legislative Ambition a Genetic Trait." *Atlanta Journal-Constitution*, February 3, 1E.

Schlesinger, Arthur M. 1957. *Crisis of the Old Order, 1919–1933*. Boston: Houghton Mifflin.

Schlesinger, Joseph A. 1966. *Ambition and Politics: Political Careers in the United States*. Chicago: Rand McNally.

———. 1991. *Political Parties and the Winning of Office*. Ann Arbor: University of Michigan Press.

Shah, Nirvi. 1998. "Election 98: House District 67: Democrats Cite Youth, Experience as Appeals." *Atlanta Journal-Constitution*, July 16, 8JA.

Shepsle, Kenneth. 1978. *The Giant Jigsaw Puzzle*. Chicago: University of Chicago Press.

Sigelman, Lee, and Paul J. Wahlbeck. 1999. "Gender Proportionality in Intercollegiate Athletics: The Mathematics of Title IX." *Social Science Quarterly* 80: 518–38.

Smith, Ben. 2002. "Multimember Districts Confusing, Challenging." *Atlanta Journal-Constitution* (DeKalb edition), May 23, 1JA.

Soule, John W. 1969. "Future Political Ambitions and the Behavior of Incumbent State Legislators." *Midwest Journal of Political Science* 13: 439–54.

Squire, Peverill. 1988. "Member Career Opportunities and the Internal Organization of Legislatures." *Journal of Politics* 50: 726–44.

———. 1992. "Changing State Legislative Leadership Careers." In *Changing Patterns in State Legislative Careers*, ed. Gary F. Moncrief and Joel A. Thompson. Ann Arbor: University of Michigan Press.

Steed, Robert P., Laurence Moreland, and Tod A. Baker. 1998. "Ambition and Local Party Activists." In *Party Organizations and Activism in the American South*, ed. Robert P. Steed, John A. Clark, Lewis Bowman, and Charles D. Hadley. Tuscaloosa: University of Alabama Press.

Stone, Walter J., and L. Sandy Maisel. 2003. "The Not-So-Simple Calculus of Winning: Potential U.S. House Candidates' Nomination and General Election Prospects." *Journal of Politics* 65 (November) (in press).

Stone, Walter J., L. Sandy Maisel, and Cherie Maestas. 1998. "Candidate Emergence in U.S. House Elections." Paper presented at the annual meeting of the American Political Science Association, Boston.

Swinerton, E. Nelson. 1968. "Ambition and American State Executives." *Midwest Journal of Political Science* 12: 538–49.

Talley, Tim. 1999a. "Committee Approves Tuition Bill." Associated Press, February 2.

———. 1999b. "House Defeats Hate Crimes Bill." Associated Press, March 10.

———. 2000. "Committee Approves Bill to Revamp Governor's Cabinet." Associated Press, February 24.

Talmadge, Herman E. 1987. *Talmadge, a Political Legacy, a Politician's Life: A Memoir*. Atlanta: Peachtree.

Taylor, Mia. 2002. "Battle of the Ages: Foes in House District 31 Say Differences in Birth Dates Is Important." *Atlanta Journal-Constitution*, August 29, 31F.

Thompson, Joel A., and Gary F. Moncrief. 1998. *Campaign Finance in State Legislative Elections*. Washington, D.C.: CQ Press.

Torpy, Bill. 1999. "Capitol Corridors." *Atlanta Journal-Constitution*, March 13, 5C.

Tucker, Harvey, and Ronald E. Weber. 1992. "Electoral Change in the United States: System versus Constituency Competition." In *Changing Patterns in State Legislative Centers*, ed. Gary F. Moncreif and Joel A. Thompson. Ann Arbor: University of Michigan Press.

*Tulsa World*. 1998. "Howe Man to Vie for Seat in House," June 25.

Tysver, Robynn. 2000. "Jockeying for Moore's Post Begins." *Omaha World-Herald*, November 11.

———. 2001a. "Bruning Begins His Campaign for the Attorney General's Job." *Omaha World-Herald*, October 10, 3B.

———. 2001b. "Legislature Begins Flow of New Bills." *Omaha World-Herald*, January 4.

———. 2001c. "Lethal Injection, Gun Bills May Perish in Committee." *Omaha World-Herald*, March 30.

———. 2002a. "Bar Ownership an Issue in Attorney General Race." *Omaha World Herald*, March 6, 4B.

———. 2002b. "Priority Bills Face Squeeze." *Omaha World-Herald*, March 18, 1A.

———. 2002c. "Senators Spar over Bruning Ad." *Omaha World-Herald*, October 26, 8B.

———. 2002d. "Some Look to Roles outside Legislature." *Omaha World-Herald*, April 21, 7B.

———. 2002e. "Two Battle for Office in Stenberg's Shadow." *Omaha World-Herald*, September 30, 1B.

van Kampen, Todd. 2002. "Bruning Will Be Stenberg Successor." *Omaha World-Herald*, November 6, 2SS.

Wahlke, John C., Heinz Eulau, William Buchanan, and LeRoy Ferguson. 1962. *The Legislative System*. New York: Wiley.

Weber, Max. 1965. *Politics as a Vocation*. Philadelphia: Fortress.

Wilson, James Q. 1962. *The Amateur Democrat*. Chicago: University of Chicago Press.

# INDEX

# ABOUT THE AUTHOR

*Ronald Keith Gaddie* earned his Ph.D. in 1993 from the University of Georgia. He is a professor of political science and faculty fellow in the Science and Public Policy Program at the University of Oklahoma. His previous books include *The Economic Realities of Political Reform: Elections and the U.S. Senate* (Cambridge University Press, 1995), *David Duke and the Politics of Race in the South* (Vanderbilt University Press, 1995), *Regulating Wetlands Protection: Environmental Federalism and the States* (State University of New York Press, 2000), *The Almanac of Oklahoma Politics* (Carl Albert Center for Congressional and Legislative Studies, 3d ed., 2001), and *Elections to Open Seats in the U.S. House: Where the Action Is* (Rowman & Littlefield, 2000). He and his spouse, Kim, like good steaks, cold beer, raw oysters, sand between their toes, and the music of Jimmy Buffett.